THE FALL OF CRETE

ALAN CLARK

CASSELL

Cassell Military Paperbacks

Cassell
Wellington House, 125 Strand
London WC2R 0BB

Copyright © Alan Clark 1962

First published in Great Britain by Anthony Blond Ltd 1962
This Cassell Military Paperbacks edition published 2001
Reprinted 2004

A CIP catalogue record for this book is available from the
British Library

ISBN 0-304-35348-5

Printed and bound in Great Britain by
Cox & Wyman Ltd, Reading, Berks.

www.orionbooks.co.uk

CONTENTS

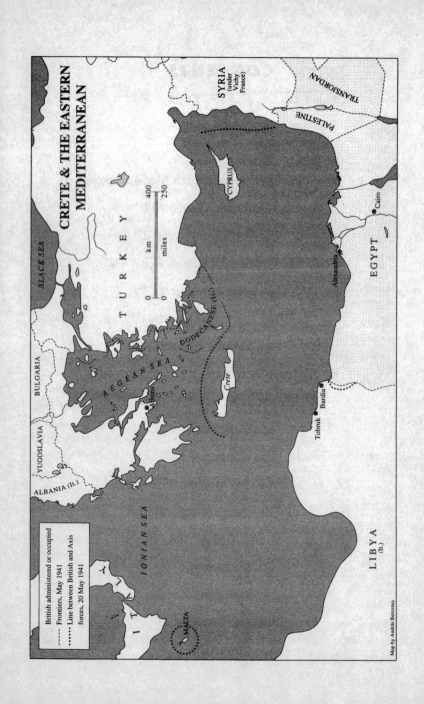

CRETE & THE EASTERN
MEDITERRANEAN

British administered or occupied

Frontiers, May 1941

Line between British and Axis
forces, 20 May 1941

BLACK SEA

TURKEY

SYRIA
(under
Vichy
France)

TRANSJORDAN

PALESTINE

CYPRUS

BULGARIA

YUGOSLAVIA

ALBANIA (It.)

AEGEAN SEA

Athens

DODECANESE (It.)

Crete

Alexandria

Cairo

EGYPT

ITALY

IONIAN SEA

MALTA

Tobruk

Bardia

LIBYA
(It.)

km   400

miles   250

0   0

Map by András Bereznay

ONE

POLICY AND FACT IN THE EASTERN MEDITERRANEAN

The collapse of France and the evacuation of the British Army from Dunkirk had, although placing Britain in a situation of immediate peril, conferred upon it an inestimable strategic advantage. For the first time in over a hundred years it was free from the wasteful complication of Continental alliances, the attrition of a 'Western Front', the expense in blood and toil of competition, in their own element, with the great land powers. A highly trained air force and a magnificent navy allowed Britain to enjoy the advantages of amphibious flexibility which had sustained her throughout so many wars with more powerful enemies.

But for Hitler the autumn and winter of 1940 were periods of fumbling, perplexity and disillusionment. 'Duce,' he wrote to Mussolini, 'in examining the general situation I reach the following conclusions: I. The War in the West is in itself won. A final violent effort is still necessary to crush England.' Ribbentrop told Molotov that 'England is beaten, and it is only a question of time before she finally admits defeat'. These judgements were, logically speaking, nonsense; and the inherent contradictions they expressed were reflected in a confusion of purpose, both political and military. There was the Wehrmacht, the most powerful and efficient army that had ever dominated Europe, but against England 'as little use as if it had been three divisions of untrained levies'. There was the Luftwaffe, also, it had seemed, all-powerful in every sphere – save one, the English skies. The Kriegsmarine? The war had been launched before the U-boat programme had got into its stride. In 1941 they were being made at the rate of only twelve a month.

The dilemma facing Hitler was threefold. Should he turn his back on England, husk that she was, and release the huge, impatient Wehrmacht on its last opponent, Russia? Or should he resign himself to many months of waiting, while manpower and materials were reallocated, until with an enormously swollen Luftwaffe he could once again challenge England? Or should he don the mask of magnanimity and consolidate by diplomacy the New Order in Europe so that to neutrals, and particularly to the United States, it would seem that, but for the empty conceit of the British, the Continent would be enjoying an orderly and harmonious peace? In the period from September 1940 to March 1941 the Germans can be seen leaning now on one, now on another of these policies. As early as July 1940 Hitler had told his Commanders-in-Chief,[1]

> In the event that invasion does not take place, our efforts must be directed to the elimination of all factors that let England hope for a change in the situation – Britain's hope lies in Russia and the United States. If Russia drops out of the picture, America too is lost for Britain, because the elimination of Russia would greatly increase Japan's power in the Far East. Decision: Russia's destruction must therefore be made a part of this struggle – the sooner Russia is crushed the better.

But Raeder, the head of the German Navy, advocated another plan – one which, with the advantage of hindsight, we see to have been much more menacing:

> The British have always considered the Mediterranean the pivot of their world empire . . . While the air and submarine war is being fought out between Germany and Britain, Italy, surrounded by British power, is fast becoming the main target of attack. Britain always attempts to strangle the weaker enemy. The Italians have not yet realised the danger when they refuse our help . . . The Mediterranean question must be cleared up during the winter months . . . the seizure of Gibraltar . . . the despatch of German forces to Dakar and the Canary Islands . . . close co-operation with Vichy . . . Having secured her western flank by these measures Germany could support the Italians in a campaign to capture the Suez Canal and advance through Palestine and Syria. If we reach that point Turkey will be in our power. The Russian problem will then appear in a different light. Fundamen-

[1] Halder, 31.7.40.

tally Russia is afraid of Germany. It is doubtful whether an advance against Russia in the north will then be necessary.[1]

Each of these two approaches made the pursuit of the other impossible, and in spite of his address to the Commanders-in-Chief in July Hitler seems to have inclined towards attempting first a diplomatic solution. In September Italy and Germany were linked to Japan by the Tripartite Alliance; Ribbentrop told Ciano that there would be 'a double advantage against Russia and against America. Under the threat of the Japanese fleet America will not dare to move'.[2] In a half-hearted follow-up to Raeder's plan Hitler pressed his overtures on Spain and Vichy France, although without making any corresponding military disposi-tions. In October he met Franco at Hendaye and they had their celebrated nine-hour meeting which drew from Hitler the comment that 'rather than go through that again I would prefer to have three or four teeth taken out'.[3] The delicate point at issue was the extent to which Franco could expect reward at the expense of the French colonies in North Africa. Hitler was meeting Pétain the following day at Montoire, and he also, Hitler hoped, might be persuaded to play an active part in an anti-British coalition. But the 'loyalty' of the administration in French North Africa would weaken if it was suspected that these territories were to be handed over to Spain at the peace treaty. The most that Hitler could promise was that 'Spain would receive territorial compensation out of French North African possessions to the extent of which France could be indemnified out of British colonies'. Franco would make no positive commitment as once again 'the Germans are trying to deal in the skin before the Lion has been killed'. From Pétain Hitler could only get an assurance of 'collaboration in principle' in return for his promise that after the War 'France will retain in Africa a colonial domain essentially equivalent to what she possesses today', and acceptance of his suggestion that Laval should be appointed foreign minister.

And so the position became more complicated, and the field of the German diplomatic commitments wider, with little to show in terms of

[1] Führer Naval Conferences, 26.9.40.

[2] Ciano, Diaries, 291.

[3] Ciano, Diplomatic Papers, 402.

3

military advantage. From the aspect of *Realpolitik*, though, the most sensitive region, that which required the greatest delicacy of handling, was the Balkans. For here the spheres of influence of Germany and Russia were in collision. Stalin had already shown his anxiety and the fact that in this area at least his policy was to act first and negotiate afterwards by his annexation of Bessarabia and Bukovina during the climax of the Battle of France. It was among this network of corrupt, flimsy and unstable states – by tradition the source of all European conflict, and in reality of vital importance to Germany as her only source of natural oil – that Hitler had to keep the peace.

The first threatening moment had occurred in August. The Hungarians wished to annex Transylvania and, noting the manner in which the Romanian government had already climbed down once, when force of arms was threatened over the 'Bessarabian problem', had mobilised their army and let it be generally known that they were prepared to go to war. It was only at the last moment that Ribbentrop managed to impose a solution, the so-called 'Vienna Award', which allowed Hungary half Transylvania immediately with a plebiscite, at an unspecified date in the future, to settle the remainder. When he saw the map depicting the new frontier, the Romanian Foreign Minister collapsed on the conference table in a dead faint, and had to be revived with smelling-salts. The government in Bucharest disintegrated and King Carol fled to Switzerland in a special train loaded with treasure, and with his mistress Magda Lupescu and her ninety-eight suitcases.

More serious, although equally typical of the Balkan scene, was an immediate demand by Bulgaria for the cession of Southern Dobrudja. Hitler once again compelled the shadow Romanians to accede, but in return he had to give them a territorial guarantee. In this way the German military commitment was brought right down to Russia's southern flank, into an area where arbitration, political pressure and the redrawing of frontiers had hitherto been a Russian preserve. So it is not surprising that the German ambassador in Moscow soon reported that he found Molotov 'reserved, in contrast to his usual manner'. The German government was accused of violating Article III of the non-aggression pact, which called for joint consultation, and of presenting the Soviets with 'accomplished facts'.

All this was extremely trying for the Führer for, even accepting the fact that war with Russia was inevitable, it was vital that this should start, not half-accidentally in the wake of some Balkan dispute, but at a time of his own choosing; and that the Russians should have no reason to suspect his intentions. So, having restored some pretence of order to the Balkan scene, Hitler resolved that there should be no further disturbances there, at least until further consultations with the Russian government had taken place at the highest level. In furtherance of this aim Hitler sent Mussolini a letter recommending that the status quo be preserved in this area 'for the time being at least'.

The text was strongly worded. Ciano described it as 'a complete order to halt, all along the line', and Mussolini found it highly unpalatable. The Duce was already upset at the prospect of the War ending before the Italian armed forces could display their prowess. He wished for a short, successful campaign against an enfeebled enemy, one in which blood would be shed, in which he could show, as he had claimed to do against the spear-carrying savages of Abyssinia, that the Italians were 'a nation of iron men'. 'It is humiliating to remain with our hands folded,' he told Ciano, 'while others write History.' The manner of 'writing History' most to Mussolini's taste was killing people. He was a man who would genuinely prefer to go to war against a defenceless victim rather than negotiate with it. He was bitterly disappointed that the end of the War and the establishment of the New Order seemed finally to have excluded this possibility.

But, in the autumn of 1940, while the Duce was grumbling to Ciano about their enforced inactivity, the Germans suffered a major military reverse: the Luftwaffe was fought to a standstill over Britain and Sea Lion, the invasion project, was, after successive postponements, finally dropped.

Mussolini was delighted. In the same week as the Sea Lion decision, on 4 October, the two dictators met at the Brenner Pass. Hitler was 'quiet', and 'thoughtful' over prospects, but Ciano wrote that 'Rarely have I seen the Duce in such good humour'. Their talk ranged over a variety of subjects; Hitler listened sympathetically to accounts of supply and administrative difficulties which were impeding the advance of Marshal Graziani's enormous army against the Suez Canal. He was reassuring over the question of American intervention, noncommittal concerning relations with the Soviets. He '. . . put at least some of his cards on the table, and talked to us about his plans for the future'. However, there was one omission from the Führer's frank résumé of current affairs – and it was to trigger a whole chain of catastrophes.

Hitler had come to realise, in the preceding weeks, that he could only preserve the crumbling Romanian policy and implement the guarantee made at the time of the Vienna Award if German troops were actually in the country. A fortnight before the Brenner meeting he had issued a directive defining the terms of a 'Military Mission':

> To the World their tasks will be to guide friendly Romania in organising and instructing her forces.
> The real tasks – which must not become apparent either to the Romanians or to our own troops – will be:
> (1) To protect the oil district . . .
> (2) To prepare for deployment from Romanian bases . . . in case a war with Soviet Russia is forced upon us.

Whether Hitler thought that the Italian Royal Family[1] would inform the west or that the information might leak out across Albania to the Soviets or, simply, that such a disclosure coming so soon after his order to 'halt all along the line' might give rise to some awkward requests from Mussolini, there is no doubt that Hitler's omission was deliberate. And when he heard of the arrival of the German troops in Romania, the Duce was furious. 'I will pay him back in his own coin,' he told Ciano. 'He will find out from the papers that I have occupied Greece. In this way equilibrium will be re-established.' He picked up the telephone and gave immediate orders to the Commander-in-Chief at Valona for the invasion to be launched that same week.

The Italian forces in Albania were hardly adequate, even on a numerical basis, but there was no time for their reinforcement, as Hitler

---

[1] They, and the Vatican, were always regarded by Hitler as serious security leaks in the Italian system and responsible, among other indiscretions, for the advance warning that had been given (and ignored) of his intended invasion of the Low Countries. In fact, this information had been communicated to the Netherlands and Belgian ambassadors by Ciano on the orders of Mussolini himself. (Wilmot, 63)

had already got wind of the scheme and had suggested an immediate conference. The Italian infantry went stumbling off into the Epirus at dawn of 28 October and when, that same day, Hitler stepped off the train at Florence, Mussolini greeted him with the words, 'Führer, we are on the march!'

Now the 'psychological and military consequences', as Hitler was to call them in a subsequent letter of reproof to the Duce, rained thick and fast. The invading Italian army was stopped short, beaten and turned tail; the Italian Navy was caught in Taranto harbour by the Fleet Air Arm and lost two heavy cruisers and three battleships; the first squadrons of Hurricanes began to appear on Greek airfields, and within weeks the Aegean and the whole of the Eastern Mediterranean up to the heel of Italy had been cleared of Axis ships and aircraft.[1] When the Spanish Foreign Minister accompanied Ciano to Berchtesgaden in November, his intransigence had markedly increased since the meeting at Hendaye. Hitler himself now became positively 'pessimistic'. He thought the situation 'must be compromised by what has happened in the Balkans. His criticism is open, definite and final'. He talked of '. . . the tendency of certain nations to avoid becoming entangled with us and to await the outcome of events'. In France, where practical considerations were uppermost, there was 'a decided strengthening of the position of those who assert that in this War the last word has not yet been spoken'.

In December the position deteriorated still further. Both Bulgaria and Yugoslavia positively rejected the invitation to join the Tripartite Alliance, and the Greeks, now handsomely re-equipped with captured Italian armaments, were trouncing the erstwhile invaders to such effect that the whole of Albania was threatened – despite the fact that the Italian Army there had been reinforced to almost three times its size at the start of the campaign. Then, in the second week of December, Wavell and O'Connor attacked Graziani at Sidi Barrani and, as Christmas

---

[1] Churchill had already evolved a plan, and had it approved by the Chiefs of Staff Committee, for an assault on the one remaining Italian position, the island of Rhodes. This was never, in fact, attempted, although the troops allocated to it (Marines of the Mobile Naval Base Defence Organisation and the Commandos of Layforce) were later, as will be seen, drawn into the battle for Crete.

passed, it became apparent that the whole of Mussolini's North African Empire stood in jeopardy.

But the most ominous of all developments was the reaction of the Russians. Invited to a conference in Berlin, Molotov showed little interest in the now distinctly unrealistic concept of 'the apportionment of the British Empire as a gigantic estate in bankruptcy'. On the first day Ribbentrop babbled speciously about 'directing the momentum of [our] Lebensraum expansion entirely southward', to which Molotov listened 'with an impenetrable expression'. When, the following morning, Ribbentrop suggested that Russia should join the Tripartite Alliance, making it a quadrilateral pact of military and economic co-operation, Molotov replied that 'paper agreements would not suffice for the Soviet Union; rather she would have to insist on effective guarantees for her security'. Hitler, who was attending to lend extra weight to the offer, found himself subjected to a close and insistent questioning on points of detail. What was to be the future of Turkey and the Bosphorus? What were German troops doing in Romania? And in Finland? What if the Soviets were to guarantee Bulgaria on the same terms as the German guarantee to Romania? 'No foreign visitor had ever spoken to him in this way in my presence,' wrote Schmidt, the interpreter, afterwards. Hitler suggested that it was time to adjourn as '. . . otherwise we shall get caught in an air-raid warning'.

The next day, when Ribbentrop was confronted once again with these questions, he complained that he was being 'interrogated too closely' and could 'only repeat again and again that the decisive question was whether the Soviet Union was prepared . . . to co-operate with Germany in the great liquidation of the British Empire'. After the conference broke up Stalin sent to Hitler a formal confirmation of the stand taken by Molotov in Berlin. Among other points he insisted on immediate withdrawal of German troops from Finland, a long-term lease of a base for Soviet land and naval forces within range of the Bosphorus, and warned of a 'mutual-assistance pact' in the offing between the Soviet Union and Bulgaria. Stalin's demands even ranged as far as an insistence on concessions from the Japanese in Northern Sakhalin.

Afterwards Hitler told Raeder that Stalin was 'nothing but a cold-blooded blackmailer'. But the die was cast. There was no longer any question of shoring up relations between the two countries for a further twelve months while the Germans completed the conquest of Britain. The Wehrmacht must attack Russia as soon as the weather was favourable – for a campaign whose probable duration was estimated by OKW, the German Armed Forces High Command, at ten weeks.

The collapse of the Italians, which had played its part in the Russo-German crisis, meant also that the Germans had to take over Mussolini's 'responsibilities' in the Balkans to secure their southern flank and this, in turn, involved the mounting of a full-scale military operation against the Greeks. But before facing this Hitler made one last effort to go down the western flank and induce Franco to allow German troops passage for an attack on Gibraltar. 'We are fighting a battle of life and death,' the Führer now admitted, 'about this one thing, Caudillo, there must be clarity.' Franco, who had received that same day [14 February] the news of Graziani's surrender at Beda Fomm, and of the bombardment by the Royal Navy of Genoa, replied that 'the logical development of the facts has left the circumstances of October [the Hendaye protocol] far behind'.

Thus were the Wehrmacht and the Luftwaffe drawn down into the Eastern Mediterranean, and a Balkan Campaign. Not as a result of a concerted plan such as Raeder had been pressing nor, as was thought at the time, in conformity with a general pattern of aggression against the remaining independent states of Europe, but following on a sequence of diplomatic miscalculations and, to the Italians, military defeats.

The question now presented itself, in the face of the threatened German intervention – what should be the reaction of the British government? The problem was a complex one. 'We often hear,' Churchill has written,[1] 'military experts inculcate the doctrine of giving priority to the decisive theatre. There is a lot in this. But in War this principle, like all others, is governed by facts and circumstances; otherwise strategy would be too easy. It would become a drill book and not an art; it would depend upon rules, and not on an ever-changing scene.' In England there was a general euphoria that had penetrated into high elements of military and political direction, brought on by the outcome of the Battle of Britain, by victorious feats of arms against the

---

[1] *The Grand Alliance*, 236.

Italians and by the military hesitation of the Germans. Now at last Britain seemed to be presented with a favourable opportunity for direct military action on the mainland of Europe; for leverage to further upset the evident confusion of the Axis.

There was also the moral aspect of the situation. The 'Allies', with the exception of a few thousand valiant Polish exiles, had simply crumbled away. Belgium, Norway, Holland, Denmark existed as little more than anthems, played in rotation, after the nine o'clock news on Sundays. The Free French could not even raise a brigade in strength. The Americans? Their entry into the war was over a year distant; the British ambassador was being pelted with rotten eggs as a 'war-monger', and the America First movement could raise a crowd of thirty thousand to hear Charles Lindbergh speak on the 'One last desperate plan of the British . . . which is to persuade us to share with England militarily, as well as financially, the fiasco of this war'.[1]

But there was one ally which had not collapsed, a poor agrarian country which had fought heroically against, and almost defeated, an attacker five or six times stronger than itself. The Greeks were the only western nation to sustain a successful land campaign against the Axis on the European continent for the first four years of the war. Let that not be forgotten. So it was quite unthinkable, morally, emotionally, ideally, for Britain to desert them at their hour of crisis.

However, while the decision to help the Greeks was unimpeachable, the manner of British intervention, its planning and execution, must be closely examined – for they were to have reactions of exceptional importance in the Mediterranean and the Far East for years to come.

[1] Shirer, 827.

TWO

THE GREEK DECISION

A strange obscurity clouds the outline of the Greek decision. In searching for the facts we find that each trail peters out or turns round to emerge at its starting point. The conferences, the memoranda, the arduous and protracted negotiations that preceded the decision are all different in emphasis and, where they overlap, they seem to contradict. Every eminent person – and they included Churchill and Metaxas, Wavell and Papagos, the Chief of the Imperial General Staff (CIGS) and the Foreign Secretary – concerned in the decision is recorded as holding within weeks, and even days, wholly opposite views as to its merits.

Every person, that is, save one. The Right Honourable Anthony Eden, as he then was, supported the whole notion of military support to Greece, by an expeditionary force lodged on the mainland of Europe, with a single-minded determination. As early as 6 January, 1941 he had written to the Prime Minister, 'Salutations on the victory of Bardia! . . . the object of this minute, however, is to call attention to a less satisfactory sector of the international horizon, the Balkans . . .'

Eden went on to discuss the situation there at length, ending with the advice that 'it is essential that our victories in North Africa should not result in any decrease of watchfulness on the part of the Yugoslavs and the Turks . . . you may wish to have all these questions answered by the Defence Committee'.

The Prime Minister at once drafted a minute for General Ismay to put before the Chiefs of Staff, which recommended that the operations in Cyrenaica be pursued no further than the fall of Tobruk. The minute ended, 'Although perhaps by luck and daring we may collect comparatively easily most delectable prizes on the Libyan shore, the massive

11

importance of taking of Valona and keeping the Greek front in being must weigh hourly with us.'[1]

In this view Churchill's own opinions were shortly to be endorsed by General Smuts, for whose strategic vision the Prime Minister had high regard, and from whom a long telegram, recommending that the Cyrenaican campaign be halted, arrived on 8 January. General Wavell, the Commander-in-Chief Middle East, was however strongly opposed to commitments on the Greek mainland. But unfortunately he chose as his first ground of objection that the German threat was not a real one, rather than that if it was real he had not the means to oppose it. To this Churchill replied, not for the last time in his dealings with Wavell, with some asperity:

'Our information contradicts idea that the German concentration in Roumania is merely a "move in a war of nerves" or a "bluff to cause dispersion of force" . . . Destruction of Greece will eclipse victories you have gained in Libya, and may affect decisively Turkish attitude, *especially if we have shown ourselves callous of the fate of allies.* You must now therefore conform your plans to larger interests at stake. We expect and require prompt and active compliance with our decisions, for which we bear full responsibility . . .'[2]

The passage in italics above would seem to indicate that political, indeed moral, considerations had supplanted the military reasoning (the extended lines of communication, the futility of further pursuing the beaten Italians, and so forth) which had been put forward by Eden and Smuts as objections to maintaining the effort in the desert. But when Wavell and Air Marshall Longmore, the officer commanding RAF in the Middle East, arrived in Athens, whither Churchill had sent them to co-ordinate 'support' to the Greeks, they found the Greek Commander-in-Chief, General Papagos, unenthusiastic. It was one of those conferences where everything is, from the outset, in agreement.

Papagos's view was that British intervention 'would not only fail to produce substantial military and political results in the Balkans, but

---

[1] *The Grand Alliance*, 14. (Valona was the chief port of Albania and at that time the object of an offensive by the Greeks – which was unsuccessful.)

[2] Op cit, 16–17. The italics are mine. AC.

would also, from the general allied point of view, be contrary to the sound principles of strategy . . . In fact the two or three divisions which it was proposed to withdraw from the Army in Egypt to send to Greece would come in more useful in Africa.'[1]

Wavell, with his own feelings of caution confirmed by the Greek attitude at this conference, told the Chiefs of Staff that he was opposed to an entry into Greece with inadequate forces as 'a dangerous half-measure', and he got permission – which had already been anticipated in action – to press on to Benghazi. But once again, whether from tact or conviction, Wavell had used language which amounted to a qualified rather than a total rejection of the idea of a Greek expedition, and the idea had taken firm root in London. In the same message that ordered the capture of Benghazi, Churchill ended by telling Wavell that 'the stronger the strategic reserve which you can build up in the Delta, and the more advanced your preparations to transfer it to European shores the better will be the chances of securing a favourable crystallisation.'

For some weeks matters remained in a state of balance, but during this period the Greek Prime Minister, General Metaxas, died, and on 8 February his successor, M. Koryzis, sent a message to the British government suggesting that 'the size and composition of the proposed force should be determined'. On 11 February the Joint Planning Staff recommended that the best response 'for the moment' was to carry through a plan for reducing the Italian Dodecanese, strengthening Crete, and assisting the Greeks by naval and air action. This recommendation was in line with that of Wavell to the Chiefs of Staff Committee on 25 January to the effect that 'the Policy of holding Crete in all circumstances should be maintained even if Greece gave way to the pressures threatening her'.[2]

But by this time the battle of Beda Fomm had been won, the Italians in Cyrenaica had been annihilated and to many British strength in the Middle East seemed greater than it was in reality.

---

[1] Papagos, 315.

[2] Sir John Dill, the Chief of the Imperial General Staff, had already gone on record twice as being in favour of consolidating in Crete and staying out of the Greek mainland. (COS 2 & 4 II '41, quoted Davin 6).

There is no doubt that Eden genuinely believed it possible to create, with the backing in this strength, a Balkan alliance of such strength that the Germans would hesitate before attacking it. By adding up the total of 'divisions' – that elastic term of military measurement, so often quoted in deception and self-deception – he arrived at a total of seventy, available to the Greeks, the Turks and the Yugoslavs. To match this the Germans had 'no more than thirty in the theatre', and it would take 'some months' to bring reinforcements from Germany.[1] But each of the three units in the proposed alliance was essential to the security of the other – the Yugoslavs to protect the northern flank, the Turks to stand on the eastern, with the Greeks in the centre. The essential first step was to bind Britain closely to Greece, with the promise and substance of military aid.

With this end in view, and doubtless fearing that if a second conference were left again to the generals they would soon agree between themselves that the project of an Expeditionary Force was impractical, Eden asked the Prime Minister that he should personally lead a fresh delegation to Athens. It had originally been intended that Sir John Dill should have gone alone but Churchill acceded to Eden's request, and thereafter the emphasis on the mission became diplomatic and political rather than military. At this stage, though, the Prime Minister still seems to have been looking at the situation realistically for, in the concluding paragraph of the letter that he wrote to Wavell informing him of the mission's purpose, he said: 'In the event of its proving impossible to reach any good agreement with the Greeks and to work out a practical military plan, then we must try to save as much from the wreck as possible. We must at all costs keep Crete and take any Greek islands which are of use as air bases . . . But these will be only consolation prizes after the classic race has been lost.'[2]

Eden's aircraft was delayed by bad weather and he did not reach Cairo until 19 February. The following day he took the chair at a conference at Wavell's headquarters at which Dill, Admiral Cunningham, Commander-in-Chief of the Mediterranean Fleet, and Longmore attended. Wavell was pessimistic, and his strategic appreciation very

[1] Churchill, *The Grand Alliance*, 59.

[2] Ibid, 149.

conservative. He thought that 'I can never see much prospect of the Balkans becoming an offensive military front from our point of view', although he recognised 'from an air point of view' they had potentialities as an offensive theatre. In any case he thought that 'our forces available are very limited and it is doubtful whether they can arrive in time'. In spite of this Eden again forced the pace, and persuaded the conference that some effort should be made. Accordingly, it was decided that the mission should propose to the Greeks that an attempt be made to defend Salonika. Cunningham took the view that 'though politically we were correct, I had grave uncertainty of its military expedience. Dill himself had doubts, and said to me after the meeting: "Well, we've taken the decision. I'm not at all sure it's the right one."'[1]

Wavell had fixed on Salonika as the vital point, for it was the hinge on which the Turkish and Yugoslav fronts, if they came into existence at all, would have to hang; and it was the only port north of the Piraeus that was capable of handling the supply train of the expeditionary force. It is also possible that by attaching to his consent conditions which he privately felt would be impossible for the Greek Army to accept – namely the defence of a line as far forward as the Macedonian passes – he thought that the whole scheme might yet fall to the ground.

However, once Eden had secured acceptance of his ideas in principle, his enthusiasm seems to have prevented him from accepting any detailed restrictions put on it at the Cairo meeting. The moment that he left Wavell he cabled to the Prime Minister that his present intention was to tell the Greeks of the help that they could be offered and to urge them to accept it as fast as it could be shipped. 'There is a fair chance that we can hold a line in Greece,' he went on, 'although present limited air forces available make it doubtful whether we can hold a line covering Salonika, which is what General Wavell is prepared to contemplate.'

The next day, after some further contemplation of the figures of men and equipment available, Eden cabled Churchill again, warning the Prime Minister that it was a 'gamble' to send forces to the mainland of Europe to fight Germans at that time, but that it was better to 'suffer' with the Greeks than to make no attempt to help them, though none could guarantee that they might not have 'to play the card of our evacuation strong suit'.

Eden may have calculated that this rapid substitution of the emotive for the strategic argument would be acceptable to the Prime Minister, but he seems to have had no illusions regarding its effects on the Greeks. For Colonel de Guingand has recounted how the next day, in the aircraft that was carrying the mission to Athens, 'I had been asked to produce a list showing totals of items that we were proposing to send. My first manpower figures excluded such categories as pioneers, and in the gun totals I produced only artillery pieces. This was nothing like good enough for one of Mr Eden's party who was preparing the brief. He asked that the figures should be swelled with what to my mind were doubtful values . . .'[1]

The conference went into session immediately on their arrival in Athens, and continued into the early hours of the morning. The Greeks were not too convinced even with figures swollen by such artifices as de Guingand mentions. They 'took a great deal of persuading' although Eden told them that Britain would be sending 'three infantry divisions, the Polish Brigade, one and possibly two armoured brigades – a total of 100,000 men and with 700 guns and 142 tanks'.[2]

Then, at last, at 3am the Foreign Secretary '. . . came in looking buoyant. He strode over to the fire and warmed his hands and then stood with his back to the fire dictating signals to his staff. They in turn looked nearly as triumphant as he did and were positively oozing congratulations. Presumably he had done his job and accomplished what he had set out to achieve. He was, therefore, no doubt entitled to be pleased with himself. But whether it was a job worth doing and in our best interests seemed to me very doubtful.'[3]

But within a fortnight of the agreement being signed things began to go badly. For Papagos, in the absence of any clear indication of Yugoslavia's attitude, was insisting on a defence of the forward line in

---

[1] De Guingand, 57.

[2] AOH 9. In these returns the anti-tank rifle was counted as a 'gun'. Less than one third of this number was actually sent.

[3] De Guingand, 60.

Macedonia – which Wavell had originally recommended – that covered Salonika. But he was having difficulty in disengaging his troops in Albania, and the British delegates soon found that they were not alone in having made optimistic estimates of the force that could be made available. Indeed, the Greek estimates proved to be as distant from reality as our own, and faced with the threat of a piecemeal destruction of the forces – the first convoy had just sailed from Alexandria and was due to arrive at the Piraeus on 7 April – the Prime Minister began to reconsider the whole problem.

On 6 April he wired Eden that '. . . We must be careful not to urge Greece against her better judgement into a hopeless resistance alone when we have only handfuls of troops which can reach a scene in time. Grave Imperial issues are raised by committing New Zealand and Australian troops to an enterprise which, as you say, has become even more hazardous.'

Eden remained unshaken in his conviction. From Cairo he replied: 'In the existing situation we are all agreed that the course advocated should be followed and help given to Greece. We devoutly trust therefore that no difficulties will arise with regard to the despatch of the Dominion Forces as arranged.'

In fact, the 'Imperial issues' to which Churchill referred were already a subject for concern. They were to assume a more oppressive gravity following on the defeat on the Greek mainland, and were to cast their shadow over the struggle for Crete. Although over 80 per cent of the expeditionary force was to consist of Australian and New Zealand troops, neither Blamey nor Freyberg were consulted during the discussions that preceded its despatch. They were simply given instructions, as unit commanders, and neither of them had a proper respect paid to his position as the leader of a national force and a principal military adviser of a government. Nor can the resentment which this treatment aroused, particularly among the members of the Australian cabinet, have been greatly assuaged by the variety of reasons which were put forward for making the expedition at all.

In these arguments we can trace the same confusion of purpose of political necessity and military expediency that plagued the whole expedition.

In a long, explanatory cable which was sent from the Dominions Office to Mr Fadden (the acting Prime Minister of Australia) on 25 February, it was contended that 'From the strategic point of view the formation of a Balkan front would have the advantages of making Germany fight at the end of long lines of communication and expending her resources uneconomically . . .' But when Menzies saw Churchill in London he was told that 'the real foundation for the expedition . . . was the estimate of the overwhelming moral and political repercussions of abandoning Greece'.

Thus it can be seen that throughout there were three sets of influences, pulling in separate directions. Eden, eager for a diplomatic coup, convinced that he could emerge as the architect of a new Balkan Coalition; Wavell and the Chiefs of Staff concerned only with the limited horizon of immediate military possibility; the Prime Minister himself leaning now towards one, now another of these attitudes, and inflamed by visions that were hardly realistic – the Balkan front of seventy divisions, the German weakness from 'having to hold down so many sullen populations', the possibility of intervention by Turkey, and so on.

This confusion of purpose had two effects. Everyone was so dazzled by the prospects of the expedition to the mainland that the one real prize that could have been taken from the Greek entanglement – the island of Crete – was overlooked.

Crete was of immense strategic importance. It lay, like a gigantic barrier reef, across the southern approaches to the Aegean. Its bulk allowed the construction of many airfields and the switching of aircraft from one to another so that some would always operate freely. It offered complete control of the narrow seas and the oilfields of Ploesti were only four hours away. Suda Bay, protected from the north by the Akrotiri peninsula, was the finest anchorage in the Mediterranean and surrounded by hills that offered perfect siting for anti-aircraft guns. But the island was very primitive. There were no railways and only one good road which ran along the northern coast. Human habitation was restricted to the coastal strips, and these were divided by the treeless volcanic ranges of the interior that rose to over 8,000 feet and were crossed along their whole length of 160 miles by only one road, or track, that ran to within a few miles of Sfakia where it petered out at the edge of the escarpment above the town. Even at Suda there was not a single crane, and the one jetty was congested by a large transit shed that stood in the middle and restricted the turn-around of lorries.

There were two other ports on the north coast – Heraklion, which could take a destroyer, and Rethymno, which could only manage small coasters – but the fishing villages in the south were useless because, although supplies and men could be offloaded onto lighters there, it was impossible to move them away without constructing new roads.

The months passed – the first British troops were landed on the island on 1 November, 1940 – and little was done to improve either the communications or the defences. From time to time a JPS paper was issued in London recommending a certain scale of garrison strength, or of AA defence,[1] or of aircraft that were to operate from Cretan airfields, but nothing was done to implement them. Between November and March there were six changes of command,[2] and the continuity of any defence planning suffered. For example, there was no co-operation between the three services regarding the siting of the airfields, and as late as 27 March, over a month after the Greek decision had been formalised in Athens, the Officer Commanding the RAF on the island was a flight lieutenant.[3] A week before, the OC signals had reported to Cairo that 'because of the ill-defined operational policy he could have no clear signals policy'. As the New Zealand historian has commented, 'his

[1] For example, the minimum envisaged by MEHQ and approved by the COS in November was 32 heavy AA, 24 light AA and 72 searchlights. The actual armament at the time that the evacuation from Greece started, when the situation was infinitely more threatening, was 16 heavy, 24 light and 24 searchlights. NZOH, 17.

[2] Brigadier OH Tidbury, MC, held command until 8 January, 1941. He was replaced by General Gambier-Parry who remained until 2 February, when he was posted to the Western Desert, and the next senior officer on the island (Lieutenant Colonel CH Mather of the 52nd LAA Regt) took his place until 19 February. From 19 February until 7 March the garrison commander was Brigadier Galloway, and when he went to Greece command passed back to Mather. On 21 March Brigadier BH Chappel, DSO came out and held the command until 26 April, when he was succeeded by Lieutenant General EC Weston, CB.

[3] NZOH, 20.

report suggests that, on the island at least, the current view was scarcely dynamic'.

Then, at four minutes to six on the evening of 25 April 5,000 men of 19th Brigade were put ashore at Suda Bay. They had come from Megara, and were the first of the evacuees from Greece. They had very little in the way of arms or personal equipment; they were dirty, ill organised, with no proper chain of command existing, 'bomb-shy' and conscious of their recent defeat. Quite suddenly the island, never a fortress, became overnight a huge field hospital, rest centre and transit camp. From being a relatively sheltered base area it became the most forward position of the Allied front in the eastern Mediterranean and one which, it seemed, would soon be subjected to the full weight of an enemy assault.

The majority of the troops that now began to pour into Crete were Australians and New Zealanders, just as they had been the majority of the expeditionary force to Greece. This brought in its train a new problem, rooted in the manner of the Greek decision, but which now threatened to plague the defence of Crete. If the island were to be properly defended, it must be fought over until the last round had been spent. There could be no withdrawal from those north-facing harbours, the air above which was already commanded by the Luftwaffe. The garrison would have to fight on in the hills indefinitely. Like Malta and Tobruk, Crete would have to hold out – whatever the sacrifices of the garrison. This was the correct, the impelling strategy.

But these men had lately been sent to Greece, in defiance of military principle, to fight a hopeless battle to which Britain was morally and politically committed. How, so soon afterwards, could political considerations be ignored and the men be sacrificed again, this time on the altar of strategic necessity? Already there was, lurking in the euphemism of Eden's, 'our evacuation strong suit'.

Here, then, were the ingredients of defeat. First an insoluble strategic dilemma that hung over the situation – the deadlock between military principle and political necessity. Second, the lack of preparation for the coming engagement, the poor communications, the absence of defensive works, the imbalance of the supplies. Third, the state of the garrison, the majority of whom had already tasted defeat at the hands of the Germans, and the attitude of their commanders, alternately fatalistic and irresolute.

There were other factors, and these suggested that the battle might, even so, be won. Crete is an island. The sea was dominated by the Royal Navy whose morale and equipment were immeasurably superior to that of the enemy and who had lately eliminated the Italian battle fleet in the night action of Matapan when they had sunk three heavy cruisers in eleven minutes. Moreover, the garrison, swollen by the daily arrivals from Greece, was now very large, far more than the enemy could put down from the air, even if he were allowed to operate in this way without interruption for days on end. Thus each in turn had command of his own element and the hours of darkness and twilight almost balanced those of the sun. Then, while the German aircrews slept and the Navy stood guard over the beaches, surely the defenders with their superiority of three and four to one could seek out and kill the enemy.

There were still some weeks and days before battle was joined, and the use to which the garrison put this time was of crucial importance.

THREE

'THE PROBLEM OF CRETE'

During the three days from 25 until 28 April a further 20,000 men from Greece were landed at Suda. They were arriving in a variety of craft – transports, landing-ships, caiques and on the decks of cruisers and destroyers. They had not always been embarked as units and in every case were without their full complement of officers and NCOs so that their discipline and cohesion were precarious. They had, moreover, been subjected to intermittent air attacks in the course of their voyage and many of them, particularly those on the decks of the warships, had suffered casualties from this.

It was usual for Suda Bay to be under more or less perpetual air attack during the daylight hours and the ships had often to heave to or put out to sea until there was a lull in which disembarkation might proceed. There were cases of men jumping overboard in the Bay and trying to swim on their own for land. Two tankers had been hit in a raid on the 24th. One of them, the 10,000-ton *Eleanora Maersk*, had been caught off Kalami point before discharging any of her cargo, and here she lay beached, and burning, for five days. Ships entering the Bay had to pass very close to the wreck and those on deck could see and hear the flames. Bodies floated in the water.

When finally the men were ashore they found that there were no tents for them – much less any sort of permanent accommodation. They were bivouacked among the olive trees on the south side of the Bay where they slept on the ground with no covering but their clothes. In the daytime the black smoke clouds from the burning tankers polluted the sky; at night it was bitterly cold without blankets or greatcoats. They had no mess gear and it was impossible to provide hot meals. Numbers of them wandered off into the countryside to forage for themselves.

'The men,' writes the official Australian historian, 'used to drinking beer, found the heavy Greek wines treacherous.' 'The discipline,' reported Brigadier General Vasey, commanding the Australians, 'is fair, on the whole. But there have been a few major incidents including an alleged murder . . . I have taken upon myself the power to convene field general Courts Martial and cases are proceeding apace.'

Other commentators were more explicit. In the report on 'The administrative aspect of the campaign in Crete'[1] we are told that 'In some cases, amongst the toughest and least trained, there was an active revulsion against military discipline and advantage was taken of the opportunities offered to avoid being brought under control. In consequence, for the first ten days at least, there were a number of men at large, many armed with rifles, living as tramps in the hills and olive groves. At night there were frequent shots if any lights were displayed. The problem of bringing these loose elements under control was difficult owing to the impossibility of giving the Military Police any lorries for rounding them up.' After some days a 6pm curfew for troops was introduced on the Suda–Canea area and it was promulgated that all men not in formed units or under camp control would be treated as deserters.

As well as a quantity of men without officers, there were soon gathered on the island a number of senior commanders with ill-defined and overlapping fields of authority. They, also, were discomfited by inadequate quarters and obstructed by shortage of staff, transport and equipment. General Weston found his seniority surpassed by General Wilson and with only nominal parity to that of General Mackay and General Freyberg. When Wavell sent a telegram to Weston, protocol obliged him to send one to Wilson also. When Wilson, as the senior officer on the island, received orders from Wavell they were couched as requests that he should act '. . . in conjunction with General Weston and General Mackay'. In the week of 20 April both Wilson and Weston submitted independent and differing reports on the practicability of defending the island.

It does seem, in fact, that Wavell had already decided to get rid of Wilson[2], and this determination will not have been shaken by Wilson's

[1] Brigadier GS Brunskill, HMSO.

[2] Unfortunately at the time of writing Wavell's private papers have not been made available to students, and so this must remain an inference from the events that follow. AC.

expressed conclusion that 'I consider that unless all three Services are pre-pared to face the strain of maintaining adequate forces up to strength the holding of the island is a dangerous commitment, and a decision on the matter must be taken at once.' Particularly as the arrival of this message was almost simultaneous with one from Churchill: 'It seems clear from our information that a heavy airborne attack by German troops and bombers will soon be made on Crete. It ought to be a fine opportunity for killing the parachute troops. The island must be stubbornly defended.'[1]

Wavell plainly saw that Wilson's statement amounted to an abdica-tion of purpose for Wilson knew perfectly well that the 'strain of maintaining adequate forces' – at least within the terms of his own preamble to this same report – was not possible. Wilson's report was dated 28 April. The following day Wavell received a report from the Joint Intelligence Committee to the effect that the Germans had enough aircraft disposed round the Aegean to enable them to land from 3,000 to 4,000 paratroops in a first sortie, and that up to four sorties in a day might be expected. The report pointed out that single-engined fighters and dive-bombers operating from Rhodes would have a substantial endurance factor over Crete itself and could be expected, by operating in relays, to give virtually continuous assistance to the enemy troops once they had landed.

The next day, 30 April, Wavell flew to Crete himself. He landed at Maleme and drove to Platanias where he saw Wilson, and they had a 'heart-to-heart talk'. Wavell explained that he wished Wilson to 'go to Jerusalem and relieve Baghdad'. Wilson took this meekly enough, although 'it came as a surprise as I had no idea what had been happening outside Greece for the last three weeks'.[2] Before the surprise could wear off, Wavell called to Freyberg who was a short distance away – they were sitting at tables on the terrace of a house in the village – and when Freyberg came over Wavell took him by the arm and congratulated him on the performance of the New Zealand Division in Greece: 'I do not think any other Division would have carried out those withdrawals so well.' He went on to say that he wanted him to take command of the

---

[1] *The Grand Alliance*, 241.

[2] Wilson, 102.

forces in Crete. Freyberg claims that 'these words came as a complete surprise'. He told Wavell that 'I wanted to get back to Egypt, to concentrate the Division and train and re-equip it, and I added that my Government would never agree to the Division being split . . .'[1] However, Wavell, doubtless fortified by the knowledge – which he had not communicated to Freyberg – that the decision was that of Churchill, ignored this protest and told Freyberg that 'he considered it my duty to remain and take the job. I could do nothing but accept'.[2]

None the less, Wavell must have been disappointed to find that, faced with the prospect of responsibility, Freyberg was showing the same misgivings as Wilson – and was more active in their diffusion. For even before they had left Platanias, Freyberg had approached Wavell again and told him 'that there were not enough men on Crete to hold it', and that 'the decision to hold the island must be reconsidered'. Shortly after Wavell had returned to Cairo he received a further communication from Freyberg, a telegraph stating that his forces were 'totally inadequate to meet attack envisaged'. The next day another telegram came, urging that 'the holding of Crete should be reconsidered' and announcing that Freyberg considered it his duty to inform the New Zealand government 'of situation in which greater part of my Division is now placed'. All this although, as Freyberg wrote later, 'The main defence problems which faced me in Crete were not clear to me at this stage.'

In his telegram to the New Zealand Prime Minister, Freyberg echoed the sentiments of his earlier communications to Wavell and concluded by saying, 'Recommended you bring pressure to bear on highest plane in London either to supply us with sufficient means to defend island, or to review decision Crete must be held.'

It may be thought that Freyberg had the intention of frightening Mr Fraser into taking political action because in this same telegram he stated that 'there is no evidence of naval forces capable of guaranteeing us against sea-borne invasion', a statement quite contrary to the facts that Wavell had put before him at their meeting at Platanias.

*

[1] Freyberg – 'Report on the Battle of Crete' quoted Long, 208.

[2] Op cit.

Now comes a strange turn of events. The date of Freyberg's telegram to the Prime Minister of New Zealand was 1 May. No record has been made public of any communications to, or by, him until 5 May. On that day he sent Churchill a telegram that began, 'Cannot understand nervousness; am not in the least anxious about airborne attack; have made my dispositions and feel can cope adequately with the troops at my disposal.'

How can this complete volte-face be explained? Churchill and Freyberg were old friends. They had first met at the Admiralty in 1914 when Freyberg had appeared with a letter of introduction, on the strength of which Churchill had secured him a commission in the Royal Naval Division. Churchill, whose own personal magnetism inspired so many, was himself occasionally vulnerable to allure of this kind. He was convinced that Freyberg was a superlatively brave man, and from this went on to endow him with other qualities for which there was less compelling evidence. In the 1920s, on a weekend that both of them spent as guests at Cliveden, Churchill asked Freyberg to show him his wounds. Freyberg stripped and Churchill counted twenty-seven 'separate scars and gashes'. In *The Grand Alliance* Churchill wrote:

> At the outset of the War no man was more fitted to command the New Zealand Division, for which he was eagerly chosen. In September, 1940, I had toyed with the idea of giving him a far greater scope . . . Freyberg is so made that he will fight for King and country with an unconquerable heart anywhere he is ordered, and with whatever forces he is given by superior authorities, and he imparts his own invincible firmness of mind to all around him.

Freyberg himself cannot have been unaware of the high esteem in which he was held by Churchill and, once he heard that he had been personally selected by the British Prime Minister, the very factors which militated against his accepting with any peace of mind an impossible command at the bidding of his superiors in Cairo – with whom he had no great personal affinities – would be reversed. For now he had been appointed by the supreme authority of the Empire. If he succeeded in his assignment, the prospects were dazzling. If he failed – well, the very circumstance of his appointment, in the light of his earlier protestations, relieved him of responsibility.

In fact, Freyberg's telegram to Churchill was completely misleading. He had not 'made his dispositions', unless by this he understood the issuing of an instruction (dated 3 May) that defined the 'organisation and rôle' of Creforce. Moreover, the supply situation, although not as bad as Freyberg claimed in his initial communications to Wavell, was only improving very gradually.

Suda Bay was virtually unusable during the daytime. The air-raid alarm system had been abandoned, and unloading was continuing in theory right up until the moment of attack. The majority of civilian crews deserted their ships on arrival and this meant that the work had to be undertaken by soldiers acting as winchmen and stevedores.[1] This arrangement was unsatisfactory enough during the day, and at night the confusion was still worse for many of the ships had been damaged by near misses and their engines had ceased to function. Thus they were without ancillary power to work cranes and lighting systems, and these could only function after a small ship had been put alongside and wired up. This in turn led to further delay and complication, and it was often dawn by the time the operation got properly underway. In the first three weeks of May over 27,000 tons of munitions were sent to Crete, but of these under 3,000 tons were landed – an appalling price to pay for the vacillation in constructing the road down to Sfakia but only, as it was to turn out, the first instalment.

The magnitude of the supply problem was, of course, itself a product of the enormous size of the garrison in relation to the means of landing and distribution available. On 3 May, when Suda was under a

[1] Even among these 'there was a tendency to windiness'. For example, the 1,005th Dock Operating Company showed 96 men – over one-third of its strength – on sick parade on the first day it was put on to unloading duties, of which the inspecting medical officer diagnosed 81 cases of 'nervous prostration'. These men had been severely bombed in Greece at the Piraeus, and the ship in which they were being evacuated to Crete was sunk by bombing. The survivors were rescued by another ship which was also bombed, although it managed to reach Suda. The men were, in any case, mostly shipping clerks from the ports of London, Liverpool and Manchester. There were only a handful of stevedores among them and the rest were quite unfitted physically for the duties which they had been assigned by the authorities, who had themselves been doubtless misled by the unit's ambiguous name.

continuous attack from 7.15am until dusk, the heaviest bombing up to that time, the labour troops were withdrawn and their place was taken by Australian volunteers commanded by Major Torr[1] who managed to accelerate remarkably the pace of unloading – even succeeding in salvaging a number of Bren-gun Carriers from a ship whose upper deck was several feet under water. These and other desperate expedients, such as the nightly use by the Navy of 30-knot warships that dashed at maximum speed from Alexandria and discharged their cargo in a three-hour turn-around, raised the general position to a level where the garrison had a reserve adequate for six weeks' continuous fighting.[2] In addition, forty-nine field guns, mostly French and Italian 75-mm and 100-mm calibre, a troop of mountain artillery with eight 3.7-inch howitzers, sixteen light tanks and six infantry tanks were put ashore in the three weeks preceding the attack.[3]

There were also 2,200 Marines of the MNBDO,[4] highly trained regulars who had not seen action in Greece, complete with all their equipment, including light and heavy anti-aircraft guns, searchlights and some long-range 4-inch naval guns for coast defence. Two more fresh battalions, the 2nd Leicester and 2nd Argyll and Sutherland Highlanders, were landed at Heraklion and Timbaki, it being General Wavell's intention that this force should constitute a mobile reserve in the centre of the island. To prevent a seaborne invasion Admiral Cunningham disposed of the most powerful fleet that had sailed since Jutland. There were four capital ships, nineteen cruisers and forty-three destroyers. These had been divided into two 'heavy' formations whose 15-inch guns cruised to the west of Crete, providing cover against the Italian battle fleet, and seven 'light' task forces, each one of them strong enough to annihilate an invading force. This meant, in

---

[1] Brigadier AG Torr, CBE, DSO. The men were drawn chiefly from engineering units and from 2/2nd Field Regiment.

[2] On 19 May the figures were: Maleme: 80,000 rations, 5,000 gallons POL (petrol oil and lubricants). Heraklion: 60,000 rations, 10,000 gallons POL. Rethymno: 40,000 rations, 5,000 POL. 'Report on Supply and Transport Services in Crete' dated 4.6.41 quoted NZOH 47.

[3] AOH 215.

[4] The Mobile Naval Base Defence Organisation.

effect, that the Germans would have to land, and to supply, their army from the air – with all the perils and uncertainties that this entailed.

So, from a purely material standpoint, there was just a possibility that the large body of troops on the island, intelligently directed, might administer to the Wehrmacht its first clear-cut defeat since the Battle of the Marne. Churchill, from the Cabinet room in London, saw the essentials of the situation with his usual clarity. In a letter to the Prime Minister of New Zealand he wrote,

> The Navy will certainly do their utmost to prevent a seaborne attack, and it is unlikely to succeed to any large scale. So far as airborne attack is concerned, this ought to suit the New Zealanders down to the ground, for they will be able to come to close quarters, man to man, with the enemy who will not have the advantage of tanks and artillery, on which he so largely relies. Should the enemy get a landing in Crete that will be the beginning, and not the end, of embarrassments for him. The island is mountainous and wooded, giving peculiar scope to the qualities of your troops.

Unfortunately, there does not seem to have been any clear plan, or central direction, whereby these qualities might best be exploited. The long frontage, with its poor communications and the enemy command of the daylight air, presented Freyberg with a dilemma. Was the defence to be linear? With, that is to say, the troops distributed in packets at every point considered to be threatened – in which case, although the enemy would be opposed at every point he landed, there was the likelihood that he would soon achieve a local superiority in numbers. Or was it to be flexible? With the mass held back ready for a counter-attack which, on a scale sufficient to dislodge the enemy, might have to wait at least twenty-four hours – perhaps until the second evening – owing to the difficulty of movement by day.

The plan adopted was a compromise. Freyberg broke up his forces into three masses, and positioned them (correctly, as it was to turn out) at the points where a German descent seemed most likely. However, he left their actual disposition to the commanders on the spot, and these adopted, without exception, a linear scheme. That Freyberg's own thinking favoured this approach is shown by his frequent references to 'wiring' as a necessary and desirable measure. After his tour of the defences on 13 and 14 May he told Wavell, 'I feel greatly encouraged by my visit . . . All defences have been extended and positions wired as much as possible.'[1] (There is no record, in any captured enemy document relating to the campaign, of their troops being impeded by the wire, but it played a not inconsiderable part in dislocating the counter-attack by the 20th and 28th New Zealand Battalions on the night of the 22nd.)

It is not possible to discern with any clarity the plan on which the defence was to be conducted. The New Zealanders were told that the essence was a spirited defence, that 'in the event of the enemy making an attack on any part of the area' they were to 'counter-attack and destroy him immediately'.[2] But the Divisional Commander laid great emphasis on the fact that 'all that concealment and defensive measures like digging and wiring could give in the way of protection must be sought to the fullest possible limit'.[3] In a lecture to 5th NZ brigade a few days before the attack Freyberg advised the men 'to stay in their positions, and not to rush out when the paratroops come down'.[4]

These latent contradictions were a reflection of an involved and overweight command structure, where there were no fewer than four separate area commanders with independent responsibilities and sub-ordinate only to Freyberg himself.[5] Although it was logical to give the Heraklion area a large measure of independence, it is less easy to understand the boundaries of the other commands.

The actual dispositions were as follows. At Heraklion, Brigadier Chappel had under him the 2nd Black Watch, the 2nd Leicesters, the 2nd York and Lancs, the 2/4th Australian Battalion, the 7th

---

[1] Long, 220.

[2] 5th Brigade, Operation Order No. 4.

[3] Puttick's appreciation, quoted, NZOH, 53–4.

[4] NZOH, 100 (report by H Gentry).

[5] In some areas, and particularly around Maleme and Suda, the men had to learn three passwords per night in order to be able to move freely, as each 'Command' had a separate security system.

Australian Medium Regiment and three Greek battalions.[1] At Rethymno, Brigadier General Vasey had four Australian battalions (2/1st, 2/7th, 2/11th and 2/1st machine-gun) and two Greek battalions. This 'sector' included the town of Georgeoupolis, which was itself only nine miles from Suda Bay. And in the Suda Sector, in a cluster of dugouts and caves in the hills to the north of Canea, Freyberg had his own headquarters.

It was in this area, stretching from Maleme airfield in the west to Georgeoupolis in the east, that the battle for the island might reasonably be expected to find its decision – yet it is in this sector that the arrangements for the command seem to have been most complicated. General Weston, who, as has been remarked, had held overall command of the garrison for two days, had remained on the island after the appointment of Freyberg, and to him the whole of the MNBDO, together with a number of ancillary anti-aircraft and coastal defence guns, remained responsible. He was now given command by Freyberg of the 'Suda area' – an artificial concept, existing in administrative rather than tactical reality and one that lay cheek by jowl with the neighbouring 'Maleme area' to which was allotted the whole of the New Zealand Division, and which was placed under the command of the Divisional GOC, Brigadier General Puttick.

Whether this arrangement arose out of consideration for General Weston's feelings, or because he had an intact staff organisation at his disposal, or because the majority of the men that he had brought out from England were in the Suda area – or from the consideration of all these factors – the effect was to seriously impair co-ordination in this vital region. To make the position still worse, Freyberg did not keep Force Reserve under his own hand in readiness for an immediate counter-offensive, but issued orders that it was 'to be administered by sector commanders'. Force Reserve consisted of the 4th New Zealand Brigade, positioned in the Karatsos area, and the 1st Welch, which was situated the other side of Canea on the neck of the Akrotiri peninsula.

Finally, one must examine the disposition of the New Zealand

[1] NZOH, 30.

Division itself, the largest coherent unit in Freyberg's Command, to which he had allocated the defence of Maleme aerodrome, the road connecting it to Canea and the inland flank approach that lay down the road from the Aghya reservoir past the prison and known as 'the Prison Valley'.

Puttick had two Brigades at his disposal, the 5th under Brigadier Hargest, which he had allocated to the immediate area of the airfield, and the 10th (less its 20th Battalion) which, under Colonel Kippenberger, had been placed in the Galatas area, where they blocked the Canea end of the Prison Valley but overlapped confusingly with Weston's sector. The 20th Battalion was not to be employed without direct authority from Divisional Headquarters, being in effect a divisional reserve that was distinct from, and in addition to, the Force Reserve that Freyberg had designated. It, too, was kept in the outskirts of Canea, where Puttick had established his own Divisional Headquarters on the extreme eastern tip of his own sector, and as far as he could possibly be from the centre of gravity, as it was to become, at Maleme. This is all the harder to understand in the light of Wavell's own warning to Freyberg during their meeting at Platanias on 30 April that 'the primary objectives of the attack are considered to be Maleme and Heraklion aerodromes'.[1]

The same curious thinning out at this vital point is evident in the positioning, by Hargest, of 5th Brigade's own battalions. He placed 21st and 23rd in a sort of stepped-up echelon in the heights above Kondomari, and his own headquarters still further east at Platanias. Neither of these units could move quickly onto Maleme airfield – they were 'wired in' and separated from it by the gully of the Sfakoriako, whose steep banks on the western side masked the whole of the 21st's firepower in that direction. Two more battalions were placed along the Canea road, to the east: the Engineers on either side of the bridge at Modhion; and the 28th (Maori) – one of the most effective fighting units on the island – at Platanias. This left only one battalion, the 22nd, for the immediate area of the aerodrome and the vital Hill 107 that commanded it. Even with this unit, the pattern of dilution was

[1] Freyberg's own report to the New Zealand Minister of Defence, 2.

maintained so that only one of the five companies available was positioned on the height, no men were placed in the western side of the Tavronitis and the vital bridge over its twin streams was virtually undefended, debouching as it did against the extreme right flank of D Company, and in the rear of No. 15 Platoon of C Company, whose three platoons were disposed around the aerodrome itself in shallow slit trenches.

The net effect of this distribution was that the total strength, at this point of maximum enemy effort, was fewer than 140 rifles – out of a garrison of nearly 30,000.

In fact, the area of the west bank of the Tavronitis, and the river mouth, had been specifically allocated to 5th Brigade by Divisional order, but on the distribution of battalions adopted there were not enough men to conform with this. Moreover, the position was still further weakened by the fact that a large and populous camp of tents and hutments, still occupied by non-combatant personnel of the Royal Air Force and Fleet Air Arm, obstructed the field of fire around the vital bridge. A request by Lieutenant Colonel Andrew, VC, the commander of 22nd Battalion, that these personnel should be placed temporarily under his command was refused. This, and other examples, underline the deficiencies of the command structure. The heavy anti-aircraft guns defending the aerodrome were controlled from the gun operations room at Canea; the majority of the Bofors were manned by Royal Marines, and as such were responsible to General Weston – although well outside the Suda area; and the various Royal Air Force ground crews and the Naval personnel who manned the long-range coast-defence guns were under the control of their own senior commanders.

Puttick made a reconnaissance on 1 May, and heard the complaints of 5th Brigade on this subject. He 'spoke of discussing the question with Creforce or General Weston'[1] but without any result it seems, for on 16 May, when Andrew suggested that the two 4-inch guns of 'Z' coast-defence battery, situated in the north-west ridge above their airfield, should include the landing strip in their field of fire, the request, although

[1] NZOH, 30.

made in person to the battery commander, was referred back to MNBDO Headquarters at Suda.

The same absence of positive leadership is apparent in the attempts to arrange cover for the vulnerable territory west of the Tavronitis. It was not until 10 May that a request was sent from 5th Brigade to Puttick, following a reconnaissance by the Brigade Major, Captain Dawson, asking for a battalion to cover the open ground west of the river. Puttick thought that the 1st Greek Regiment, at that time garrisoning Kastelli some twelve miles to the west of Maleme, should be brought further in towards the perimeter, but permission had first to be obtained from the Greek authorities. When this was obtained 'Puttick had his doubts about the wisdom of the move at so late a stage'.[1] 'It was decided' – but by whom is not plain – 'that 23rd Battalion must take over the additional task of repelling any landings on the beaches west of the Tavronitis.' This was a most impractical solution as the men of the 23rd had just become thoroughly dug in in their allotted positions above Dhaskaliana, and the move would entail seriously weakening these, besides stretching their lines of communication round the bulk of 22nd Battalion and Hill 107. Shortly after these orders were issued they were, in fact, cancelled, and the only reinforcement that was sent to the area was one section of 21st Battalion that was sent with a week's rations to a high point west of the river, and 'in the event of landings it was to report back by telephone'.[2] The significance of leaving this vulnerable region unguarded will be appreciated in due course.

In the realm of strategic decisions, as distinct from the purely tactical questions cited above, the Chiefs of Staff Committee in London, Middle East Headquarters in Cairo and the Prime Minister himself were all active. The most important of these concerned the air defence of the island. At the end of April the number of serviceable aircraft at the disposal of the Royal Air Force in this theatre had sunk to a low point that was never touched subsequently. For his commitments in Libya, Syria, Iraq, Cyprus, Egypt and Crete itself, Air Marshal Longmore

[1] NZOH, 60.
[2] NZOH, 63.

disposed of ninety bombers and only forty-three single-engined fighters. Of these, twenty-three bombers and about twenty fighters were at Maleme and Heraklion, but the aircraft and crews were the remnants of the squadrons evacuated from Greece[1] and completely worn out. The fighters had been used for daily convoy protection, and were all in a dangerously unserviceable condition. There were only twelve Hurricanes among them, and the American Brewsters were only to be flown 'in an emergency'.

So it can be seen that the Joint Planning Staff in London were nothing if not optimistic when they recommended the retention of two fighter squadrons on the island, and their reinforcement by a third from Egypt.[2] When Air Marshal Longmore received this recommendation, he flew to Crete and carried out an inspection in person. This led him to the belief that 'Suda Bay could be kept open by a squadron of Hurricanes at 100 per cent strength, and with 100 per cent replacement rate and reserve of pilots'. To maintain a squadron of Hurricanes at this level would hardly have been possible anywhere in the Middle East at this time and, even if it had been, it is hard to see how long it would have lasted against the scale of the enemy attack as envisaged in the JIC report.[3] When, on 27 April, these figures were presented to Portal, the Chief of the Air Staff, he shifted some of the responsibility over to the Navy, saying, in COS committee, that 'if the Navy attached great importance to holding the island, the risk of keeping forces for its defence should be taken; otherwise it would better to keep the fighters in Egypt'. The Chiefs of Staff decided to 'seek further information' and referred the question back to Wavell who, in turn, asked the Admiral Commanding the Mediterranean Fleet, Cunningham. Cunningham's appreciation did not arrive until 1 May, and then was a muddled affair recommending that 'we should maintain on the island a force strong enough to keep the enemy out until adequate AA and air defences could be established'.

---

[1] Consisting of 30 Squadron (14 Mk I Blenheims), 203 Squadron (9 Mk IV Blenheims) and remnants of 33, 80 and 112 Fighter Squadrons.

[2] JPS paper, 49, dated 21.4.41.

[3] This showed enemy air strength in the Aegean at 315 heavy bombers, 60 long-range fighters, 270 single-engined fighters and 240 dive-bombers.

In the meantime, however, Portal had had second thoughts, and at the COS committee of 5 May he was 'emphatic' that 'it would be dangerous to maintain an active air defence over the island at the expense of the Western Desert and elsewhere. The soundest course was to rely on AA, dispersion and concealment . . .' But the effect of this decision was quite spoilt by the contradictory recommendation that ran parallel with it, namely, '*and at the same time to maintain a ground organisation which would permit aircraft to fly in from Egypt* if a seaborne attack was attempted.' Freyberg, however, who had fixed on the concept of 'one squadron of Hurricanes at 100 per cent strength, with 100 per cent replacement' as the best that he would be likely to get, was continually badgering MEHQ for its fulfilment, and mentioning his need 'for a few extra fighters' in such messages as he sent to London (including that of 5 May to the Prime Minister).

On 8 May, Longmore's final report was submitted to COS London, and stated that the condition of the Cretan airfields was such that casualties would be high from lack of repair facilities, and that lack of cover made dispersion of aircraft difficult. He was against the permanent stationing of squadrons, but *thought that the airfields might be used as advanced landing grounds for fighters.*[1]

All this while the fighters from Maleme and Heraklion were being steadily depleted in sortie after sortie against the German bombers. By 13 May the Hurricanes were reduced to six and the remaining Gladiators, three in number, had been grounded as they were outclassed in combat. Their pilots were getting rudimentary flying training in the Hurricanes at sundown of each day after the Messerschmitts had returned to Rhodes. Freyberg was still asking for his '100 per cent Squadron', and in some way seems to have succeeded in presenting this as one of the conditions upon which he had undertaken to defend the island, for on 17 May, in defiance both of Portal's opinions as expressed to the COS Committee and of Longmore's own views as expressed to Portal, a further ten Hurricanes were landed at Heraklion. In the two days following all but two of them, and a further four of the original flight, were shot down or rendered unserviceable for one reason or another. Compelled to land on

[1] My italics. AC.

a poorly prepared strip at higher than recommended speeds, the aircraft would overshoot or damage their undercarriage. There was a scarcity of coolant fluid for the Merlin engines and of lubricants for servicing the airframes and control cables. The shortage of Browning .303 ammunition meant that they often went into action with only six, or even four, of their eight machine-guns loaded.

In fact, their crews were trying to dispute, on a smaller scale and over a foreshortened period of time, the same sort of issue as was at stake in the Battle of Britain – the control, that is to say, of the daylight air over an island threatened with invasion by a land power – but these pilots were outnumbered not by three or four to one but by forty or fifty. They had no communication with the controllers on the ground, there were no radar stations to help them to locate the enemy or to advise them when a raid was ending, when it was safe to refuel or desperately urgent to scramble. And so, in spite of all their bravery, they lost the battle.

On 19 May Beamish, the Air Officer Commanding, finally managed to persuade Freyberg that the retention of the remaining aircraft (now reduced to three Hurricanes and the three grounded Gladiators) was a useless sacrifice of brave men and valuable machines, and they were flown back to Egypt on that same evening.

Beamish himself, in his report subsequent to the battle, says that 'the intention was that the Royal Air Force should return in greater numbers and at a later stage', and this is certainly borne out by Portal's and Longmore's supplementary recommendations to the effect that airfields should be kept open and ground crews preserved. It may seem impertinent to compare this with the refusal of the French General Staff to obstruct the Ardennes in 1940 so that their cavalry should not be impeded, but the effect on the forthcoming battle was equally disastrous. The hesitation by the Chiefs of Staff, in the face of Portal's ambiguous directions and Freyberg's insistence on whatever HQME could spare him, simply meant that nearly half the Hurricanes available in the Eastern Mediterranean at that time were destroyed piecemeal while a decision – if it can be called that – was reached; that a large number of non-combatant personnel remained on the island where they obstructed its defence; that it was never clearly put to the garrison, as it might have been several weeks before the attack, that the battle was to be fought as a matter of policy under conditions of complete enemy air superiority, with all that this implied in terms of tactical training in movement and attack by night, concealment and so forth; and, finally, that no effort was made, or indeed permitted, to mine and obstruct the three landing grounds. More than any other single factor, this decision contributed to the defeat that was to follow.

One other matter on which the Chiefs of Staff and Headquarters Middle East were concerned, and which directly influenced the defence of Crete, was the question of tanks. This is second in importance only to the decision concerning the mining and demolition of the airfield runways, and the fact must be set out at some length.

In the days before the invention of the bazooka and the *Panzerfaust*, lightly armed infantry had virtually no answer to the tank, even at close quarters. At very short ranges the German anti-tank rifle, a two-man affair not unlike a monstrous elephant gun, was effective against their tracks, but as a general rule it was even less formidable than its British counterpart which could, at least, penetrate the armour of some of the lighter Italian tanks. Even the standard German anti-tank gun, the 37-mm which fired a shot of slightly less than two pounds in weight, was of very little use against the British 'I' (for Infantry) tank and the newly introduced Valentine.[1]

This same 37-mm gun, together with a 75-mm mountain gun that had a negligible muzzle velocity, were the only field pieces that the German Junkers Ju 52 transport aircraft could carry – and then only in a dissembled state. Hence, until the invaders had established proper unloading facilities they would be acutely vulnerable to armoured attack.

None the less, the provision of adequate tank strength to the garrison was subject to the same fumbling and indecision that characterised the attitude to the air defence. It is hard to find any evidence that the matter was being treated with urgency in Cairo. The provision of armour is not mentioned in Wavell's letter to Churchill and COS dated 29 April, nor in that to CIGS dated 2 May.

[1] The German execution in the Western Desert was done at this stage by the (*Pak* 38) 50-mm guns 'long' tank-mounted and, of course, at a later stage by the legendary 88-mm and a number of captured Russian 76.2-mm (from which was developed the long-barrelled 75 mounted in the Panther). AC.

This may have been because Wavell thought himself to be seriously short of tanks at this time. Another German armoured division (15th Panzer) had just been identified in the Western Desert, and as he had telegraphed Churchill on 20 April, 'the best I can hope for by the end of the month is one cruiser regiment less one squadron, and one "I" tank regiment less one squadron, to assist defence of Matruh. During May I may get another thirty to forty cruisers out of the workshops to make another weak unit, and some "I" tanks which will probably be required for the close defence of Alexandria against possible raids – there are only two regiments of cruiser tanks in sight for Egypt by the end of May, and no reserves to replace casualties.'

On receiving this news, Churchill had conceived, planned and persuaded[1] his Chiefs of Staff to authorise Operation Tiger, a daring gamble by which the fast ships of convoy WS7, due to sail in two days' time for Suez by the Cape, were to be loaded with cruiser tanks and pass through the Mediterranean. The Chiefs of Staff had been unanimous in their recommendation against the scheme and in their forecast of the direct results if it were implemented. But the Germans were taken by surprise and the convoy passed through the Narrows on 8 May with the loss of only one ship.

By this bold stroke the whole balance of tank strength in the Middle East was reserved as the convoy contained no fewer than 99 Mk IV and Mk VI cruisers and 180 'I' tanks. Churchill, the moment the news came that the ships were safe within our own fighter umbrella, suggested to the Chiefs of Staff that one of them, the *Clan Lamont*, should make for Suda Bay and there discharge at least twelve 'I' tanks. But 'My expert colleagues, while agreeing that tanks would be of special value for the purpose that I had in mind, deemed it inadvisable to endanger the rest of the ship's valuable cargo by such a diversion.'

This was the third time in as many weeks that Churchill had been in direct conflict with his military advisers: the instructions to Admiral Cunningham to use the whole Mediterranean Fleet in bombarding Tripoli[2]; the decision to run Tiger through the Narrows; and now the

---

[1] For Churchill's own account of this see *The Grand Alliance*, 217–21.

[2] The correspondence, *The Grand Alliance*, 212–21.

case of the *Clan Lamont*. On the first two occasions Churchill had been vindicated, and his audacity been amply rewarded, but this time he compromised. He suggested that if it were '. . . thought too dangerous to take the *Clan Lamont* into Suda, she should take twelve tanks, or some other ship should take them, immediately after she has discharged her cargo at Alexandria'. This was not done. Wavell replied that he had 'already arranged to send six infantry tanks and fifteen light tanks to Crete'. However, these were not new vehicles drawn from Tiger but 'battered ancient hulks'[1] without proper cooling systems for the guns, drawn from the workshops without being properly refitted or even having their wireless equipment reinstalled.

It is one of the lesser ironies of the war that, after all the skill and courage that was put into the operation of Tiger, the results should have been so utterly negative. Even the small packet of armour that might have altered the scale of events in Crete was never sent, and the remainder was squandered in the ill-conducted Battleaxe offensive in the Western Desert.

In spite of Wavell's assurance, it is plain that Churchill remained uneasy about the tank strength on the island.[2]

All my information points to Scorcher [code name for the coming invasion of Crete] any day after 17th. Everything seems to be moving in concert with that and with great elaboration. Hope you have got enough in Colorado [Crete] and that those there have the needful in cannon, machine-guns and armoured fighting vehicles. It may well be that in so large and complicated a plan zero will be delayed. Therefore reinforcements sent now might well arrive in time and certainly for the second round, should enemy gain a footing. I should particularly welcome chance for our high-class troops to come to close grips with these people under conditions where enemy has not got his usual mechanical advantages . . .

And the following day: 'I am increasingly impressed with the weight of

[1] Colonel Farran, *Winged Dagger*, 84.

[2] *The Grand Alliance*, 246.

the attack impending upon Colorado especially from the air. Trust all possible reinforcements have been sent.'

Wavell replied that 'reinforcements include six "I" tanks, sixteen light tanks, eighteen AA guns, seventeen field guns, one battalion . . . etc' but he was, in fact, making the same consignment of tanks do duty a second time, though without making this clear – particularly as the numbers quoted had been slightly altered in this second reference.

Wavell, in contrast to many others who held high, or supreme, commands during the war, was an absolutely first-class soldier with great strategic acumen and tactical flair. Had he personally been in command of the island garrison, it is my belief that Crete would have been saved. Having said this, the immense burden of his duties at this time must also be emphasised. There was a more or less simultaneous emergency arising in no fewer than five separate theatres, each of which was the responsibility of a subordinate with military gifts markedly inferior to Wavell's own, and with which he had repeatedly to concern himself. In the Western Desert there stood Rommel, poised, it seemed, for a descent on Alexandria; in Abyssinia the campaign against the numerically superior Italians dragged on; in Iraq the revolt under Rashid Ali threatened to give the Germans access to the oilfields by the northern flank and collapse the whole position in Asia Minor; in Syria stood the army of Vichy France, hostile, actively co-operating with the Germans[1] and stronger in numbers and artillery than our whole army in the Middle East. All this was aggravated by disorganisation, the losses, the memories of defeat that followed the evacuation from the Greek mainland.

It may be asked against this background whether Wavell really believed that Crete could be held and, further, did he appreciate the opportunity that the battle might offer? One further pointer to his attitude, besides the affair of the tank consignment, may be found in his provision of artillery to the garrison. The only guns that were sent to them were captured Italian ones, together with some French 75-mm weapons. There was not a 25-pounder standing idle at the Artillery Depot at Tel el Kebir throughout the month of May, and while the question of supplying the Cretan garrison

[1] Halder's diary (GS 41) records that the French had agreed to give the Luftwaffe refuelling and overflight facilities.

was being discussed another thirty-six had been issued to the Australian Field Artillery regiments, which were in reserve at Matruh, in exchange for their old 18-pounders. Like the tanks, these guns might have made the vital difference to the battle – particularly as Freyberg had wired on 8 May that he had 'ample artillery personnel available, also sights and directors without stands'. But, of course, if Wavell was privately convinced ('Experience shows that German blitzes take a good deal of stopping,' he had written to Churchill five days before the attack) that the island would be lost, then his reluctance to supply the garrison with modern equipment is understandable.

As we examine the documents, the messages that passed back and forth between Freyberg and Wavell, the Prime Minister and the Chiefs of Staff and the Dominion Governments, it emerges that only one man, Churchill, saw the impending battle for what it was – not an isolated rearguard action, or even a battle which, for good or ill, must take its place in the pattern of the Mediterranean campaign – but a head-on collision, as he himself wrote, with 'The very spearpoint of the German Lance'.

Afterwards Churchill recorded that 'In no operation did I take more personal pains to study or weigh the evidence or to make sure that the magnitude of the impending onslaught was impressed upon the Commanders-in-Chief, and imparted to the General on the scene.' He even sent a special memorandum to Wavell to pass on to Freyberg, setting out his own views on how the battle might be conducted.

But the sheer weight of historical circumstance was against him. Just as two successive disputes over Tripoli and Tiger made the Prime Minister reluctant to force a third over the *Clan Lamont* and its cargo, so did the insistent tone of his recommendations to Wavell seem almost mild beside their parallel, and still more urgent, correspondence over the measures required to crush Rashid Ali in Iraq. 'I have consistently warned you,' Wavell was writing, 'that no assistance could be given . . . to Iraq in present circumstances, and have always advised that a commitment there should be avoided . . . My forces are stretched to the limit everywhere, and I simply cannot afford to risk part of them on what cannot produce any effect.' Two days later, 'Your message takes little account of realities. You must face facts.' Even after the military situation had been transformed in Britain's favour Wavell was still grumbling that '. . . in order to avoid a heavy military commitment in a non-vital area, I still recommend that a political solution be sought by all available means'. The Prime Minister, as so often, was proved right, but it is against this acrimonious background that the exchanges of Crete must be read. Here, in principle at least, they were almost in agreement.

And so, as the warm May days passed and the German bombardment of the island mounted in intensity, the garrison prepared: 'wired' themselves in; sited their captured Italian field-pieces; and awaited the men who had dropped on the fire-swept *glacis* of Eben Emael – the very flower of the Third Reich.

FOUR

THE FLOWER OF THE THIRD REICH

'The German air corps', wrote Churchill, 'represented the flame of the Hitler Youth Movement, and was an ardent embodiment of the Teutonic spirit of revenge for the defeat of 1918.'

In 1941 British Intelligence believed that there were 'up to four' parachute divisions in the Corps but, in fact, there was only one, the 7th. It had seen service in the Netherlands and, lately, in an almost unopposed drop on the Isthmus of Corinth. However, although one brigade had had bitter, though brief, combat experience at Schipol on May 10 and 11 1940, the division had not yet seen action as a whole. Thus, although it was superbly trained, there was a chance that it might be disconcerted by a resolute and ingenious adversary.

Hitler was obsessed by the idea of parachute troops. The very idea of these iron, ruthless men in their skull-tight helmets and strange futuristic apparel, floating down from the blue, loaded with death, in clouds of evil many-coloured blossoms – all this mated with the synthesis of Valkyrian mysticism and the original martial flair that characterised Hitler's attitude to military affairs. 'That is how the wars of the future will be fought,' he told Rauschning, 'the sky black with bombers, and from them, leaping into the smoke the parachuting storm-troopers, each one grasping a sub-machine-gun.' His thoughts turned constantly to the men of this, his elite division, yet he could not bear to risk them in any operation that presented a serious military problem. Thus they had never achieved anything that the conventional infantry and panzers of the Wehrmacht would not, in the fullness of time, have themselves achieved unaided. This, in turn, meant that OKH, the governing body of the Wehrmacht, was lukewarm about the parachutists and no additional divisions had been provided for. And so the wheel came round full circle – the very scarcity, the isolation, the elite character of the one existing division made Hitler all the more hesitant to risk it in a serious operation.

It was not until 1943, when he was already showing the first signs of bitterness at the 'failures' of his soldiers and the paratroopers were fighting as infantry – at Monte Cassino – that he paid them the highest tribute that was in his power. In a conversation with Speer, Hitler said, 'The paratroopers are the toughest fighters in the German Army, tougher even than the Waffen SS.'

But, in 1941, the Führer's reluctance to subject his favourite unit to a real trial of strength was a complicating factor in the formulation of General Staff plans. As early as 25 October 1940, after the cancellation of Sea Lion, General Halder, Chief of the General Staff, had suggested that 'mastery of the Eastern Mediterranean was dependent on the capture of Crete, and that this could best be achieved by an air landing'. Hitler dismissed the idea at that time, although he recognised the strategic importance of Crete and supported an appreciation, written by Jodl that same week, which suggested that if and when the Italians invaded Greece it was essential for them to occupy Crete so as to forestall a landing there by the British.[1]

However, during the winter the backbone of the Italian fleet was crippled by the Fleet Air Arm at Taranto, and such brief encounters that occurred with their surface ships showed the Italians to be timorous and incompetent. They had no air arm worthy of supporting such a landing, much less one capable of initiating and sustaining it, and their army had been severely worsted by the Greeks. Consequently, by March of 1941 it had become necessary for the Germans seriously to concern themselves with events in the Mediterranean.

A word should be said here about the background to German policy in the Middle East in this year. The most important factor is a negative one, namely, this: there was no real plan. Nowhere in documents captured since the war is there any evidence of a properly worked-out scheme, delineated stage by stage at staff level, for a campaign in the Eastern Mediterranean and Asia Minor. Instead, the whole thing was a make-shift of improvisation. With the exception of the campaign in Greece, which was little more than a pre-Barbarossa exercise for Army Group South, the military operations all bear the same stamp of inadequate

[1] *Entwürfe*, General Greiner, Vol 1, 167.

matériel, an uncertain flow of supplies and a succession of political compromises – with the Vichy French, the Arab League, the various pretenders and nascent puppets of Palestine, Persia and Iraq. It is the case that no individual of influence or on the General Staff, with the exception of Raeder, cared for the notion of a Mediterranean campaign. Hitler would speak excitedly of the swastika flying 'over the Minarets from Cairo to the Persian Gulf', he dabbled with the Grand Mufti, and flew in millions of forged English pounds to Iraq and Rashid Ali, but there was no system in these actions. This is because for the first time he was abandoning the strategy of the indirect approach in the exciting prospect of a head-on collision with the one remaining land-power, Soviet Russia. With this in sight, operations in the Balkans and Mediterranean became of secondary importance – significant only in so far as they safeguarded the German rear and flank. In November 1940, Hitler had written to Mussolini, '. . . I must have my German forces back in the spring, not later than May 1.'

The whole of the OKW was occupied with the task of deploying the 137 German, Finnish and Romanian divisions that were to attack simultaneously along the Eastern Front, and for Hitler himself the 'sacred' moment in his drive for mastery of the world had come. Now could dissimulation be cast aside, and the Bolsheviks finally liquidated and the Slavs reduced to the status of a huge labour pool for the services of the German Empire – '*Slaven sind Slaven*'. The result of this was that the attack on Crete must – however well planned, amply provided, and devotedly executed by its commanders – be, in a strategic context, a *Blitz* in isolation to which, if checked, there could be no follow-through.

There were, however, two factors – one strategic, the other personal – that influenced the decision to attack Crete. The first was the supposed threat to the Ploesti oilfields from Royal Air Force bombers based on Cretan aerodromes. This had already been a consideration at the time of the campaign on the mainland and was revived in reports from General Lohr, GOC 4th Air Fleet, to the effect that complete fighter protection could not be guaranteed from Greek airfields and recommending physical occupation of the island. The second factor was constituted by the taste and personality of the Reichsmarschall, Goering. The 7th

Parachute Division was a component of XI Air Corps and, as such, owed its ultimate allegiance through the hierarchy of the Luftwaffe to its Commander-in-Chief, Goering – even though for the purposes of a particular campaign it might be operated through the Wehrmacht chain of command.

Goering was as enthusiastic about the paratroopers as was Hitler, but less scrupulous over the prospect of shedding their blood. He was a law unto himself. He held, and frequently proclaimed the view, that the Luftwaffe was capable of fighting and winning campaigns without assistance from the Army. This theory had suffered an unwelcome setback the previous year in the Battle of Britain, and he was anxious for any opportunity to reverse the decision. The prospect of the Russian campaign held no great appeal for him for in that the rôle envisaged for the Luftwaffe was purely one of short-range co-operation with the Army. Thus, when, on 15 April, General Lohr submitted a tentative plan for an airborne attack on Crete Goering grasped it with both hands.

The plan was conceived by General Student, the commander of XI Air Corps, and had taken shape at a series of conferences during the first week of April between Suessmann, the commander of the parachute division, and the Chiefs of Staff of the Luftwaffe and of XI Air Corps. In spite of their preoccupations with Barbarossa and the Balkan campaign, OKW seem to have been favourably impressed by the decisive character and the economy of the scheme. For they had to consider that, secondary theatre or not, the Mediterranean was still commanded by the British Fleet, and the three fortresses that ran along the Southern flank of the Axis – Gibraltar, Malta and Alexandria – were still firmly held. Jodl and Keitel sent for Student and tried to persuade him that the energies of XI Air Corps would be more profitably expended against Malta. Student replied that 'Crete with its long northern coast-line favoured invaders from the air, while in Malta attacking troops would have to contend with a quick switch of reserve forces'.[1] Goering had put the plan to Hitler on the day after it had been received from Lohr (16 April) and while he was considering it he further encouraged Student to resist the suggestions of

[1] Student, *Kommando*, 312.

Keitel. Together he and Student discussed the possibility of a sequence of quick, 'leap-frog' assaults, of which the next was to be on Cyprus, with a final descent on the Suez Canal.

Hitler took five days to consider the plan. On 21 April he saw Student and Goering together and questioned them closely. 'It sounds all right,' he commented, 'but I don't believe that it's practical.'[1] Goering then became 'very excited' and expounded at length on the stepping-stone plan. However, the prospect of one commitment leading to another did not appeal to the Führer, and the interview closed with him unconvinced. Student was dismissed first, and flew back to Athens in a dejected state. But in the days following Goering continually raised the subject with Hitler, and finally his intervention – all the more effective for being, in matters of high strategy, so rare – was successful. On 25 April Hitler issued Directive 28: 'An operation with the object of using Crete as an air base against Britain in the Eastern Mediterranean'.

From this day the planning rapidly gathered momentum, and the allotment of forces grew in weight and diversity. Student's task in collecting and allocating units was greatly simplified by the presence in Greece of the twenty-six divisions that had completed the Balkan campaign under the command of von Brauchitsch, and the fact that Goering's support allowed a carte-blanche selection and rapid distribution of all units responsible to OKL, the governing body of the Luftwaffe. In addition to the parachute division, Student was allotted the whole of 5th Mountain Division and elements of 6th Mountain Division. He also managed to put his hands on an armoured regiment and a motorcycle battalion from 5th Panzer, an engineer battalion and two light anti-aircraft units.

Already under the command of XI Air Corps were nine transport groups, each containing about sixty Junkers Ju 52 aircraft. This robust, ugly, slow – the cruising speed at sea level was 130mph – and utterly reliable aircraft was the German counterpart of the DC 3 Dakota, which served the Allies in so many theatres. Designed originally as a bomber-transport, it was one of the very first aircraft to be delivered to the Luftwaffe when the arm was rebuilt in defiance of the Versailles Treaty in

[1] Student, Interrogation (Liddell Hart), 1945.

1935. It had been used as a bomber in Spain, and was still used to supplement the main bomber striking force, where no resistance was expected – for example, two groups from XI Air Corps had assisted in the unopposed bombing of Belgrade on 5 and 6 April. The chief use of the Ju 52, though, was now as a transport. In this rôle it could accommodate within its angular fuselage fifteen fully armed men or 4,000 pounds of freight. In the last weeks of April over 500 of these aircraft were hurriedly rounded up from the scattered airfields where they had been assisting von Brauchitsch's supply train and sent back to their maintenance bases in Austria for refitting.

Equally important to Student was the allocation to Operation Mercury – on Goering's personal order – of the whole of VIII Air Corps, commanded by Wolfgang von Richthofen, with its famous Stuka groups, trained in close support, which had spearheaded the invasions of Poland, the Low Countries and Greece itself. The Corps consisted of three groups of Dornier Do 17 bombers, two groups of the new twin-engined dive-bomber, the Junkers Ju 88, one group of obsolescent Heinkel He 111 bombers, three of single-engined fighters, Messerschmitt Bf 109s, three of twin-engined fighter-bombers, Bf 110s, and a variety of Fieselers and Do 17s without bomb-bays for reconnaissance work. Backbone of the Corps, and still the glamour crews of the Luftwaffe, were the 150 single-engined Junkers Ju 87 Stuka dive-bombers: the same dreaded Stuka, whose evil silhouette, high, square tailfin, fixed undercarriage and jowly cooling nacelle, had become a sign of ill-omen to refugees on crowded roads the length and breadth of Europe. The Stuka had things very much its own way in the first two years of the war. Once only in the opening days of the Battle of Britain did they meet with real opposition, and Goering had withdrawn them immediately. They, like the paratroopers, had been cosseted. Its slow speed, restricted ceiling and formalised bombing technique combined to make the Stuka so vulnerable that its use, like that of the Ju 52, was impractical against serious resistance. But the pilots relished their reputation as instruments of terror – many of them fixed special sirens to the undercarriage struts which emitted a fearful wail as the aircraft went into a dive. They seem to have taken a special pleasure in attacking defenceless open targets, such as civilian refugees, hospital ships and trains, schools, churches and so forth.

THE FALL OF CRETE

The Stukas were based on the island of Scarpanto. Phaleron and Eleusis were used by the twin-engined bombers. The Ju 52s of XI Air Corps were distributed at Corinth, Megara, Topolion, Dadion and Tanagra. The Germans estimated the duration of the campaign at ten days, starting with an assault on 17 May. However, due to the impassability of the roads and the non-existence of the railway system, it was necessary to bring the 2,500,000 gallons of aircraft fuel by sea in small boats down the Adriatic coast from Trieste, and the last consignments did not arrive until the 19th. The attack was accordingly set for the following day, 20 May.

In contrast to the efficiency of their material preparations, the operational plan of XI Air Corps was defective in a number of ways. The Germans were ill served by their own intelligence system. With a characteristic lack of comprehension for the sentiments of their victims, they thought the attitude of the Cretan population would be one of 'sympathy towards the Axis, or at least, of neutrality for the sake of better terms'.[1] Various attempts were made through Admiral Canaris's intelligence service to contact pacifist circles on the island. Again, in spite of constant daylight reconnaissance patrolling, the enemy intelligence picture of the strength of the garrison was highly inaccurate. One estimate put it at only 'three battalions of infantry, with 30 light tanks [the Germans used to call the Bren Carrier a "light tank"], 30 AA guns and about 40 heavy machine-guns with nine coast-defence guns in emplacements'. Even the most pessimistic estimate put the strength no higher than 'two infantry Brigades, an artillery regiment, and an unknown number of troops evacuated from Greece and of questionable fighting value'. Student said afterwards that 'our information about the enemy was scanty. Sometimes British strength was put as high as 100,000 yet our pilots reported that the island appeared lifeless.'

One must assume that it was on this basis that XI Air Corps formulated their plan for the assault because, on any other reckoning, it involved a very serious over-dispersion. Student proposed no fewer than seven simultaneous landings, and listed Kastelli, Maleme, Canea, Georgeoupolis, Rethymno, Heraklion and Askifou, in the centre of the

[1] NZOH, 84.

island, as objectives for the first day. This meant that the air support would be correspondingly thinner at each place and both von Richthofen and Lohr raised objections. Lohr wanted to concentre the whole weight of the parachute division, and the follow-up with the 5th Mountain Division, against Suda–Maleme. When Student referred the dispute to Goering, OKL advised a compromise solution which, on the basis at least of the defenders' estimated strength, held out the most promise. This was for a landing in the Maleme–Canea area at first light, with 'consolidation' during the morning, followed by a switching of VIII Air Corps support to the secondary landing at Rethymno and Heraklion, timed for 4.15pm that same day.

General Lohr divided the command of the operation as follows: he retained to himself the overall command of both land and air forces, which were themselves responsible to Student and von Richthofen, respectively. The actual attack frontage was divided into three groups: West – under Major General Meindl; Centre – under Suessmann; and East – under Lieutenant General Ringel. This meant that Group West and half of Group Centre would be in action on the morning of the assault, Group East and the remainder of Group Centre, not until the afternoon.

Lohr was still convinced that the *Schwerpunkt* must be at the western end of the island, against the airfield at Maleme, and he allotted it to Meindl, who was the commander of the crack 1st Assault Regiment. These men were glider-borne storm troopers, an elite within an elite, who were kept separate even from 7th Parachute Division. They had trained at Hildesheim, in Silesia, and they were not brought into Greece until 10 May, when the first elements arrived at Salonika by train. They were moved only at night, and with all badges and other insignia removed; their special equipment was moved separately in sealed containers; their paybooks gave no indication of the bearer's unit; and even the singing *en route* of their special regimental songs was banned.

The effect of this was that their use came as a complete surprise for, although the same precautions were enforced in respect of the whole of 7th Division, the difficulties of concealing the movement of over 12,000 men were insuperable. So from the profuse and invaluable reports submitted by Allied agents in Greece, there was built up a picture of the

German order of battle that was, with the one exception cited above, remarkably accurate.

The Assault Regiment was made up of four battalions, each of four companies. The 7th Parachutists and the 5th Mountain Division each had three regiments divided into three battalions and three companies to each battalion. In addition, the parachutists had an anti-tank, a pioneer, and a heavy machine-gun battalion. It was arranged that specially trained engineers would drop with the first companies, with the task of removing explosive charges, forestalling demolitions and salvaging captured equipment, particularly vehicles. This thoroughness extended even to providing for containers of captured vehicle spares, taken from dumps abandoned during the retreat in Greece, to be dropped in the first morning.

The parachutists wore leather jerkins and special round crash helmets with canvas camouflage covers. Every man had a greenish-coloured knee-length camouflage cape over his uniform and rubber-soled boots that laced halfway up the calf. They were generously padded at knees, chest and shoulders with heavy stitched rubber and canvas ribbing – rather like wicket-keeper's pads – which they discarded with their parachute harness on landing. The majority of men dropped with only pistols and long-handled knives as weapons, collecting their sub-machine-guns and heavier weapons from separate containers. They were organised so that each section had over double the firepower of a British Bren group, with one light machine-gun (Solothurn), eight tommy-gunners (Schmeisser) and two champion sharpshooters with special long-barrelled Mausers with telescopic sights to compensate for the limited range of the tommy-guns. The sharpshooters wore special goggles to protect their eyes during the descent. The companies from the anti-tank battalion were distributed among the infantry, and those in the first waves brought anti-tank rifles with them. These were useless against the 'I' tanks, but could immobilise the Mark VIs by knocking the bogeys out of alignment. They were also useful for shooting through the walls of houses, built-up parapets and so forth. Four flame-throwers and their crews were also distributed among the Assault Regiment, as were a company of heavy, and of light, mortars. Every man carried rations for two days, special Wittler bread wrapped in silver paper, processed chocolate and rusks, tartaric acid, sugar and thirst-quenchers. Each company had a portable water-sterilising apparatus, and provision had been made for supplying Group West with 1,500 gallons of fresh water a day by air. Besides a profusion of ordinary medical supplies dropped with the medical officers and orderlies, the NCOs carried hypodermic syringes containing a caffeine–sodium salicylate solution with which to inject themselves or others suffering from extreme fatigue.[1]

On their last evening the men were issued with beer and brandy by their quartermasters, 'and the bottles did not long remain full'. Then,

> As it grew dark we were transported in lorries to the airfield, where we were greeted by the ear-splitting roar of 120 air-transports as they tested their engines in preparation for the take-off. Through clouds of dust, we could see red glowing sparks flaring from the exhausts of the machines, and only by this light was it possible to discern the silhouettes of our men. Flashing the pale green beams of their torches in order to indicate their whereabouts, the 120 officers and NCOs of my battalion tried their best to make themselves heard above the thundering of the engines . . .

Although, in many cases, the men were not told their destination until they were actually in the aircraft, their morale seems to have been very high – with a few exceptions. Max Schmeling, the champion boxer, who later made great play of his exploits in Crete, reported to his commanding officer that he had a terrible case of diarrhoea, but the reply he received, though practical, was hardly comforting. ' "You can report sick, my dear fellow, when we get to Crete," I told him. "Our medical staff is flying with us." '[2]

The first of the transports were airborne shortly after 5am and as they rose out of the red fog of dust that covered the runways the men re-read

---

[1] The men were also supplied with pervitin, or benzedrine tablets, but apart from this there is no evidence to suggest that they were 'doped' – subjected, that is to say, to an unnatural degree of chemical stimulation. AC.

[2] Von der Heydte, 14.

to themselves the 'Ten Commandments of the Parachutist' which each had sewn to the inside of his pack. These were a curious, highly Germanic mixture of sentiment, mysticism and good tactical principles.

1. *You are the chosen ones of the German army. You will seek combat and train yourselves to endure any manner of test. To you the battle shall be fulfilment.*
2. *Cultivate true comradeship, for by the aid of your comrades you will conquer or die.*
3. *Beware of talking. Be not corruptible. Men act while women chatter. Chatter may bring you to the grave.*
4. *Be calm and prudent, strong and resolute. Valour and the enthusiasm of an offensive spirit will cause you to prevail in the attack.*
5. *The most precious thing in the presence of the foe is ammunition. He who shoots uselessly, merely to comfort himself, is a man of straw who merits not the title of parachutist.*
6. *Never surrender. To you death or victory must be a point of honour.*
7. *You can triumph only if your weapons are good. See to it that you submit yourself to this law – first my weapons and then myself.*
8. *You must grasp the full purpose of every enterprise, so that if your leader be killed you can yourself fulfil it.*
9. *Against an open foe fight with chivalry, but to a guerrilla extend no quarter.*
10. *Keep your eyes wide open. Tune yourself to the topmost pitch. Be as nimble as a greyhound, as tough as leather, as hard as Krupp steel, and so you shall be the German warrior incarnate.*

As the transports flew out across the shining Aegean they met the first of the returning bombers, silver specks thousands of feet above them. And then, after an hour's flying, Crete appeared. A thin black spine of rock in the blue, with smoke from the bombardments thickening the haze.

FIVE

THE ATTACK ON MALEME

The order of jumping was, first, Regimental commanders, then, Battalion and Company leaders, then junior officers and first-class parachutists. After them descended an immense stream of young parachutists.[1]

The Ju 52s came in very low, under 400 feet, and the defending New Zealand infantry could plainly see the aircraft's gunners in their positions amidships. They were in tight formation, three or five at a time, below the elevation of the 3.7-inch AA guns, but easy targets for the Bofors, which kept up a continuous fire, slamming out alternate tracer and incendiary until the barrels jammed with heat. 'They were sitting ducks,' a sergeant of the Royal Marines said afterwards, 'you could actually see the shot breaking up the aircraft and the bodies falling out like potato sacks.' When the transports reached the dropping zones the men spilled out, pulling the ripcords immediately, and the sky was filled with colour – 'like the balloons coming down at the end of a party'. Officers' parachutes were violet or pink, other ranks black, medical supplies yellow, arms and ammunition white.

And so battle was joined. Along the whole length of shore from Maleme to Canea and up into the hills of Akrotiri could be heard the shrill clatter of small-arms fire and the jagged slap of the mortar. The air bombardment had died down but the Stukas and Bf 109s cruised overhead, waiting for the recognition Vereys that were to assist them in identifying friend and enemy. Over the landscape were scattered the limp silk canopies of the parachutes, hanging from trees and houses, caught in telegraph wires, lying half-submerged in reservoirs and ditches.

The Germans landed a number of photographers with the first wave, and from their pictures we get a vivid impression of those early hours.

[1] Student, *Kommando*, 313.

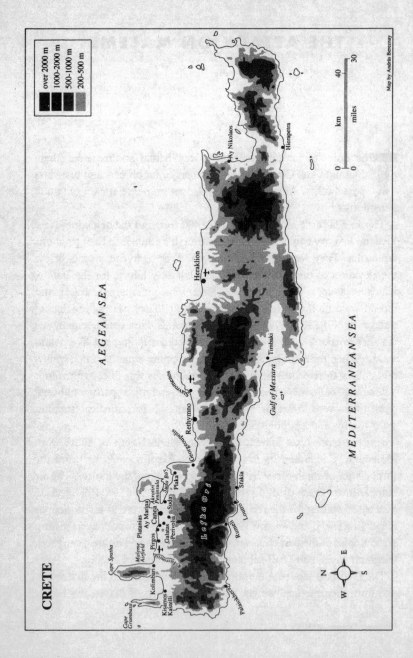

CRETE

over 2000 m
1000-2000 m
500-1000 m
200-500 m

AEGEAN SEA

MEDITERRANEAN SEA

Map by András Bereznay

km
0   40
miles
0   30

Cape Spatha
Maleme Airfield
Cape Grumbusa
Kolimbari
Kisamos
Kastelli
Platanias
Ay Marina
Canea
Pirgos
Galatas
Perivolia
Suda
Akrotiri Peninsula
Sud' Ba's
Plaka
Stavromenos
Rethymno
Georgeoupolis
Heraklion
Ay Nikolaos
Hierapetra
Timbaki
Gulf of Messara
Lefka Ori
Slakia
Rumeli
Louro
Palaiochora

The young parachutists, with their smooth blond faces, eyes narrowed to slits, stalking warily among the olive groves, searching for their officers and for the rubber-padded canisters that held their heavy weapons; crawling in file along steep-sided ditches, and over the glaring white pebbles of the dried water-courses that intersect the coastal plain. There are moments of desperate urgency as they break down the doors of houses, heap stones and timber against the windows, struggling to make the buildings ready for defence as the minutes slip past. Brief glimpses of elation as they discover and unpack the containers that hold mortars and heavy machine-guns; and of sudden confusion in the leafy olive groves – the first encounters, usually at point-blank range, with the defenders.

The Germans followed the same landing pattern as they had in Holland, but a copy of their parachute training manual had been captured during the assault on Ypenbourg aerodrome in May 1940, and its contents thoroughly disseminated throughout the British Army. 'The loss was never reported,' Student[1] complained. 'If we had known we should have followed a quite different plan.' This oversight was to have a profound effect on the early stages of the battle because as a result the enemy landings were directly and immediately opposed at almost every point. The only exceptions to this rule were in the case of those paratroops who were landed on the western side of the Tavronitis and to the south of Kolimbari. This area had, as has been seen, been left undefended by the dispositions of the New Zealand Division. Here dropped the II Battalion (under Major Stentzler), the IV Battalion (Captain Gericke) – which also included the two supplementary companies of the Assault Regiment with heavy weapons, anti-tank guns (20-mm and 37-mm) and some mountain howitzers – and the Muerbe detachment, whose task was to reconnoitre westwards to the direction of Kastelli and guard the invaders' rear.

These troops formed the western arm of Meindl's pincer attack on Maleme airfield. The eastern hook was made up of the four parachute companies of Scherber's III Battalion that were to land along the coast road between Pirgos and Platanias. The centre of this three-headed attack were the glider detachments of Major Braun and Major Koch.

[1] Student, Interrogation (Liddell Hart), 1945.

These great, square-fuselaged aircraft, with their immense wing span, had flown silently in at fifteen minutes before zero and landed along the western flank of 5th Brigade in the flat mud and shingle of the mouths of the Tavronitis. The pilots touched down wherever there was a clear space, letting the gliders plough on through bushes, olive trees and the shallow stone walls until their momentum was exhausted, and then disgorging their load of fifteen fully armed infantry, taut with the anticipation of combat. Other gliders carried 20-mm guns, partially assembled with high- and low-angle mountings for anti-tank work, motorcycles, trench mortars and flame-throwers. This compact, balanced force, the cream of XI Air Corps, with its command structure intact and the men landing not singly but as complete fighting formations, were indeed the very tip of the lance, and they had been assigned tasks which matched their quality: Braun, the seizure of the road bridge over the Tavronitis, and the neutralisation of the Bofors battery at its mouth; Koch the capture of Hill 107.

Each commander divided his detachment into two, but all four of them ran into serious trouble almost immediately. Plessen's detachment was fired on by the Bofors as it came in and one glider was set alight in the air, another being hit at point-blank range by one of the guns firing at zero elevation just as it came to a standstill. They also suffered severely from the Bren guns of C Company of the New Zealand 22nd Battalion which was dug in on the western edge of the airfield at a distance of 300 yards. Unfortunately, two of the Bofors battery were unusable owing to their situation for the Germans had crossed the coastline some miles to the west, then wheeled and brought the gliders in on a downstream approach where they were in dead ground to these guns that had a seaward field of fire. The personnel of the battery had been issued with rifles but they had no ammunition and were quickly overwhelmed when the Germans mounted their attack. However, in spite of this initial, if costly, success and a numerical superiority of nearly two to one, the Germans could make no impression against the resolute New Zealanders of C Company, and after the failure of his first assault Plessen himself was killed while trying to make contact with Braun's men to the south.

The nine gliders of this group landed exactly where intended, in the dry bed of the river just above the road bridge, but here they came under vicious small-arms fire from D Company in positions directly above them, the machine-gun bullets tearing into the canvas sides of the gliders and causing fearful casualties while they were still lurching along the ground. Braun himself was killed before he had even stepped out of his glider, and the regimental headquarters which had been riding with him was quickly withdrawn to Stentzler's dropping zone at Ropaniana. Under heavy fire the survivors made their way downstream to the bridge, and here they were able to take advantage of the dead ground screened by the Royal Air Force encampment buildings and to force their way across. They penetrated as far as the edge of the airfield and took a number of unarmed prisoners *en route*.

Major Koch had divided his group into two, each of about fifteen gliders, that landed on the two opposite slopes of Hill 107. But here, too, the spirited resistance of the New Zealanders was decisive. Instead of the converging movement that had been planned, the Germans found themselves pinned down by the defenders on the crest of the hill, who switched their machine-gunners energetically from one side to another. The group on the north-eastern side was also under cross-fire from 21st and 23rd Battalion positions on Vineyard Ridge on the other side of the Xamoudhokori road, and within a couple of hours had disintegrated as a coherent unit, although individual snipers continued to skulk there for days afterwards. Koch himself, who was with the group on the south-western side, was fatally wounded in the stomach while attempting to rally his men, and the survivors withdrew to the bed of the Tavronitis, carrying the body of their dying commander among them.

So, the situation confronting Meindl, the commander of Group West, who, at the age of 49, parachuted himself onto the battlefield less than two hours after zero was highly delicate and uncertain. The isolated encounters which had so far taken place had led to negative achievement and severe casualties being suffered by his advance guards, and it was plain that intelligence had seriously underestimated the spirit and numbers of his opponents. Still more disquieting was the news, or lack of it, from the eastern arm of the pincer – Scherber's III Battalion.

The fifty-eight Junkers of this group had come straight in from the north as it was believed that by then the glider troops and the preliminary bombardment would have silenced the AA. In the event they came under heavy fire from Bofors batteries at Pirgos and at the bridge below Modhion; several aircraft were shot down and the formations began to lose cohesion. Instead of dropping their crews in a compact strip along the coast road, the various companies were scattered over about four miles, falling among the terraced vineyards and the steep, rocky slopes of the foothills to the south of the coast road.[1] The units were too scattered to give each other proper support and, as their ill-fortune would have it, fell either directly upon or within easy range of the positions occupied by the 21st and 23rd Battalions.

'Suddenly they were among us. I was watching the 21st Battalion area and a pair of feet appeared through a nearby olive tree. They were right on top of us. Around me rifles were cracking. I had a Tommy gun and it was just like duck shooting.'[2]

The Battalion commander, Lieutenant Colonel Leckie, himself killed five paratroopers in those first minutes; the adjutant shot two without so much as rising from his desk. Many of the Germans had no idea where they were and their officers, including Scherber himself, had been killed in the air. Within a couple of hours the force was broken. Only the 10th Company, which had landed among the houses in the valley below Modhion, were still giving trouble, and even they had suffered over 60 per cent casualties – the majority of these inflicted by the machine-gunners of the New Zealand Engineers, dug in on the slopes just above the bridge, who picked the Germans off as they landed on the flat roofs and were still struggling with their parachute harness. Those that fell in the streets were harried 'by the entire population of the district, including women, children and even dogs; those Cretans would use any weapon, flintlock rifles captured from the Turks a hundred years ago, axes, and even spades'.

For these defenders the equipment situation was soon to be improved. Punctually, at eleven o'clock, the first of three flights of Ju 52s appeared and, after some uncertain cruising back and forth, dropped a large

---

[1] XI Air Corps report attributes this to the pilots' fear of dropping the men into the sea. There were also cases of unit commanders, alarmed at the evidence of defence activity on the shoreline, urging the pilots to fly further inland before dropping.

[2] Report by Captain Wilson, quoted NZOH, 123.

quantity of supplies, including a number of heavy machine-guns, hand-grenades, mortar bombs and a vast amount of tommy-gun ammunition – which was useful in keeping in commission the very large number of these weapons which had been taken from the enemy.

The effect of this repulse was that the German attack on the airfield had already been stopped short in its original form for it no longer had any of the converging attributes of a pincer, but must take on the character of a set-piece assault from one direction only – the western bank of the Tavronitis. And it was with an attack of this kind that the defending 5th Brigade should have been best suited to deal, in terms of its numbers, disposition and temperament. However, before examining the New Zealand reaction some note should be taken of the operations of Group Centre and their effect on the battle of Maleme.

Group Centre was numerically the strongest of the three, and its operations were directly commanded by General Suessmann, who was also CO of 7th Parachute Division itself. His assault on the Canea–Suda area was timed to be simultaneous with that against Maleme, and here also the German plan was for a converging attack from dropping zones on the two flanks, preceded by a glider assault whose task was to neutralise the AA batteries.

However, the gliders were fewer in number than at Maleme and their intended dropping zones were too far apart (over three miles) for them to render each other effective support, even had they been in greater strength. As it was, the northern group, under Captain Altmann, came under heavy fire as it approached the Akrotiri peninsula and the formation became scattered. Several of the gliders crash-landed on the rocky foreshore and those that penetrated inland found that the AA battery that they had been sent to attack was a dummy. Their crews were quickly rounded up by the Northumberland Hussars operating in tracked Bren Carriers, and they suffered over 50 per cent casualties in the first three hours. A few remnants held out on the rocky summits of the peninsula until lack of supplies forced their surrender two days later but, in essence, this threat to Canea, and to Freyberg's own headquarters from the rear, was eliminated by midday on the morning of the assault.

The second group, Gentz's detachment, had lost one of its gliders over the sea, but the remaining eight came down exactly within their target zone – the emplacements of No. 234 Heavy AA battery at a crossroads on the Mournies–Canea road. They overwhelmed the garrison, shooting all but seven of them,[1] and then attempted to fight their way south to the wireless station. Later on a counter-attack by a scratch force of Royal Marines drove them back to the battery position with heavy losses, and here they were contained during the remainder of the day. (During the night the survivors, three officers and twenty-four men, broke out and made their way south-east to join the main body of parachutists who had been dropped in the Prison Valley.)[2]

It had been the German intention that the main body of parachutists should drop in the Prison Valley, with a supporting drop (Heilmann's battalion) at Karatsos and the coast road. These two thrusts, along the axes Platanias–Canea and Alikianou–Canea, were intended to converge on and lead to the fall of the town, the capture or dispersal of Creforce Headquarters and the paralysis of the island's defence system 'at least by the fourth day'.[3] But the main body of transports had been routed over the Akrotiri peninsula and came under heavy fire from the AA batteries there. Instead of being dropped in a compact group on the high ground to the east of Galatas, Heilmann's battalion were scattered over the length of the range of hills Monodhendri–Karatsos and confusingly intermingled with the battalions of von der Heydte and Derpa. 'The moment we left the planes we were met with extremely heavy small-arms fire. From my aircraft we suffered particularly heavy casualties and only three men reached the ground unhurt. Those who had jumped first, nearer to Galatas, were practically all killed, either in the air or soon after landing . . . Approximately 350 men of my battalion survived the initial landing and organising period.'[4]

The German situation was further complicated by the death of

---

[1] Some accounts tell that men were machine-gunned in the slit trenches where they had taken refuge from the preceding air bombardment.

[2] Student himself tells that 'they went past the battle headquarters of a British general [*sic*]. In a critical moment it was the excellent English spoken by Gentz that won through.'

[3] Student, *Kommando*, 391.

[4] CSM Neuhoff, quoted NZOH, 142.

Suessmann. His glider, containing a large proportion of Parachute Division staff and their essential administrative impedimenta, lost its wings shortly after take-off and crashed on the island of Aegina, killing all its occupants. Command passed to Colonel Heidrich, CO of the 3rd Parachute Regiment, and in the brief but critical interregnum that followed the scattered companies of II and III Battalions suffered severely by adhering to the original plan and attempting isolated attacks on their original objectives.

It is interesting to note that the German soldier, for all his qualities, was definitely not at his best under these conditions. The undoubted bravery and endurance, the imaginative training and tactics of the German infantry were at a discount. Why? Because, it may be suggested, the orderly structure, the conventional military pattern which, however adverse, would evoke these qualities, was absent. The same men who fought with such incredible and heroic obstinacy at Cassino, Avranches, Stalingrad and Walcheren seemed by some alchemy of military circumstance to be altered in character – by the ingredients of a situation where the chain of command, the concept of the battle as a whole, existed only in obscurity. One observer wrote, 'They do not run to form at all. Some were so tough that they just never gave in, and having assembled in small parties, fought on hopelessly until we killed them. Others appeared to be very resentful of the reception they had had on the way down (they had been told to expect no opposition) and after wandering helplessly for 48 hours, more or less gave themselves up with cries of "Give me water!" '[1] It was just as Churchill had foreseen. The parachutists, for all their youth, their fitness, their indoctrination, the elaboration and efficiency of their equipment, were hardly a match for the grizzled, bomb-blasted New Zealanders or the valiant Greeks with their five rounds per man. It was only when fronts had formed, when the attack resumed a conventional pattern, that the innate superiority of the German soldier in terms of discipline, training and leadership of NCOs and junior officers could once again assert itself with confidence.

So it was that in the first hours and days the invaders either hung about in a condition of apprehensive indecision –

[1] Buckley, 176.

It was an eerie feeling, and we were almost relieved to hear the sound of fighting on the heights of Galatas, which were at least a token that we were not entirely alone in this hostile world. The gnarled, crippled olive trees around us looked like deformed and evil beings, laughing and mocking us as if to say: 'Go on farther, right ahead, you alien intruders! And the further you go, the farther you advance towards your destruction!'[1]

– or they butted their heads against the defenders' positions in a series of hopeless piecemeal attacks.

We advanced to attack the hill of Galatas [presumably Cemetery Hill]. We proceeded, without opposition, about halfway up the hill. Suddenly we ran into heavy and very accurate rifle and machine-gun fire. The enemy had held their fire with great discipline and allowed us to approach well within effective range before opening up. Our casualties were extremely heavy and we were forced to retire leaving many dead behind us . . . This first attack on Galatas had cost us approximately 50 per cent casualties about half of whom were killed.[2]

Earlier that day an isolated attack by the 7th Parachute Company on the same position had been beaten off with such heavy losses that 'the company ceased to exist' and its commanding officer was killed. Yet the position was held by no more than a scratch force of New Zealanders, the Petrol Company of Composite Battalion. 'The rifles were without bayonets, and five fewer than the men who needed them, and besides rifles there were only two Bren guns, one Lewis machine-gun and an anti-tank rifle. The men were for the most part drivers and technicians and so ill-trained for infantry fighting.'[3]

It is satisfactory to record that the same fate overtook the 10th Parachute Company, who had landed directly on the undefended area of the 7th General Hospital and 6th Field Ambulance. Here they forced the Commander, Lieutenant Colonel Plimmer, to surrender, and then

---

[1] Von der Heydte, 69.

[2] Neuhoff, Interrogation, NZ Div, 1944.

[3] NZOH, 158–9.

shot him. They also shot about twenty of the patients and forced the remainder out of bed, using them as a screen in their advance against the 18th Battalion positions at Evthymi.[1] However, they were completely isolated from the rest of their battalion, and as this became apparent during the afternoon many of them surrendered while, of those that attempted to fight their way across to the Prison Valley, the majority were killed.[2]

As the morning wore on the reports came back to Lohr's and Student's headquarters at the Hotel Grande Bretagne in Athens. 'My early impressions were that the start of the operation was favourable,' Student wrote afterwards. But this was based simply on the reports from the Luftwaffe debriefing of returning aircrews. These showed that the preliminary bombardment and parachute drops had followed the planned time schedule, and that losses in the air had not been too heavy. The crews of the Ju 52s were naturally not anxious to admit that their formations had been broken up, and that the drops had often taken place outside the area designated.

But 'later reports were not so good'. By 3pm it was apparent that only one substantial inroad had been made in the defenders' positions – the bridgehead on the eastern bank of the Tavronitis. And there were only two bodies of troops intact and responding to central control, namely the battalions of Stentzler and Gericke west of Maleme and the rump of Heidrich's 3rd Parachute Regiment in the Prison Valley. Suessman, Scherber, Koch, Braun and Plessen were all dead, Meindl and Derpa severely wounded. 'It was obvious,' wrote Student, and he was hardly overstating it, 'that the British were stronger and tougher than expected.' But at that moment there was nothing he could do but hold his breath and leave the conduct of the battle to the commanders on the spot for nearly half the parachutists remaining at the disposal of XI Air Corps were at that moment emplaning for the assault on Rethymno and Heraklion. Would the resistance there be as fierce, or had the defenders

[1] For a comprehensive discussion of culpability in this incident see Appendix III to the New Zealand Official History.

[2] On the coast road at this spot the Germans, with characteristic lack of tact, have erected a memorial to the dead of II Battalion.

denuded the island of troops so as to be able to concentrate at Maleme? And what might occur during the critical three hours while von Richthofen's Air Fleets deserted the Canea area to support the afternoon attacks?

In answering the last of these questions first, we must look at the handling of the New Zealand Division and in particular of its 5th Brigade.

SIX

THE CHAIN OF COMMAND

The pattern of the German landings, and of their repulse, meant that, even as early as the morning of the assault, the whole weight of the enemy force was impinging on the one New Zealand Brigade, the 5th, that was distributed at the extreme western tip of Creforce's front, on Hill 107 and around Maleme airfield. It is true that there was a large number of enemy in the Prison Valley, but they were hardly in contact with the defenders at this stage, while still attempting to recover their posture after the scattering and piecemeal destruction of many of their leading companies. The remainder of the detachments that had landed in the coastal region were no longer of any serious fighting value. Fifth Brigade sector was the only point where there was contact with the enemy as a coherent, centrally directed force, and in that sector only one battalion, the 22nd, was carrying the weight of the assault on its shoulders. The New Zealanders had been outnumbered from the start, and as the fresh troops from Gericke's and Stentzler's battalions began to come into action, after forming up undisturbed on the west bank of the Tavronitis, this disparity became increasingly serious. They had to withstand two attacks during the morning, each one preceded by dive-bombing from three squadrons of Stukas, and although they held their ground the position of the outlying platoons was gradually deteriorating. Under a blazing sky the men were suffering from thirst and exhaustion. Ammunition, particularly mortar bombs and hand-grenades, was becoming dangerously short, and the wireless batteries were running down so that communication between the different companies was becoming uncertain and erratic. Indeed, by midday the Headquarters Company had lost contact with its fellows although, with its more powerful apparatus, it could still speak with Hargest's headquarters at Platanias.

To the men on the western perimeter and on Hill 107 it was plain that the enemy was hourly becoming stronger and more aggressive, for his patrols now stretched in an almost continuous line from Ay Nikolaos to the shore. Through field-glasses the New Zealanders could see other groups safely out of range up the valley or over by Ropaniana. They were now under a continuous fire from the heavy mortars and mountain guns which the enemy had leisure to unpack and assemble, and receiving attention from flights of aircraft every ten minutes or so. All that they could hope for was the strength to hold their positions until reinforcement should reach them – a time which should not, at any rate, prove later than two hours after dusk.

In fact counter-attack routes for 21st and 23rd Battalions had already been reconnoitred, and the two battalion commanders, Lieutenant Colonels Allen (21st) and Leckie (23rd) had been ordered to hold themselves in readiness to move immediately to support the 22nd Battalion. Neither Allen nor Leckie, however, made any move to do so, and they do not appear to have noticed Andrew's distress flares, in spite of the fact that this manner of communication had been decided on many days before the battle. At 11.30 Allen sent out a reconnaissance party in the direction of the Tavronitis, but it was only a platoon in strength, and it is hard to see what it was intended to achieve. And even when this platoon returned at 4pm and reported that Vlakherontissa, deep on Andrew's southern flank, was strongly held by the enemy, this was not reported to Brigade Headquarters and does not seem to have been regarded either as a serious symptom in its own right or as a matter which came within the responsibility of 21st Battalion. Both Allen and Leckie were thus able, by confining their perspectives to their own immediate 'wired-in for all-round defence' areas, to send back to Brigade Headquarters messages (sent at 11.45am by 23rd Battalion, and 1.30pm by 21st) that the situation in their own areas was well under control.

Their policy of making no positive move towards relieving 22nd Battalion received official endorsement in a message from Brigade Headquarters, timed 2.25pm. 'Glad of your message of 11:40 hours. Will not call on you for counter-attacking unless position very serious. So far everything is in hand and reports from other units satisfactory.'[1]

[1] 23rd Bn WD NZOH, 124.

The wording of this message is very odd, and for two reasons. First, it seems strange to have relieved 23rd Battalion of any obligation to take up the rôle for which it had been intended, or rather of redefining this rôle in terms of a final act of desperation. Second, it shows a curious interpretation of the reports from Andrew and 22nd Battalion if these were really considered 'satisfactory'. As early as 10.55am Andrew had reported that he had no communications with his outlying companies. A further report at noon told of the almost continuous bombing to which the battalion was being subjected, and also mentioned the heavier weight of metal which the Germans were beginning to deploy. It should have been plain to Hargest, even at as great a distance as his Brigade Headquarters at Platanias, that the centre of the fighting was at Hill 107 and to the west of Maleme, if only because from all other directions the sound of firing was abating and it was in that region that the enemy aircraft were most active. Moreover, 5th Brigade with its powerful transmitters was being used as a sort of telephone exchange by outlying units, and throughout the morning was relaying requests for searching artillery fire in the region west of the Tavronitis and the road bridge.

As the afternoon wore on the messages from Andrew showed an increasingly serious situation. At 2.55pm he reported that his Battalion Headquarters had been penetrated. An hour later he told Hargest that his left flank had given way, and that the need for at least some reinforcement was now urgent. Finally, at 5pm Andrew asked Hargest point-blank when he could expect the pre-arranged counter-attack by the 23rd Battalion, which all his men were confidently expecting to come in when the light began to fail.

Hargest did not reply immediately, but came through about twenty minutes later to say that 23rd Battalion '. . . was itself engaged against paratroops in its own area.'

It is impossible to understand the intention, if any, behind this message which was a complete travesty of the facts. Twenty-third Battalion had accomplished great slaughter among the men of Scherber's III that morning, but by the evening its activity had been reduced to minor patrol activity against snipers. Whatever the purpose, however, this message had an immediate and disastrous effect on Colonel Andrew, who thereupon decided to counter-attack himself with such oddments as he could scrape together and the one trump left in his hand – two 'I' tanks, the only two west of Rethymno – which had remained concealed in an almond grove to the north of Hill 107 throughout the day.

Tanks, as has been earlier mentioned, were the one weapon against which the parachutists had no answer. Yet, as on so many occasions in the short history of the arm, the British ignored, or misunderstood, its importance. It has been seen how the provision of adequate armoured strength, urged by Churchill, was thwarted by the evasions and muddle of Headquarters in Cairo. And now, before the battle was a day old, the few that were available were to be committed, not as part of a concerted counter-offensive planned at Divisional level and executed in strength, but as a piecemeal effort by a harassed local commander. At a quarter past five the two tanks obediently started up their engines and trundled out of the camouflage pits in which they had lain concealed, setting off down the road towards the Royal Air Force camp and the Tavronitis bridge. They were at thirty-yard intervals, and almost immediately the leader began to draw fire from enemy small arms, the machine-gun bullets clanging harshly as they bounced and ricocheted off its armoured flanks. The sound of their tracks and engines were immensely heartening to the hard-pressed infantry, particularly to the isolated companies of Captains Johnson and Campbell that were still holding out, though in a sadly depleted condition, to the west of the airfield and below the road bridge. Both these units had by now exhausted all their mortar and heavy machine-gun ammunition and had been reduced by casualties to less than half strength, but as they heard the tanks advancing they believed that the counter-attack for which they had been 'keeping the door open' was at last being put in. Those still dug in above the Royal Air Force huts could hear 'The Jerries . . . shouting and screaming orders to each other all over the place, some of them tried to manhandle a small gun [probably an airborne 20-mm] into position, but we soon put a stop to that'.

Andrew's attack was from the outset gravely handicapped by shortage of infantry. The German breach at the road bridge had split his force into three parts, isolating Campbell's men to the south, the bulk of Johnson's on the western perimeter of the airfield and his own headquarters with A and B Companies that were grouped around Hill 107. He felt unable to detach men from this force owing to the strength of the enemy on this flank at Vlakherontissa, and the only men sent to accompany the tanks on their forlorn expedition were two sections of Johnson's company, which were detached from the main body, and six gunners from the Bofors battery whose English officer 'pleaded to be allowed to join in' – a total strength of twenty-six soldiers. They advanced strung out in a line with their right resting on the second tank, and almost immediately came under a withering fire from the parachutists who were lodged in the Royal Air Force camp and others who had crept forward along the dried-up drainage culverts that ran down to the canal here. After a few minutes the tank stopped. It found that 'its two-pounder ammunition would not fit the breech block, and its turret was not traversing properly'.[1] It lay still for some minutes, then turned and withdrew. Some of the attacking infantry went on in an attempt to catch up with the leading tank, but they suffered so severely from the enemy machine-guns that after about a quarter of an hour the survivors (only eight in number, the English artillery officer among those killed) were compelled to give up.

In the meantime, the leading tank, unaware of the developments behind it (it will be recalled that the tanks had been sent out from Egypt without wireless sets) pursued its course down the slope, through the southerly tip of the Royal Air Force camp and down into the bed of the Tavronitis. Here, for a few moments, it paused. It was under fire the whole while from the Germans on three sides, and was hit many times, although without effect. Then it turned right and crept slowly up the bank of the river, passing under the road bridge and crushing a mortar crew that were dug in under one of the pylons. Trundling on for about 300 yards along the gully, it gradually sank lower into the mud and finally bogged down. The crew now found that the turret on this also would not traverse properly and so they abandoned it.

So ended the only aggressive move made by 5th Brigade on the day of the assault, and in this way were immobilised the only two heavy tanks in the whole Suda–Maleme region.

---

[1] NZOH, 110. How it came about that these defects were not discovered in training or before the attack has not been made clear. AC.

The immediate result was that Lieutenant Colonel Andrew seems to have lost faith in his ability to defend his positions and, more serious, he decided to abandon Campbell's and Johnson's companies to their fate because he had been unable to make contact with them for several hours and 'it seemed probable that Johnson's had lost over two thirds of its strength' while 'according to one report' Campbell's men had been wiped out.

In actual fact, although they had suffered very severe casualties, both these groups were still full of fight and holding up an enemy force many times their number. Moreover, A and B Companies around Hill 107 were still completely intact. From the confusion of that evening and night – the broken wirelesses, the abandoned telephone logs, the conflicting evidence of survivors and the general fallibility of human memory – it is hard to piece together the facts of a decision which was of critical importance. From 5th Brigade Headquarters War Diary we know that Andrew spoke to Brigadier Hargest shortly after 6pm, told him of the failure of the tanks and warned that he might have to withdraw. To which Hargest replied, 'If you must, you must.'

Andrew later contended that by 'withdraw' he meant regroup on B Company ridge, which was a spur of ground below Hill 107 and overlooked by it. Even after taking into account Andrew's exhaustion, his disappointment at the failure of the counter-attack and his feelings of being abandoned by Brigade, the soundness of this decision is open to question. Hill 107 was the key to the whole region, and his men were already established there. A move up to a piece of ground unprepared for defence and overlooked by the Hill, for the sake of putting a few extra hundred yards between himself and the enemy, is hard to understand.

After thinking over Andrew's decision, Hargest decided to send him some reinforcements – two companies, in fact, one from 23rd Battalion and one from the Maoris – and after another interval he was in touch with Andrew and told him this. For some reason, which again has never been fully explained, Andrew 'expected companies almost immediately from the gist of the message' although he must have realised that the Maoris had an approach march of over eight miles, which they could hardly be expected to cover in less than three hours. The result of this misunderstanding was that as the evening wore on, with no sign of the promised companies, Andrew began to withdraw his men from Hill 107 and the eastern perimeter of the airfield.

Shortly after nine o'clock the first of the companies arrived – that from 23rd Battalion. Andrew, his own men now being grouped on the ridge below, sent them up to his former positions on Hill 107, his idea being to hold it as an 'outpost' while waiting for the Maoris to arrive. But the Maoris had taken the wrong turning on their way up and got hopelessly lost, getting involved in a battle with some parachutists who had dug in to a group of houses on the coast road and taking twenty of them prisoner. During this further period of waiting Lieutenant Colonel Andrew again changed his mind – the deficiencies of 'B Company Ridge', as it was referred to, being increasingly apparent. He ordered the company from 23rd Battalion off Hill 107 again, and to cover the withdrawal of the whole of the force 'into the lines of 21st and 23rd Battalions'.

In effect this decision meant giving up the airfield and the ground that commanded it. It also meant the final abandonment of the men fighting to the west. We are often told of the many occasions on which Hitler's refusing permission to withdraw aggravated the perils of his armies. But we hear less frequently of those occasions where a timid and premature retreat by the Allies surrendered to the enemy objectives for which he might have been made to pay dearly, or which a resolute defence could have denied him altogether. Certainly there can be few more obvious examples of this than the evacuation of the positions around Maleme airfield for by this one move the whole balance of force on the island was altered.

All that day the German parachutists had been desperate men. The incessant air attacks, the profligacy with which the parachutists expended their ammunition, the fact that being scattered they appeared to be more numerous than they were in reality, seemed, perhaps, to some of the New Zealand commanders to give the enemy a uniformly aggressive character which was not supported by the facts of his situation. For the parachutists had achieved none of their objectives; they had suffered immense losses and in an operation where speed of movement was essential they were still, on the evening of the assault, in the positions from which they had started, unable to penetrate a screen of one and a half companies of New Zealand infantry.

These men, the companies of Campbell and Johnson, which Andrew assumed to have been 'wiped out', were 'still full of fight, although their ammunition was lower than their spirit'. D Company, situation below the Royal Air Force camp and along the canal, was reduced to about forty, but 'the surviving men were in excellent heart in spite of their losses. They had NOT had enough. They were first-rate in every particular way, and were as aggressive as when action was first joined'.[1]

Campbell was confidently expecting his positions to be used as a hinge for a second counter-attack during the night, and when a Marine gunner strayed into his headquarters with the news that the Battalion had withdrawn he refused to believe him. It was not until after midnight that he and his CSM came upon Battalion Headquarters while searching for water and found it deserted. It was a great shock to the whole Company, and dashed their spirits, when Campbell told them the news on his return. He broke the Company up into three groups and sent them off to filter through the mountains to the south. Captain Johnson, whose position on the coastal side of the airfield was even more exposed and isolated than that of Campbell, held on until 4.20am while trying repeatedly with small patrols to make contact with any of the Battalion. Finally, at first light, he decided that the others had withdrawn and he also took his men down through the hills to 21st Battalion. The Germans were absolutely exhausted and offered no interference with either of these movements. Johnson made his men take off their boots and hang them round their necks, and as the men crept out of their positions they could hear the enemy snoring.[2] There can be little doubt that had Andrew launched an attack with all his companies that night, instead of moving them in the opposite direction, the line would have been restored and the enemy driven back to the western side of the Tavronitis.

Yet it is hard not to feel some sympathy for Colonel Andrew, disastrous though his decision was. He had received no support or understanding from his senior commanders. He had been left to fight this

[1] Report by Captain Johnson.

[2] Captain Johnson's report, quoted D 119.

vital battle completely on his own. Freyberg himself had fixed on
Maleme airfield as the danger-point as early as midday, and had allotted
his whole reserve (less one battalion) to Puttick to use in a counter-attack
there.[1] But that is as far as things got. Puttick's reports from Hargest had
been 'cheerful and confident', and he did not feel it necessary to make use
of the reserves. That night the copy of the Operation Order of the 3rd
Parachute Regiment, which had been captured during the afternoon, was
presented to Freyberg in translation and showed Maleme as the priority
objective. Even then there is no trace of any urgency either in the
dissemination of this intelligence or in the measures adopted to cope
with it. If Freyberg is culpable for his lack of incisive leadership, for
'suggesting' courses of action rather than ordering them, for 'offering'
reserves, the real blockage seems to have been further down the chain of
command.

A partial explanation has been offered to account for this by Major
General KL Stewart, CB, DSO, at that time Brigadier CGS to the New
Zealand Division. 'A striking feature of the battle,' he has written, 'was
the tendency for senior commanders to stay at their Headquarters.

'It was Brigadier Puttick's custom to fight his battles from his
Headquarters and Crete was no exception. There were occasions when
he authorised his GSO (Lieutenant Colonel Gentry) to make decisions
on his behalf at conferences in the forward area. Here, naturally, he was
under pressure from the various unit commanders and without such
prestige as Puttick possessed for enforcing his decisions. I do not suggest
that Brigadier Puttick's presence at these conferences would have altered
the turn of events, but I do suggest that his harassed subordinates would
have been glad to see him.

'Had Brigadier Hargest gone to his forward Battalions himself instead
of sending his Brigade Major (Captain Dawson) there might have been a
different story to tell. Surely he would have vetoed the withdrawal of
22nd Battalion from the airfield. Surely he would have launched a
counter-attack, and his presence would have inspired his troops at a time
when inspiration was needed.'

Those who followed the practice of allowing subordinates to fight the

[1] AOH, 225.

battle and take the immediate tactical decisions were only following the example of the C-in-C himself. Although Freyberg seems correctly to have appreciated the pattern of the German attack, there is no evidence that his grasp of the situation was firm enough to co-ordinate his subordinates, with their differing qualities. This negative character of his leadership had two results, relating directly to the qualities, or lack of them, among his Brigade and Divisional Commanders. The imbalance threatened by the German pincer, imperfectly developed though this was on the first day, was exaggerated by the hesitant optimism of Hargest and Puttick on the one hand and on the other by the vigour and urgency of Inglis and Kippenberger, the Brigade Commanders on the opposite flank.

Colonel Kippenberger, who the following year was to hold command of the New Zealand Division, was probably the best fighting officer on the island. He commanded the under-strength 10th Brigade, positioned around Galatas and at the neck of the Prison Valley – the flank route to Suda. They had been under considerable pressure throughout the morning from the scattered but aggressive companies of 3rd Parachute Regiment, but in contrast to his colleagues of 5th Brigade Kippenberger sensed that the Germans were off balance. He realised, too, that time was of the essence, that the hours were vital. Behind him was 4th Brigade, commanded by Brigadier Inglis, who shared his views. As early as 10.40am Kippenberger had been urging preparations for a counter-attack, and as soon as Inglis heard that he had been put under Puttick's orders he at once asked for permission to put this plan into operation. Inglis proposed to Major General Stewart, who as Freyberg's CGS had brought him the news, that both the 18th and 20th Battalions should be put in immediately, drive the enemy out of the prison and down the valley towards Alikianou, and that here they should wheel north (the route had previously been reconnoitred) and surprise the enemy on 5th Brigade front in a dawn attack. Stewart agreed that this was a sound plan, but told Inglis that he must put it up to Puttick. The orders could not come direct from Creforce Headquarters (whose representative he was). The two men then parted, Stewart returning to Freyberg and Inglis journeying to Puttick's headquarters to put forward his plan.

Puttick, however, 'did not like' the sound of Inglis's scheme. On being pressed, he said that he would telephone and refer it to Freyberg but made Inglis leave first. One may assume that when he got through to Freyberg, Puttick presented the plan in an unfavourable light. If he had believed that there was any likelihood of Freyberg accepting it he should have made Inglis remain while the orders were amplified. At any rate, shortly after Inglis returned to his own headquarters he received a message to the effect that 'General Freyberg did not approve the counter-attack'.

Thus was cast away the last opportunity of dislodging the Germans while they were still disorganised and, in the light of Hargest's inertia at Maleme, one that offered a good chance of eliminating both lodgements. As we look back we can see that this operation would have got underway while VIII Air Corps were occupied with close support for the landings at Rethymno and Heraklion. It was to be the one afternoon during the whole battle when the sky was clear of enemy aircraft. Most unfortunately, what followed was to repeat almost without variation the pattern of events at Maleme: a series of requests from the commanders on the spot, couched in tones of mounting urgency; vacillation and inertia at Divisional Headquarters; a muffling of reports from the firing line so that their full import never penetrated to Freyberg; and, partly owing to all these things, a strange absence of leadership, incisive or otherwise, from the C-in-C. Then, finally, the orders – but too late and for operations on a scale quite inadequate for any result of importance.

At 2.15pm Kippenberger, who had not heard of Puttick's rebuff to Inglis, again contacted Divisional Headquarters saying that 'a vigorous counter-attack would clear the prison'. After a local enemy attack during the afternoon, which was beaten off, Kippenberger again 'pressed for infantry with which to counter-attack . . .' At 5pm a report came through that some of the Engineering Battalion had been taken prisoner, and from this it was inferred (erroneously, it transpired) that the enemy was preparing a landing ground in the Valley. At this Inglis once again returned to Puttick and urged him to authorise some action. The most that Puttick would allow, though, was for 19th Battalion to go forward 'in full strength if situation permits' but otherwise with only two companies. To support them he allocated one troop of C Squadron 3rd Hussars, thereby halving in numbers, and almost eliminating in terms of effectiveness, the tank strength which had been patiently waiting at the fork of the Galatas–Karatsos road.

Even if 19th Battalion had attacked in full strength it would hardly have been adequate for the rather vague terms of the Divisional order. In any case, 'Puttick did not expect much from this attack beyond assistance to 10th Brigade morale and a cautionary lesson to the enemy'.[1] As it was, the attack was only made at half-strength and Colonel Kippenberger himself was not even informed of its coming. The first that he heard of it was when 'three light tanks of the 3rd Hussars came into the village. They said they were going to attack at 8.30pm, but they were not at all clear what their objective was.'[2]

The attack was late in starting. The tanks – Vickers lights and so vulnerable to mortars and heavy machine-guns – were held up for some time by an enemy roadblock just outside Galatas. By the time this had been cleared by the infantry of 19th Battalion, it was already dark. It was not for another two hours that the attackers were even up at the start-line in Kippenberger's forward positions, and when they reached there it was decided by him and Blackburn, the 19th Battalion commander, that the attack itself had begun too late, was too weak to be successful and should therefore be cancelled.

Colonel Heidrich, however, was by now 'in a state of some nervousness'.[3] Of his regiment, I Battalion was battle-worthy but exhausted and was too far away at Perivolia (he had sent orders for it to withdraw and help him to form a defensive front south of Galatas). II Battalion had had very heavy casualties, III Battalion was dispersed and in part destroyed and the Engineer Battalion reasonably strong but too distant in the altered situation he had already recalled. He felt that the initiative now lay with the defence and that a heavy counter-attack was inevitable.

In this Heidrich was assuming an opponent of his own temper, and one who would act promptly and forcefully on the simple principle that the initiative should be seized as soon as opportunity offered.

[1] Puttick's Paper, quoted NZOH, 168.

[2] Kippenberger, *Infantry Brigadier*, 57.

[3] From XI Air Corps report, quoted NZOH, 172–3.

SEVEN

AN ISOLATED INCIDENT

T wenty-six miles west of Canea, on Kisamos bay, lies the tiny port of Kisamos Kastelli. As has been seen, the ground west of the Tavronitis had been left undefended by Freyberg but it was felt that Kastelli, where there was an unfinished airstrip and whose single crumbling wharf was the nearest point on the island to enemy territory, should be granted some 'nominal' defence.

It was entrusted, therefore, to the 1st Greek Regiment, a motley collection of about a thousand souls, who had come from the town itself and the outlying hill villages and waited patiently outside the recruiting office some three weeks before, making their mark on the enlistment forms and then being packed off for some perfunctory drilling to a large disused factory that was their temporary barracks.

Their armament was pathetic. There were fewer than 600 rifles and for each of these only three rounds of ammunition. This meant that nearly one third of the strength were without firearms. Moreover, the rifles were of many different kinds and ages, and in many cases the ammunition supplied would not fit. Two antique machine-guns that appeared had to have their belts built up by hand from single cartridges scrounged from among the whole unit.

But these men had qualities which, as their compatriots had already demonstrated against the Italians, were worth many tons of military equipment. They had unquenchable spirit. They were fighting on their own soil for their own homes. Behind them was a whole tradition of mountain valour, of guerrilla banditry, of rock and field craft and marksmanship that ran in the blood. The men armed themselves with axes and curving Syrian knives. Ancient shotguns and flintlocks that had seen service in the Venizelist fighting were brought out, grenades were fabricated from dynamite, with scatter charges of rusty nails and broken glass. To stiffen this magnificent rabble there were also in the town a strong detachment of Cretan gendarmerie, their erstwhile opponents but now united in defence against the invader, and a few New Zealand officers and NCOs sent there by Puttick to 'train' the Greeks and bringing with them a couple of Bren guns and some ammunition.

These last were under the command of Major TG Bedding, a physical training instructor from Pahautanui. He divided the Greeks into two 'battalions', positioning them west and east of the town, and constituting the gendarmerie as a form of mobile reserve in the centre, to which he attached himself and his own party. He could hardly be expected to deny the port to the enemy for any length of time. His orders were merely to put up a token resistance and then withdraw to the south, making his way round through the hills to link up with the 6th and 8th Greek Regiments in the Alikianou sector.

But it was in a very different spirit that the defenders awaited the German attack.

Student had allocated Kastelli to the Muerbe detachment, a force of seventy-four parachutists under Lieutenant Muerbe, who had instructions to reconnoitre aggressively to the west, seize the port and report and block any move by the defenders towards Maleme that might take Meindl's troops in the rear. The parachutists were all in their teens and twenties. With the exception of Muerbe and two of his sergeants who had dropped at Corinth, they had no previous combat experience, but they were trained to the standard of the rest of the Division and were eagerly looking forward to the fighting which, it had been predicted, would be light as 'only a token resistance is to be expected from irregulars among the inhabitants . . . they have no heavy equipment'. In contrast, the Germans were equipped not only with their standard quota of tommy-guns and long-barrelled Mausers with telescopic sights but also had extra mortars and heavy machine-guns. It was arranged that there should be a supplementary ammunition drop at 11.30am in response to a prearranged code of recognition signals.

The Muerbe detachment dropped at 8.15am. By 11am there were only seventeen alive, and they were in the town jail.

From the first they had met with ill fortune. They had dropped in two groups to the east of the town, landing more or less among the positions of the A Battalion formed by Bedding. The Greeks killed many of them in the air, and then stalked those that had landed by creeping on their stomachs along the drainage culverts or behind the stone walls of the olive and almond groves that intersected the area. They knew the whole region perfectly, each fold in the dead ground, each well and house and cluster of bushes. When they were up on the enemy group, they would rise from the earth and charge. With no ammunition remaining, they would club the Germans to death or knife them. Within minutes Bedding and his party had brought up their Brens and could give some covering fire, and as the Greeks took the tommy-guns and Solothurns from their dead foe their own firepower increased by leaps and bounds. The Germans were in great confusion. Soon, as they heard and felt their own weapons being used against them, they started firing on each other, turning their mortars in the direction of the sound, once familiar and encouraging, of their own machine-guns.

Within an hour of their landing the only survivors were in a desperate condition, walled in at a cluster of farm buildings just south of the coast road, surrounded and under continuous fire. Bedding advised against a direct attack on the position owing to the firepower of the enemy, but the officers of the gendarmerie overruled him, and at half past ten the Greeks made a wild charge, chanting an Evzone war-cry. 'Casualties were heavy,' Bedding wrote in his report, 'largely owing to failure to use cover', but the position was carried and the few unwounded survivors made prisoner. Bedding thought it prudent to confine them in the town jail for their own safety, 'as a good many of the inhabitants were gunning for them'.[1]

In this way, a picked detachment of the Hitler youth – trained and measured to the last ounce, carrying every weapon that technology could provide, indoctrinated since childhood, whose machine-guns could fire at the rate of 300 rounds a minute, with five different choices of grenade and 2,000 pounds of tracer and armour-piercing ammunition per man, and special rations and stimulants and water and wireless and binoculars and rangefinders, and all the weight of von Richthofen's

---

[1] There are three separate sets of figures for strengths and casualties in this engagement. They only differ slightly. I am using the German, from XI Air Corps report. AC.

air fleet behind them – were, in the space of a few hours, defeated by the valour of those whose soil they had attacked. How different might the course of history have been if, a year before, the inhabitants of the West had shown the same fierce courage when their villages were invaded.

For two days the men at Kastelli enjoyed an uneasy peace. They had no communication with the rest of Creforce, and the BBC news bulletins were their only source of information regarding the course of the battle. During those two days, with the battle for Maleme in the balance, the Germans had no troops or any inclination for another trial of strength with the 1st Greek Battalion, but on 23 May some advance guards of the 5th Mountain Division, which had been landed fresh at Maleme in the preceding forty-eight hours, began to probe westwards. These were men of the 95th Engineers' Battalion under Major Schaette. That evening they encountered 'snipers' (the outlying positions of 1st Greek Regiment) and, presumably, they also came upon some of the unburied corpses of Muerbe's men because 'atrocities were reported'. It is likely that the Germans drew this inference from the fact that some of their dead had been killed, not with bullets but with knives and clubs, and they assumed that this had been done after capture. At all events, with Puttick's withdrawal to the wadi Platanias and the security of Maleme now firmly established, the Division, in the words of its diarist, 'decided to advance in all possible strength against these bestial hordes'.[1]

The following day, at 9.30am, the Stukas appeared. For over an hour they circled the town at leisure, machine-gunning the streets, stacking up in grids at 4,000 feet, and peeling off in a dive, one after the other, sirens screaming, to release their bombs. The majority of aircraft were dropping clusters of 50-kg high explosive but others were picking out the prominent buildings and aiming for them with single 1,100-pounders. One of these scored a direct hit on the jail and the prisoners escaped. They made straight for Bedding's headquarters, which was nearby and had also been hit, taking him and Second Lieutenant Baigent prisoner just as they were on the point of leaving to rally the garrison against the

[1] This somewhat melodramatic language should not be allowed to obscure the fact that an XI Air Corps Strategic Appreciation had now fixed on Kastelli as the only port that could be captured within a reasonable time where armour might be landed. AC.

impending attack. A rescue attempt organised by Lieutenants Campbell and Yorke was driven off, and Campbell was killed.

While confusion reigned in the centre of the town the Germans, now in considerable strength and supported by a number of anti-tank guns, were advancing from the east. Many of the garrison had drifted back towards the town when the bombing started out of concern for their families. The others soon exhausted their ammunition, and over 200 were killed in hopeless charges. By midday the Germans had fought their way into the centre of the town, and proclaimed its capture.

This, however, was premature. The B Battalion that Bedding had organised was still more or less intact at the western end of the harbour and around the jetty. With the help of the weapons taken from Muerbe's men, which had been distributed among them, they held out here for another two days while the Germans systematically blasted every house from under them with the anti-tank guns. It was not until 27 May – by which time the whole defence of the island had collapsed – that the few surviving Greeks slipped away into the hills, and the Germans had the use of the harbour.

Infuriated by the delay, and by the humiliation inflicted on the Parachute Division, Schaette declared that the Greeks were *franc-tireurs* and therefore not entitled to the honours of war. The Germans took no prisoners. They selected over 200 men from among the inhabitants and shot them in the square as reprisals for the alleged 'mutilation' of Muerbe's men.

This action is all the less excusable when we learn that both Bedding and his erstwhile prisoners-turned-captors assured Schaette that they had been properly treated. Later the Germans made a judicial investigation of the whole affair, and a report was submitted by the Chief Medical Inspector of the Luftwaffe. The substance of this was that 'Judge Rudel, a member of the enquiry commission in Canea, said . . . that all interrogations had revealed a total of six or eight cases of mutilation in Kastelli, about fifteen more scattered elsewhere, and only two or three at Rethymno. From all investigations it appears that no enemy soldiers had been guilty of mutilation. The crimes were all attributed to fanatical civilians. Judge Rudel emphasised the fair way in which the British and New Zealanders had fought; they had protected German prisoners whenever possible, and had saved them from the wrath of civilians, even going so far as to fire on the mobs.'[1]

The incident at Kastelli illustrates very typically the German character in war. Humiliation at defeat, at surrender to an enemy from an inferior peasant race; then the barbarity of revenge excused by trumped-up charges; then remorse, the adopting of a judicial posture, the magnanimity of the New Order.

This last phase was of short duration. Bitterness left by the repressions conducted by Schaette's group lasted throughout the war. The region was never completely pacified and arms taken from Muerbe's parachutists were still being recovered from dead guerrillas as late as 1944.

[1] Quoted in Long, 240.

EIGHT

EVENTS AT RETHYMNO AND HERAKLION

Rethymno was the point selected by XI Air Corps for the left flanking assault by Group Centre, 2nd Parachute Regiment under Colonel Sturm. Sturm's orders were that the airfield should be seized on the evening of the assault and that the whole force should then wheel right-handed along the coast to take the defenders of Suda in the rear. He had divided his large and well-equipped force into three. That on the western side, under Captain Wiedemann, consisted of the whole of III Battalion, two troops of airborne artillery (with two types of 37-mm gun, a long-barrelled anti-tank weapon and a mountain howitzer, and some heavy mortars) and a company of heavy machine-gunners. This group was to land in the village of Perivolia and seize Rethymno town. Sturm himself was to drop with his headquarters and one and a half companies in the centre, more or less on the airfield itself, where he could co-ordinate the converging attack. The eastern group, under Major Kroh, was made up of the remainder of I Battalion, together with the regiment's heavy weapon detachments, which included some flame-throwers and motorcycle combinations and another machine-gun company. Kroh's task was to march westwards against the airfield immediately on landing.

The whole made up an extremely powerful and well-balanced force that outnumbered the defenders, as well as far surpassing them in terms of equipment. For the area had been allotted to two weak Australian battalions, the 2/11th (West Australians) under Major Sandover and the 2/1st under Colonel Campbell, who was also area commander. The garrison had no anti-aircraft guns whatever and only seven mortars, none of which had base-plates. Their field artillery amounted to four old Italian 100-mm guns and four American 75-mm weapons that had no sights and had to be aimed through the barrel.

But the Australians had one great quality. They were free men. The comparison between the free and the indoctrinated regiment has been made so many times and in such differing and inappropriate contexts that today it seems a cliché with little validity. But the defenders of Rethymno were the genuine article, accustomed since birth to the independence, the quickness of reaction, the self-reliance that comes from life in range or bush. Men from a young and vigorous country, with the arrogant certainty of right, of the fact that victory would be theirs in the end. The Germans have no such conviction. They have won too many battles, lost too many wars. In their mythology there is always that dark corner when the limit of endurance is reached, when surrender cannot be avoided and may even be honourable, when the Valkyrian barque sinks beneath the dark waters of the Rhine and the souls are confined to that nether region of Grunel and Mephistopheles.

These moral factors were reinforced by physical circumstance. The Australians were perfectly positioned, while the German drop was muddled and, due to confusion at the airfields in Greece and losses that morning at Maleme, it got out of phase with the preliminary bombardment. In placing his men Campbell had ignored the town and given only light protection to the beaches. He regarded his primary task as denying the enemy the use of the airfield, and for this purpose the two battalions were sited to perfection on the two hills (referred to as A, the eastern, and B, the western) that rose on either side of the wadi Pigi and embraced the flat ground below and to the north of them on which the airstrip lay. Sandover's 2/11th was put on Hill B, Campbell himself and the 2/1st opposite, and between them were the two Greek battalions, the 4th close in and the 5th back in the hills around Adhele village. The town of Rethymno itself was left to the vigorous and well-trained Cretan gendarmerie.

The men were concealed so skilfully that when, on the 16th, a low-flying Henschel reconnaissance plane was shot down by small-arms fire the photographs it carried showed that only one of the defenders' positions had been located (it was altered forthwith). This excellent camouflage and the absence of anti-aircraft guns deluded the Germans into thinking that the area was virtually undefended, and when the preliminary ground-strafing began at 4pm it was a haphazard affair, directed mainly against civilian targets on a terror principle, and doing no damage to the defenders.

The strafing continued for about fifteen minutes and then there was a short lull before the first of the transports could be heard approaching. These, twenty-four in number, crossed the coast some miles east of the Australian positions at Refuge Point and then flew slowly along the shore to their dropping zones, drawing a tremendous fire from the defenders' machine-guns. As the minutes passed more and more Ju 52s appeared, but they were sometimes flying in loose formation, or even singly, and it was plain that the enemy timetable had gone awry. The drop dragged out to over half an hour and at its height there were counted 161 transports in the air at the same time, unloading and searching for their zones. Two collided and crashed and at least seven were shot down by Brens, which the Australians were operating from high-angle tripods. Others were filled with bullets at point-blank range and only two or three men jumped from them. Still others turned and flew out to sea, trailing smoke. Not only were the separate drops of the three groups out of phase with each other but in many cases there were intervals of up to a quarter of an hour between attacks by the parachutists on the same spot so that the later arrivals were jumping into places where they could see their comrades who had gone before already dead and the weapon containers lying unopened. This was particularly the case on the right flank, where load after load of Kroh's detachment fell directly on top of the eastern fringe of 2/1st Battalion positions on Hill A. There were four Vickers guns here, and they killed literally scores of enemy in the air. They used up their ammunition and the guns jammed with heat. Gradually, one by one, they were overcome until after two hours of fighting the Germans had eliminated them all and forced the surviving crews and the remainder of the infantry platoon that had been dug in there to withdraw over the crest of the spur. In spite of their losses, the Germans were in very great strength at this point because in the confusion of the drop two companies that should have been put down on the western flank jumped here instead, and as this was also the Heavy Weapons Detachment zone they had a profusion of mortars, armour-piercing machine-guns, light howitzers and anti-tank guns. The Australians counter-attacked at dusk but by then the parachutists had filtered down the terraced slopes of the ridge and kept up an intense fire from among the vines and almond groves. Two 'I' tanks were sent down the coast road to give weight to the left flank of the attack. Both got stuck when they tried to leave the road and the attack was called off.

On the two other sectors the Germans had much the worst of the day. In the centre they were forced to take cover immediately on landing and were so disorganised by their casualties that they never became a serious threat, falling back to a line among the dunes and tussocks along the beach. On the left they had also suffered severely and, furthermore, were short of the two companies that had been dropped in error in the 2/1st positions. That evening the Australians rose from their positions and drove the demoralised enemy back down the slopes of Hill B and into the maze of vineyards in the flat country around the village of Perivolia. They took a large number of prisoners. Once, in a clearing, they came across a complete stick of twelve parachutists, every one of whom had been riddled with bullets as he came down. From the dead body of a lieutenant they took the enemy signal code which Major Sandover, acting as his own GSOI, translated, so that the next day his men laid out the various requests for mortar and small-arms ammunition – in each case having their requests met within half an hour.

Thus it can be seen that at midnight the position at Rethymno had developed the same pattern as at Maleme. The Germans had been seriously upset by the strength of the defence and had been repulsed at every point save one, but at this point they were able to exert a powerful leverage and one which carried a threat to the whole area. Here, however, the resemblance ends for Campbell, far from considering a withdrawal in the face of the enemy strength at Hill A, could think only in terms of immediate attack on the enemy with the object of driving him off the crest at dawn.

Kroh himself was well aware that in this sector (he had no communications with the others) he was, due to the dropping error, over-strength but had, none the less, failed to reach any of his preliminary objectives. His men kept up a vigorous patrolling all night, which forced back some of the Australian outposts, and he, too, had planned an attack at maximum possible strength for first light.

So it was that a few minutes after dawn the two forces met head on in no man's land. The Australians were the first to start, by minutes only, and they ran straight into the intense fire that the Germans put down to support their own advance. They lost heavily and all their officers were wounded in the first 100 yards. A fierce enemy cross-fire aggravated the confusion and soon parties of parachutists had worked their way behind the Australian screen and were attacking their rear with grenades. Captain Moriarty, who had been sent up with another company and some Bren Carriers in case reinforcements were needed, found that the attackers had been driven back beyond their original starting point, and he telephoned back to Campbell that the situation was 'very desperate'.

On getting this news, Campbell set off in person for the neck of Hill A, taking with him the last remaining reserves. They followed a sheltered route along the bed of the wadi Bardia and their approach, which occupied about forty minutes, went unnoticed by the enemy. On arrival he ordered Moriarty to drive the enemy off the hill immediately.

Moriarty organised his force, which had now swollen in numbers but was still numerically inferior to the enemy, into four columns which attacked with great dash, bypassing the German positions on the crest and filtering round into the rocky gullies on the north side, each one of which was the chosen route of a separate column. By attacking in this way on such a wide front, and with such vigour and ingenuity, there is no doubt that the Australians deceived Kroh into believing that they greatly outnumbered him, and he felt himself in danger of being cut off from the coast road. The Germans were exhausted by their activity during the night and the failure, as it seemed, of their dawn attack. They had been further demoralised by an attack from a flight of their own aircraft, which had preceded Moriarty's advance and killed sixteen of their number.

By midday the German force on Hill A had been broken, many prisoners being taken as well as a large quantity of arms and ammunition of all kinds. The survivors of the enemy force drifted back to the coast road, where some of them were captured while changing into Greek uniforms. During the day the remainder were rounded up – among them the luckless Sturm, who had never managed to get control of the force that was nominally his. Kroh and those elements of his group which had not been cut off by Moriarty's attack withdrew eastwards to the headquarters of the Heavy Weapons Detachment in a large olive-oil factory at Stavromenos.

Throughout the day the enemy on the left flank made no move against Hill B or to assist their comrades north of the airfield, but contented themselves with digging in around the village of Perivolia.

Thus, on the evening of the 21st Campbell had every reason to congratulate himself. The enemy force had been split into two groups, both of which were unable to give each other mutual support, and the threat to the airfield had been removed. He ordered that on the following day the two remaining enemy lodgements should be eliminated.

It was planned to assault the olive-oil factory at 10am after a short bombardment by the 75s, but as zero hour approached Captain Moriarty, who was to lead the attack, was killed by a sniper while doing a final reconnaissance. Observation showed that the 75-mm ammunition was proving too feeble to do much damage to the factory walls and Campbell postponed the attack until the evening. To strengthen it he had brought up over 200 Greeks from the 5th Greek Battalion who were to make a charge from the south simultaneously with the Australians coming in from the west. But at the appointed hour the Greeks did not move, although the Australians played their part. The result was that this attack also was a failure. It was plain that the Germans, with their greatly superior firepower and functioning now as a compact force under unified command, were still formidable – in a defensive rôle at least.

On the other side of the airfield the 2/11th were having much the same experience. With the help of some captured enemy mortars they forced back the German outpost line, dislodging the paratroopers one by one from the scattered houses that they were holding on the eastern outskirts of Perivolia. During the afternoon the Australians laid out a signal asking for bombs on the village and the Stukas obliged at 5pm. But as the Germans fell back the 2/11th found the ground became more and more unsuited to infantry attacks with the small numbers at their disposal. The Germans were resting their right flank on St George's Church, a huge structure of granite blocks surrounded by a stone wall, and from here they could sweep the open ground that fell away towards Perivolia while from observation points in its tower they could draw warning of any preparations for a fresh attack.

Like the olive-oil factory in the east, this building was to hem in the

ABOVE General Bernard Freyberg addressing Australian troops on Crete before the German attack. *(IWM HU 17833)*

BELOW German troops in Greece prepare for embarkation onto Junkers Ju52 transport aircraft. *(IWM HU 39539)*

ABOVE Two Ju 52s sweep over Crete as they prepare to disgorge their paratroopers; they were slow, lumbering aircraft, highly vulnerable to ground fire. *(Süddeutscher Verlag)*

RIGHT One German paratrooper's view of another as both land near Heraklion. *(Süddeutscher Verlag)*

OPPOSITE ABOVE A Ju 52 goes down in flames over Heraklion: initial German losses of both aircraft and men were high. *(IWM A4143)*

OPPOSITE BELOW A Royal Air Force reconnaissance photograph of Maleme airfield: the landing ground is strewn with wrecked German aircraft. *(IWM CM 879)*

OPPOSITE ABOVE Colonel Bruno Bräuer, commander of the German 1st Parachute Regiment, directing operations at Heraklion. Note the habitual cigarette holder. *(IWM MH 12797)*

OPPOSITE BELOW German paratroopers assembling and checking their equipment in a Cretan olive grove. *(Ullstein)*

ABOVE Setting up a heavy machine-gun: the attacking German forces were lavishly supplied with such weapons. *(IWM MH 12853)*

LEFT British troops on Crete. Much of their equipment had been abandoned during the evacuation from Greece. *(Camera Press)*

OPPOSITE ABOVE German paratroopers on the attack: two grenades have just exploded in front of them. *(Süddeutscher Verlag)*

OPPOSITE BELOW British prisoners under guard: some 18,000 Allied troops were left on the island. *(Bundesarchiv)*

LEFT A column of British and Commonwealth troops retreats towards Crete's southern coast and evacuation at Sfakia.

BELOW British shipping burns in Suda Bay, where it was repeatedly bombed by the Luftwaffe. *(Camera Press)*

ABOVE Some of the 15,000 Allied troops evacuated from Crete arrive at a quayside in Egypt. *(Camera Press)*

BELOW German forces marching through Heraklion after its capture. *(Ullstein)*

Australians with their light infantry weapons, while at other points, and by other men, the mastery of Crete was decided.

Even so, and in spite of their handicaps – weak in numbers, in ammunition, in food and in armament – the Australians never lost the initiative. Every day they attempted an attack. They brought over two anti-tank guns captured from the Heavy Weapons Detachment at Hill A and used them to systematically reduce the church with armour-piercing ammunition. On the 26th, the very day that Freyberg told Wavell that the men under his command had reached the limit of their endurance, they finally captured the olive-oil factory after manhandling their 75s into positions where the remaining shells could be fired off at point-blank range. On the following day, after storming the church, they had transferred their remaining strength – including the two 'I' tanks, now repaired and manned by Bren Carrier crews – and were attempting a final attack on Perivolia.

The tanks broke down again, and the two attacking forces got separated, but some idea of the spirit of the men who were engaged can be gained from this account of Captain Honner, a company commander with the 2/11th:

> [One platoon had broken into the German position, but was now cut off] . . . that left me only one thing to do – attack to help Roberts out of trouble or to complete the success he had started. I knew I'd have to lose men, but I couldn't lose time. A section from 14 Platoon, nine men, was ordered to move to a low stone wall fifty yards ahead round a well about twenty-five yards from the German front line, to cover with Bren fire our attack across the open. They raced along the low hedge to the well. The leader, Corporal Tom Willoughby, was nearly there before he fell. The man carrying the Bren went down. Someone following picked it up and went on until he was killed and so the gun was relayed until it almost reached the well in the hands of the last man, and he too was killed as he went down with it. Eight brave men died there – Corporal Willoughby, Lance Corporal Dowsett, Privates Brown, Elvy, Fraser, Green, McDermid and White. The ninth man, Private Proud, was hit on the tin hat as he jumped up and fell back stunned into the ditch.

91

The walled town of Heraklion, a centre of Minoan civilisation, lying below Dicte, the birthplace of Zeus, is the largest settlement on the island of Crete. In 1941 it also possessed the most comprehensive port facilities and the best aerodrome, with a four-directional runway pattern.

The defenders were under the command of Brigadier Chappel, and amounted in numbers to almost a division's strength, though lacking heavy arms in any quantity. There were three first-class battalions of British regulars, the 2nd Black Watch, the 2nd Yorks and Lancs, the 2nd Leicesters, and two Australian, the 2/4th and the 7th Medium Regiment, armed as infantry. There were also three Greek battalions. Brigadier Chappel adopted the same plan as had Campbell at Rethymno, ignoring the town (or rather entrusting it to the Greeks) and concentrating his best troops around the airfield.

The whole area of the airfield and port is completely dominated by two hills that rise steeply from the plain at about a thousand yards' distance from the coast road, and it was upon these two, nicknamed East Hill and The Charlies, that the defence of the region was hung. Twelve Bofors were dug into pits around the airfield perimeter, and all the field guns (nine 100-mm and four 75-mm) were ranged onto it and grouped to the south-west, under the lee of The Charlies. Chappel had placed his two 'I' tanks one at each end of the airfield and his six light tanks at the tip of East Hill with instructions to move out and attack the enemy the moment he landed.

It can thus be seen that the whole essence of this intelligently planned defence was that of concentration and aggressive reaction at the decisive point – a very different policy to that adopted at Maleme. This contrast was emphasised by Chappel's orders that the defenders were not to give away their position by firing until the Germans had actually landed in strength.

Against Heraklion the first wave of Group East consisted of four battalions – the whole of the 1st Parachute Regiment commanded by Colonel Brauer, who also held overall command on the first day, and II Battalion of the 2nd Parachute Regiment with some supporting heavy units and an anti-aircraft machine-gun company.

Shortly after four o'clock on 20 May the intermittent ground-strafing, which had started at dawn, began rapidly to gather in weight and intensity. Soon over fifty Stukas could be counted in the air, stacking up for their dives or reforming in squadrons before returning to their fields at Scarpanto. However, due in large part to the effective positioning and camouflage of the defenders, the bombardment, though noisy and nerve-racking, did little other than warn them to expect the parachutists at any moment[1] (news had already been received of the morning's drops at the eastern end of the island).

It was not until 5pm that the first of the Ju 52s appeared. They came in from the north-east and followed the coastline to their dropping zones. An Australian corporal has described how

> I was spell-bound by the futuristic nature and the magnificence of the scene before me. It wasn't long before they were coming in along about five miles of coastline and as far as the eye could see they were still coming. They were about 100 feet above the water and rose to about 250 feet as they came over, dropping their parachutists, dived again and turned back to sea. I saw many Huns drop like stones when their parachutes failed to open. I saw one carried out to sea trailing behind the plane with his parachute caught in the tail. The men all had black 'chutes; ammunition and guns were dropped in white ones.[2]

In addition to the Australian Bofors, there were some 3-inch naval AA and some pom-poms manned by Royal Marines. All the guns were 'sited to perfection' and did considerable execution among the cumbersome transports. At least fifteen wrecks were counted that evening and it is probable that a further 200 among the attackers were killed as they dangled from their parachutes or while they still struggled to free themselves on the ground. Less than three hours remained before dusk and the departure of von Richthofen's squadrons, and in that short period the Germans found

---

[1] The effect of air attack on the defenders of Crete, in general, has been much emphasised, particularly by General Freyberg in his report on the battle, but this is not borne out in all the reports of *particular* instances. For example, the Australian Official History records that in the 2/4th Battalion, 'no man was struck by a bomb fragment or a bullet fired from the air during the whole operation at Heraklion'. This foreshadowed what came to be a general experience of those attacking trained infantry in mountainous territory as, eg, the Allies in Italy or, still later, in Korea.

[2] Corporal NM Johnstone.

their confusion multiplying. Losses among the Ju 52s had already been so heavy that over 600 men of Group East had to be left behind. Many of the transports, which had already made several runs to Maleme during the morning, broke down while taxiing and had to be manhandled out of the way. Refuelling was slow, and blinding dust rose in clouds and obscured the runways. Co-ordination was lacking between fighters and transports, which were being sent off in the wrong order and late. The effect of this on the German landing pattern was very serious. For example, the drop of I Battalion was stretched out over two and a half hours. Half of them were put out more or less over the positions of the Black Watch on East Hill, where the 'configuration of the ground necessitated jumping at 200 metres'[1] and suffered severely from rifle and Bren fire as they floated down. All the officers except Captain Burckhardt were killed during or soon after the landing. The other hand of the Battalion fared even worse, falling on Buttercup Field, an open space immediately to the west of the aerodrome, and enfiladed by the positions of the 2/4th Australians dug in around The Charlies. Within twenty minutes the group had been annihilated. Only five men escaped, by swimming along the coast and joining the remnants of Burckhardt's companies at East Beach.

The I/1st Battalion was landed too far to the east, and during its approach march was unaware of the fate of its sister unit. Colonel Brauer, the commander, found his task further complicated by the fact that only one company was landed at the right time and he and his staff did not themselves arrive until nearly three hours after zero. He had immediately set off with what men he could muster, but it was not until one o'clock on the morning of the 21st that Brauer reached the edge of the East Wadi, and here he came upon not the II/1st Battalion which it was his purpose to reinforce but the vigorous and well-directed fire of the Black Watch. In the darkness only one German platoon, that commanded by Count Blucher, managed to filter round the spur of East Hill and establish itself within range of the airfield.

On the western side of the town the III/1st Battalion had landed late and widely dispersed. A portion of it under Major Schulz penetrated during the late evening as far as the town wall where they were held at

[1] XI Air Corps Report.

bay by the Greek garrison. The II/2nd Battalion was only landed at half-strength (two companies had to be left in Greece owing to the shortage of transports) and in an undefended area some miles to the west. They took no part in the fighting on the first day.

The effect of this was that the Germans had neither the number nor the cohesion required to press their original attack plan. None the less, Brauer, without the authority to modify these instructions, set about improvising a concentric attack in obedience to them. The evident strength of the Black Watch persuaded him that to delay this attack, even for hours, might be fatal, and so the Germans came in piecemeal during the night instead of waiting for the day and air support. On the western flank Schulz had been sent a message 'to attack airfield Heraklion with all available forces' but this does not seem to have been received, in spite of having been transmitted by wireless every fifteen minutes. However, Schulz did intercept a VIII Air Corps signal to the effect that Heraklion was to be attacked between nine and ten on the morning of the 21st and decided to delay his own assault until after this bombardment. By that time Brauer had accepted defeat at the hands of the Black Watch and withdrawn his men to the high ground on the far side of East Wadi, and a sortie with the 'I' tanks had killed Blucher and eliminated the small lodgement that his platoon had made.

Von Richthofen's squadrons duly appeared at 10am and ranged un-opposed over the town for over an hour, but when Schulz came in to the attack, he found that the bombing had made little impression on the defenders. The Germans attacked in two columns – that under Becker through the North Gate, with the harbour as its objective, and that commanded by Egger through the West Gate. Becker made some progress in the first hours. His men fought their way through to the quay and occupied the old Venetian Fort, but Egger's detachment soon became dispersed by heavy street fighting against the Greek population – themselves well armed with German weapons that had been distributed during the night. A succession of fierce counter-attacks drove them across the town and up against the remnants of Becker's men at the western end of the harbour. Here, claims XI Air Corps Report, 'A major of the Greek Army offered the surrender of the town, but the British forced the Greeks to fight on, and advanced with strong forces from the east and south [in actual fact a platoon of the Leicesters and a platoon of the Yorks and Lancs]. Because of lack of ammunition the battalion was forced, under cover of darkness, to fall back to its starting place west of the town.'

With this defeat, on the evening of 22 May, the failure of the German assault on Heraklion was complete. For the following four days, until the outcome of the critical battle at Maleme was certain, the parachutists at Heraklion made no aggressive move, contenting themselves with reprisals against those of the civilian population that were in their area and issuing ultimata to the effect that the town would be 'destroyed' unless it surrendered forthwith. The Luftwaffe was active, making bombing attacks on the town at least twice a day, but the 2/4th Australians had captured a number of German Vereys and broken their signal code, so attacks and supply-dropping in the combat area were confused[1] and in some places discontinued completely.

By the evening of the third day the Heraklion garrison had buried over 1,300 Germans. Their own dead[2] amounted to less than fifty, and to the numerical ascendancy with which they had started the battle (eight battalions against two) were added a quantity of excellent equipment and a tremendous rise in morale. Unfortunately, this impetus seems to have petered out in the days that followed, which saw little action on a scale wider than mere patrolling. Two 'I' tanks[3] that had made the journey over the hills from Timbaki were loaded onto a lighter and sent to Suda Bay, but for four days the large, victorious force at Heraklion stood idle. Creforce HQ, hampered by poor communication and preoccupied by the urgency of the struggle in its own vicinity, seems to have overlooked the

[1] For example, the 2/4th asked for, and received, 'machine-guns, wireless sets, mortars, a motor-cycle and side car, chairs and tables, a tent, and much food and ammunition'. AOH, 284.

[2] Australian and British units only. No figures are available for the Greek forces.

[3] It is interesting to note the very different performances of these two tanks from the other 'I' tanks on the island. They made the difficult journey over the mountain from Timbaki on their own tracks, and were then sent by sea to Suda. Here they became involved immediately in the retreat, and covered the different rearguard actions that were fought on the hill road that wound back to Sfakia. They received no maintenance whatever, yet functioned perfectly until the end when they were scuttled by their own crews. The contrast is easily explained – these were the only *new* tanks (from the Tiger convoy) on the island. In this light it is of interest to speculate on the outcome had Churchill's wishes been followed.

potentials of the situation at Heraklion (namely an elimination of the enemy between that town and Rethymno and a linking up of the two forces), and in the absence of clear instructions Brigadier Chappel seems to have confined his own perspective to that of the orders given him before the battle developed.

On the night of the 26th/27th Chappel asked Freyberg, through Cairo, whether he should attack and open the road to the west or the south. But by that time the main issues had already been decided elsewhere.

NINE

THE SECOND DAY AT MALEME

The headquarters of XI Air Corps were at the Hotel Grande Bretagne in Athens, and it was to this place that, during the late evening and night of 20 May, the first detailed reports on the course of the battle were brought. No feat of imaginative power is required to picture the scene in those ornate, rococo suites, with their high ceilings and Edwardian décor, the long trestle tables stretching across the floor, the wall maps hanging from gilt cornices, the heavy nineteenth-century furniture strewn with telephone apparatus, duplicating machinery, papers of every kind and developing baths for the aerial photographs that arrived hourly.

It was in three rooms on the second floor looking out on the square that the actual Oberkommando was situated. Here were Student, his intelligence officer, Major Reinhardt, and two ADCs. On that evening there were also present Lohr, commander of IV Air Fleet, with overall responsibility for the whole operation, and Ringel, commander of 5th Mountain Division, and their ADCs.

In his writings, and under interrogation after the war, Student has described his feelings at this time, and the tension that pervaded the conference. The air was heavy with foreboding. Student could assume from the number of senior commanders who had already been reported as killed or seriously wounded that his losses were very heavy. The beloved Assault Regiment, the very elite of the 7th Parachute Division itself, had been virtually annihilated. Of the gliders that landed at Akrotiri and Galatas, there was no news. Aircraft reported that there was 'no sign of concerted activity' in these areas. He knew that Plessen, Braun and Koch had all been killed at Maleme, that the divisional commander and his entire staff had perished and that one complete battalion (Scherber's) had simply disappeared. From air observation it was clear that any men who remained in the area of the shore from

Pirgos to Canea were scattered and without leadership, and the units at Maleme and the Prison Valley had failed to attain their objectives. Student had one hope remaining that afternoon – that the unforeseen strength of the defence against Group West meant that Heraklion and Rethymno had been left unprotected – but now this assumption was shown to have been groundless. The attack on both these places had been stopped dead, and at Rethymno he was unable even to make contact with the commander, Colonel Sturm. It further appeared that these casualties had been suffered to no purpose. For his men were everywhere, as in some terrible frustrated offensive of the First World War, at their starting point. The one exception, the bridgehead over the Tavronitis, was but a fraction of the gains that had been confidently expected from the desperate extravagance of the first day's *Blitz*.

There were other, internal, grounds for anxiety. These were to be found in the complicated hierarchic rivalries of personalities and private armies within the Third Reich. Operation Mercury was a Luftwaffe affair in conception and, in the opening stages, in execution. The Wehrmacht were unenthusiastic. Even the Führer had so little confidence in the outcome that he had told Goebbels that there was to be no mention of the battle over Berlin Radio 'until the outcome was absolutely certain'.

Student knew that the Wehrmacht were only waiting for the situation to worsen fractionally before exerting pressure at General Staff level to have the whole operation called off and, indeed, this possibility was already being covertly mentioned. At a quarter to midnight, when the corrected casualty figures for I and III Battalions of 3rd Parachute Regiment came in, Reinhardt asked Student if he should start any preliminary studies of the problem of 'breaking off' the engagement if this should be thought 'advisable'.

For Student it must have been a dreadful moment. If he did this, and accepted defeat, he would have expended the Führer's most cherished force. He would have let down Goering, his superior and protector. He would be utterly discredited. In his dilemma he was alone. Neither Lohr nor Ringel could offer him much sympathy. Lohr was an airman, with little understanding of land operations. He was impatient to move, with the whole of IV Air Fleet, to take part in Barbarossa. Ringel was an

Austrian, an infantryman. He had a motto, 'Sweat saves blood', and with it a conviction in favour of the indirect approach. Moreover, he was of the Wehrmacht. The idea of putting his highly trained mountain division into this unconventional and, it seemed, disastrous frontal attack on a heavily defended fortress cannot have appealed to him.

Student, however, was a commander of the highest calibre. He had two attributes that are seldom found together. He had a fresh and unconventional approach to problems, together with a calm and thoughtful manner. That is to say that his processes of thought, although unrestricted by military conservatism, were at all times reasoned and analytic. 'I decided,' he wrote afterwards, 'to concentrate all our forces against one spot. We selected Maleme because here, at least, we could see a glimmer of light.' To Group West therefore, Student allocated his remaining parachutists, only half a battalion strong, with instructions that they were to be held in readiness for a drop the following day. He turned to Ringel and said, 'You will be flown to Crete tomorrow.'

And then, having committed the last reserves that lay under his own hand, the man who was to face and surmount, only in reverse, a crisis of similar gravity in the British airborne attack at Arnhem three and a half years later, retired to sleep.

Student would certainly have slept less soundly, and it is conceivable that he might have altered his decision to press the attack, had he known that at that very moment his campaign plan was being read out to Freyberg by the light of a hurricane lamp in the quarry tunnel that was Creforce Headquarters. For the full text of the Operation Order for the 3rd Parachute Regiment had been captured that afternoon and sent up to the intelligence section there. This document was of immense importance for not only did it show the strength and intended direction of the enemy thrusts, their order of battle, armament and supply position, but it was plain from reading its preamble that the Germans had grossly underestimated the strength of the defenders and that they had already committed virtually the whole of their airborne force.

In actual fact, the Operation Order was only discovered by chance. The intelligence staff were a scratch body under a Major Blunt, who had lately been the military attaché in Athens. There was no G 3 (I), but four separate intelligence officers, each of whom pursued independent, although not necessarily complementary, researches. Their work was arduous for with the collapse of Scherber's attack and the rounding-up of prisoners in the coastal region whole truck-loads of documents were being brought back to the Quarry, and it was difficult for each one to be closely examined. At about ten o'clock that night the Order was discovered by Geoffrey Cox, who was not really one of the IOs at all but a subaltern who had been given the task of producing the *Crete News*, a daily paper for the troops. On the day of the assault he had left his desk in Canea and got himself attached to a platoon of 20th Battalion which had spent the day mopping up the glider troops of the Altmann detachment who had landed on the Akrotiri peninsula. That evening, on his way back to Canea, Cox had called in at Creforce Headquarters in the hopes of being given some fresh active assignment for the following day, and here he had come across the Order which had been placed with a pile of documents that were waiting despatch to MEHQ in Cairo. He at once began to translate it, with the help of a pocket German dictionary that he had used while working as a journalist in Vienna before the war and still carried, and as its importance became apparent he was taken to Freyberg's cave, where he read it aloud.

Of all the points that emerged from a study of the Order, the most crucial, and the most urgent, concerned the vulnerability of the enemy to an immediate counter-attack. Yet during that same night the first and finest chance for this was being allowed to slip by. After the withdrawal of 22nd Battalion from Hill 107 and its perimeter around the airfield the battalion commanders held a conference at which Lieutenant Colonel Leckie presided. There is no record of proceedings but the decision – 'to hold our positions next day'[1] – was a disappointing one. Between them they had two fresh battalions and the survivors of a third – a force stronger than that which was to achieve so much the following night. The enemy were exhausted and had suffered heavy casualties during the day. They had not yet had time to reorganise in their new positions, and these were in many cases still interlocked with the men of C and D Companies who were at that time still holding out in good heart. However, the commanders on the spot, in the words of the official New Zealand

---

[1] 21st Bn report, D 185.

historian, 'were caught off their judgement, forgot the policy of immediate counter-attack on which the whole defence plan rested, and thought in terms of how to hold their present positions'.

Nor does Hargest seem to have seen anything amiss in the lethargic attitude of his battalion commanders. He did not report the withdrawal to Puttick until 3am and made no move to visit the area himself. He sent first for Andrew, who had arrived (still without any sleep) in a Bren Carrier at 5am, and told him that there was no hope of pulling 22nd Battalion out of the line to reorganise and that he must fit himself in with the 1st and 23rd, then he had sent his Brigade Major, Captain Dawson, back in the carrier with Andrew to 'discuss the question' of organising the new positions for defence. When Leggatt, Andrew's second in command, had first visited Hargest at half past two that morning and told him that 'we are officially off Maleme', he found the Brigadier 'asleep and in pyjamas. He was absolutely surprised and unprepared.'[1]

This seems to summarise adequately Hargest's first reaction to each fresh twist in the pattern of the engagement. His reluctance to leave his headquarters has already been discussed above, but he should not carry the blame alone. The lack of vigorous, decisive leadership is as marked in this vital sector on the second as it was on the first day, and it forces a painful conclusion. This is that the qualities of the senior officers of the New Zealand Division (with the exception of Inglis and Kippenberger) were not suited to the new methods of warfare, and an inadequate complement to the bravery of the men and the tactical skill and resourcefulness of the junior officers and NCOs. Men like Hargest, Puttick and Andrew were brave – Andrew had won a VC in the First World War – they were calm and they were experienced. But this was 1941. The war was hardly a year old. 'Experience' still referred to the battles, the drawn-out linear deadlock, of 1914–18, when there was time to consider every decision, when flanks were all-important, when the rear was always secure, when the reserves should never be used in the opening hours. The irony of Crete was that the overall command lay in the hands of the men to whom these ideas were least

[1] 22nd Bn OH.

sympathetic. Freyberg had a reputation for dash and vigour. It was for these qualities that Churchill had selected him. It is to be regretted that he did not give them free rein in this his first, and last, independent command.

What went wrong? Why was Freyberg's leadership so hesitant and negative and his fighting qualities wasted? A combination of circumstances suggests itself. First, there was the isolation, the vague political overtones, that go with every supreme command. Freyberg was in communication with London as well as Cairo. He had responsibilities to the New Zealand Government. It is possible that doubts that he had earlier so freely expressed concerning the feasibility of the operation still lurked. He was beset with problems of administration, handicapped by a small and inexperienced staff. Second, there was the purely physical difficulty of communication. The shortage of wireless equipment, the broken telephone lines, the enemy aircraft that shot at individual runners in daylight hours, all aggravated the difficulties of transmitted orders and receiving up-to-the-minute reports. Third, a certain diffidence that may have originated in the terms of his appointment. Because Freyberg, a man who lived not in New Zealand but in Britain, had been promoted over the heads of other and more senior claimants – Puttick among them – to command the New Zealand expeditionary force at the outbreak of war. He may now have felt that they should be allowed to fight their own battles without interference.

Whatever the reason, the result was that the preparations for the counter-attack proceeded at a snail's pace. At 11.15 Hargest suggested to Puttick that the Maori and another battalion should make an attack 'towards Maleme' after dark. Puttick said that he would put the idea to Freyberg, but he did not consider the situation sufficiently important to warrant a visit in person – even so short a distance as 5th Brigade Headquarters – and he refused Hargest's request for another 120 men to guard his lines of communication if 20th Battalion were to go forward.

When Freyberg was consulted he suggested a conference at Creforce Headquarters that afternoon which would be attended by all the New Zealand Brigadiers, Weston and Vasey, who commanded the 19th Australian Brigade at Georgeoupolis. The conference finally sat down at 4pm. No record is available of the proceedings, but the results show

THE FALL OF CRETE

the disadvantages that follow when policy is formed not by orders from the top but by a flow of contradictory suggestions by a committee of subordinates. The facts were before them, plain and alarming – namely the German possession of Maleme and the rate of enemy reinforcement there. The first units of 5th Mountain Division had already been identified and it was plain that with one more day's intake at the airfield the Germans would achieve a local numerical superiority, and with two days' they would approach an overall parity. It was absolutely essential that they be denied the use of Maleme immediately. Once this was done, the other enemy lodgements would wither away.

Freyberg still had a large force at his disposal. He had over 6,000 men[1] in the Suda area, excluding the New Zealand Division (which was itself not fully engaged). In this number were two absolutely first-class battalions in the 1st Welch – which had only taken part in the mopping-up operations at Akrotiri and had suffered no casualties – and 2/7th Australian, veterans of Bardia, never defeated in battle and one of the finest fighting formations in the Middle East. In spite of this strength there does not seem to have been any serious consideration given to the advisability of attacking with more than two battalions. Although the day had been allowed to pass without making any plans for their movement, it would still have been possible to use the 18th and the Welch as well as the 20th and Maori, putting two or three in at once and bringing up the others to relieve the 5th Brigade, thus allowing Hargest's men to take part in a general forward movement.

[1] The units available together, with their approximate strengths, were as follows (D 195):

19th Australian Brigade (2/7th and half 2/8th Bn about 1,000).

1st Welch (854).

1st Rangers (417).

Northumberland Hussars (279).

106th RHA (307).

2/2nd Australian Field Regiment (554).

2/3rd Australian Field Regiment (300).

16th Australian Inf Bde Composite Battalion (443).

17th Australian Inf Bde Composite Battalion (387).

Royal Marine Unit (300).

'Royal Perivolians' (700).

Dock Defence Force (RN, RM, Australian and NZ, about 600).

However, none of the brigade or area commanders was anxious to release troops to someone else's battle (the operation was to come under Puttick's command) and pleaded the necessity of guarding against the threatened sea invasion and the importance of safe-guarding communications against the isolated enemy parties that still survived here and there. These arguments ignored the salient fact – that, if the airfield was not recaptured, the frustration of the seaborne invasion and the preservation of communications were academic points, for the island would surely be lost.

However, they seem to have carried the day because it was finally decided that two battalions would be used: the Maoris, who were on the spot, and the 2/7th, who would be brought over from Georgeoupolis (which was not threatened from the sea, being protected by the Suda boom). At this point, though, Brigadier Vasey objected. He contended that taking away his best battalion and placing it under Puttick would leave him with no troops under his command except the 2/7th Field Ambulance and a detachment of engineers, as he had already lost the 2/8th to Inglis and was cut off from the 2/1st and 2/11th who were at Rethymno. He asked that he might be allotted an area where he might command the 2/7th and 2/8th as a combined force. This reasonable request was acceded to, but at the cost of settling on a compromise solution which, for such a relatively small body of men, was so complex as to be almost unworkable in practice. The final plan was for the 2/7th to move in lorries from Georgeoupolis to the 20th Battalion area, where they were to de-bus and hand their vehicles over to 20th Battalion. These last would then use the lorries to drive up to a position on the right of the Maoris whence the two would move off to the attack at a time somewhat optimistically scheduled for 'between 10 and 11pm'.

The effect of this decision, apart from calling for a manoeuvre which could hardly have gone off without a hitch on a peaceful night exercise, was to commit one of the finest units on the island to a rôle on this the most critical night of the battle which was little more than that of acting as chauffeurs and ballast.

That morning Walker, the commanding officer of 2/7th, had worked out a plan for cutting eastwards and taking the Germans at Rethymno in the rear – a move which, combined with the pressure of 2/11th, would probably have opened the road and, by uniting the two forces, should have removed any misgivings that Freyberg may have felt about using the bulk of available forces in his counter-offensive. Deprived of this prospect, Walker told Inglis as they left the conference that he did not like the new plan, 'an attempt to bring forward by night a battalion that lacked its own transport, was eighteen miles away, and not connected to Headquarters by telephone, in time for it to relieve another battalion that was to make an attack that same night'. Inglis, however, replied (and his brusqueness may suggest the mood in which the officers finally quitted the conference), 'that a well-trained battalion could carry out such a relief in an hour'.[1]

At the same moment that Puttick, Freyberg and the brigade commanders were sitting down to the conference at Creforce Head-quarters, the Germans resumed their forward movement. The remnants of the Assault Regiment, reinforced by three companies of Stentzler's battalion, moved down from the southern edge of the airfield, under the lee of Hill 107 and against the positions of the 23rd Battalion. Pirgos and Maleme village had been subjected to a heavy bombardment by Stukas, starting at 3pm, and the advancing troops encountered little resistance[2] until they had crossed the valley and were advancing up the slope. At about 150 yards the New Zealanders opened fire with Brens, rifles and a number of captured Spandaus. Within a few minutes the attack was broken and the enemy withdrew, leaving over 200 dead in the valley.

In a parachute drop that was simultaneous with the frontal attack the enemy was even more roughly handled. Once again the parachutists – the last, now, that were left of the whole of 7th Division – landed strung out along the coast, falling almost directly into the positions of the Maoris and the Engineer Battalion.

'At one stage I stopped for a minute or two to see how things were

---

[1] Long, 234–5.

[2] Some of the remnants of 22nd Battalion were still holding out in isolated positions. XI Air Corps report speaks of 'a lone New Zealand Sergeant' (believed to have been Sergeant J Woods) who killed five of the enemy before being captured.

going and a Hun dropped not ten feet away. I had my pistol in my hand and without really knowing what I was doing I let him have it while he was still on the ground. I had hardly got over the shock when another came down almost at top of me and I plugged him too while he was untangling himself. Not cricket I know, but there it is.[1]

At the height of the battle the enemy started landing Ju 52s on the beach, but the majority of these were so riddled with bullets before they had come to a standstill that scarcely a man was left alive and fit to get out. Of six transports that crash-landed in front of one Maori platoon, only twenty men survived and all were taken prisoner. Within an hour there was no organised resistance left and the isolated parties that remained were being hunted down and killed at close quarters:

> I ran over to the Mill race and saw a German in the mouth of a filled-in well firing a tommy-gun. Told Jum Tuwahi to lie on the bank and shoot at him and calling to a soldier to run out with me and we would rush the man from the other side. We did that. As we got up to him he crouched down, shamming dead. I told the Maori to bayonet him. As he did so he turned his head away, not bearing the sight. Tuwahi had now joined us and we rushed out among the Germans scattered every 15 to 20 yards . . . One at about 15 yards, instead of firing his tommy-gun started to lie down to fire. I took a snap shot with a German Mauser. It grazed his behind and missed between his legs. My back hair lifted, but the Maori got him (I had no bayonet). We rushed on . . . some tried to crawl away . . . a giant of a man jumped up with his hands up like a gorilla and shouting "Hants oop". I said: "Shoot the bastard" and the Maori shot him. That was because many others were firing at us and a Spandau from further off. Suddenly bullets spluttered all round my feet . . .[2]

Student's reason for dropping these two companies behind 23rd Battalion lines seemed logical enough. He has since explained that when the first reports were brought in from patrols, showing that 22nd Battalion had abandoned its position during the night, he assumed that

[1] Report by Captain Anderson, NZOH, 189.

[2] Report by Major Dyer.

this, and the absence of a counter-attack at dawn, must mean that the defenders had no reserves left – otherwise it was inconceivable that they should not have been committed to an immediate counter-attack. Now, with the repulse of the Assault Regiment and Stentzler's men, and the slaughter of his remaining parachutists, the position seemed, if anything, worse than that on the evening of the 20th. Now there was no doubt that the defenders still had ample strength remaining, and that this strength would shortly be committed in a sweeping counter-blow. He, on the other hand, had no parachute reserves left whatever, for two companies had been dropped on Maleme that morning and the last two and a half had been committed as support for the afternoon attack. Around him in Athens Student could feel confidence evaporating. Lohr's staff were stressing the dangers of continuing to operate with the presence of an intact enemy force in the rear at Kastelli; they reported strong enemy troop concentrations at Palaiokhera (in actual fact these were German flank guards). Lohr himself refused Student permission to go to Crete in person 'in case the pattern of fighting there should suddenly change'. But Student believed, as he told Reinhardt, that 'it is to preserve my head in case it should be wanted at an enquiry'. There was still no mention of the battle on Berlin Radio. Moreover, Student now learned that even Goering was getting uneasy and that he and Hitler were attributing Student's acceptance of such heavy casualties to the fact that he 'must still be suffering from an old head wound'.

There was only one fact left to comfort him. That evening the convoy that was to make a landing on the beaches had sailed. In the boats were over 2,000 men and a quantity of heavy weapons, including 50-mm anti-tank guns. If they could be safely put ashore the tide of battle might still be turned.

TEN

AT SEA

Naval historians will agree that no British fleet has had so wide or so diversified responsibilities, or been exposed to such risks or suffered so protracted an ordeal, as that of Admiral Cunningham's in the first six months of 1941.

It was the concern of this fleet to sustain the garrison of Malta and maintain an offensive squadron there; to blockade the Libyan coast; to supply the isolated fortress of Tobruk; to maintain a standing patrol of heavy warships against the Italian fleet which outnumbered it; to hold itself ready for such hazardous operations as the Admiralty might order in the way of bombarding enemy ports and running convoys through the narrows; and, lately, to escort an army of 50,000 men to Greece and, within the same month, to evacuate them.

At the beginning of May the general state of the fleet was giving Cunningham some concern. All the cruisers and destroyers were in need of refit – their stay in port was so short that there had not even been time to clean the boilers. The engines, gun mountings and turrets, and the steering gear were all in need of overhaul. Even more important, none of the crew had had any leave. In a letter to the First Sea Lord dated 3 May Cunningham said, 'Pridham-Whippel and myself had noticed signs of strain among officers and ratings, particularly in the anti-aircraft cruisers and also in the destroyers. The former have had a gruelling time ever since the move of the Army to Greece started on 4 March, never a trip to sea without being bombed.' Anti-aircraft ammunition was beginning to run low, not only in the ships themselves but in the depots ashore. On 13 May Cunningham was writing to the Admiralty that '. . . since 20 April between one third and one half of the main items in the Mediterranean Fleet had been expended. The remaining stocks of 5.25-inch and 4.5-inch were now down to only three quarters of the outfit required . . .'

This was particularly serious as it was, of course, from the air that the main threat came. The crews seldom had the satisfaction of a ship-to-ship encounter. The Italians would run away the moment they sighted so much as one English destroyer; surface engagements were brief and, often, frustrating and inconclusive. Instead, the crews had to endure, day after day in those narrow seas, attacks from the mounting power of the Luftwaffe, without any fighter cover whatsoever. The aircraft-carrier *Formidable*, which had managed to give some protection to the Malta convoys with its eight-gun Fulmars, was unserviceable. Losses during the bombardment of Tripoli and escorting the Tiger convoy had reduced her strength to four.

During the evacuation of Greece the strain on the Navy had reached what, at the time, had seemed to be very near breaking point. In the two days 21 to 22 April twenty-two ships had been lost from German air attacks, and it was painfully clear that daylight movement in the Aegean was possible only if ruinous losses were to be accepted.

The *Slamat* episode had reinforced this – and another lesson whose application was to have painful consequences during later evacuations. This ship, a Dutch merchantman, had been embarking troops at Nauplia on the night of 27 April. She had been warned that the latest time of sailing that would allow her to clear the Antikithera channel by daylight was 3am, but rather than leave some troops behind her captain had waited until 4.15am. *Slamat* was caught by the dive-bombers at seven o'clock while still north-east of Cape Malia, hit three times and set alight. The destroyers *Diamond* and *Wryneck* were sent to her assistance, arriving just as she capsized. They also were attacked while hove-to and picking up survivors, and were forced to get underway again, *Wryneck* being damaged by near misses. Shortly after midday the two destroyers were again attacked and this time both suffered direct hits almost immediately. On *Diamond* the bomb landed aft and exploded her cargo of depth charges, blowing off her stern; *Wryneck* was struck amidships and holed in her keel. Both ships sank in a few minutes and only one officer, forty-one ratings and, from over 500, eight of the soldiers who had embarked on the *Slamat* survived.

The lessons from this disastrous episode were clear. First, troopships had to stick rigidly to their embarkation schedules, even if this meant forsaking a large number of soldiers who had not got on in time. Second, it was not possible to stop and pick up survivors in the closed inshore waters of the Aegean without, at the very least, cover from the guns of many other warships. Third, the operation of single vessels, or even pairs, was too dangerous in daylight. The only hope lay in the commitment of a whole squadron complete with anti-aircraft cruisers that could give mutually supporting fire.

Now a moment had arrived when, despite the risks of whose gravity he had lately been so sharply reminded, and of the condition of ships and guns, Cunningham was being asked to commit his fleet to a maximum effort in the waters north of Crete. He was told that 'the island could be held against airborne attack only' and that it was the duty of the Navy to guarantee it against a seaborne landing. To this end Cunningham divided his fleet into three parts. The Battle Fleet (forces A and A I, with the *Queen Elizabeth*, *Barham*, *Warspite* and *Valiant*, two cruisers and sixteen destroyers), under Vice Admiral Pridham-Whippel and Rear Admiral Rawlings, was stationed to the west of Crete, where it could intercept the Italian heavy ships if they should attempt to give support to a landing convoy. The task of directly repulsing the invasion fleet was left to the cruisers. These were divided into two Forces – C, under Rear Admiral King, with which sailed *Naiad*, *Perth*, *Calcutta*, *Carlisle* and four destroyers, and Force D, under Rear Admiral Glennie, with *Dido*, *Orion*, *Ajax* and four destroyers.

It was planned that until the enemy invasion fleet sailed the two cruiser squadrons should remain to the south of the island during the day and at dusk sweep the northern coast on converging routes, Glennie passing through the Antikithera channel and turning east and King entering by the Kaso Strait and bearing west.

The first day, 20 May, passed off without incident for Glennie – largely on account, it may be thought, of the Luftwaffe's preoccupation with supporting the parachute landings in their most vulnerable phase. King's squadron bombarded Scarpanto, and had a brush with some Italian torpedo boats, on four of which it inflicted damage. But at dawn on the 21st, when the ships were once more on a southerly course, they were attacked by high-altitude bombers and *Juno* was hit in one of her magazines. She blew up and sank in two minutes. Cunningham's nephew was among those drowned.

During the 21st it became plain that the enemy were planning to attempt a landing that evening. The Admiralty Intelligence on Crete, under the Naval Officer in Charge, Captain JAV Morse, was of a very high standard of efficiency, and co-ordinated with reconnaissance Sunderlands based in Egypt and with a host of informants among the Greek population at the ports on the mainland. Morse heard at midday on the 21st that a large enemy flotilla[1] had put to sea and notified C-in-C Mediterranean Fleet immediately. Glennie and King were thereupon ordered to turn about for the north coast of Crete. They were instructed to sweep close inshore during the night and then, if no contact had been made with the enemy, to work northwards into the Aegean during the day, 'on a wide zig-zag to locate enemy convoys'.

Cunningham knew that to send ships into the Aegean in the daytime was to invite disaster, and it is some measure of his assessment of the crisis that he should have ordered them to sail there. From the moment that they were sent into those narrow, land-locked waters for fourteen hours of cloudless daylight the cruiser squadrons were committed into the lap of death.

Throughout the late evening of 21 May Glennie's force steamed along the north coast of the island, passing Cape Kisamos an hour after dusk and then setting course for Suda, running at 27 knots – near maximum speed. White luminous foam ran from their wake. In the twilight the jagged outline of the Lefka Ori could be seen to starboard. The shore was without light and lifeless, and from it a hot wind blew the scent of pine needles.

At a quarter past eleven, as they were nearing Canea, the radar on *Dido* picked up first one signal then a whole cluster of shadows and 'blips'. The two groups were closing at over 35 knots and within the next ten minutes Force D found itself in the centre of the enemy convoy, now only eighteen miles from the shore. The interception had been perfect.

The enemy flotilla consisted of about twenty caiques and four or five coastal steamers, escorted by the Italian destroyer *Lupo* and four torpedo-

[1] The German Admiral South-East disposed of two flotillas made up of steamers and motor-vessels, together with two destroyers and twelve motor-torpedo-boats. In fact, both of them sailed on the 21st, although it was thought at the time that only one was at sea as that for the Canea area turned back during the morning and was sent out again during the afternoon.

boats. The ships carried a battalion of Ringel's 5th Mountain Division (III Bn of 100th Regt), part of an anti-aircraft regiment and a number of different heavy weapons detachments, including light lorries, motorcycle combinations and some tanks. There was also an artillery detachment with 50-mm anti-tank guns. The total strength of the troops carried is given by XI Air Corps report as 2,330.

Into this group Glennie's ships charged, 'with zest and energy', as he wrote in his report. A wild mêlée followed, with the English destroyers ramming one after another of the caiques, sinking by gunfire the steamers and threshing this way and that in water crowded with drowning soldiers and enemy crews who were clinging to rafts and pieces of wreckage. The whole area was brilliant with flares and criss-crossed with tracer and pom-pom fire. For two and a half hours the enemy convoy was hounded until it had been thoroughly shattered and dispersed, and then Glennie called his ships together and they turned west, with a good night's work behind them.[1]

Glennie had taken it upon himself to withdraw to the south for he felt that with the convoy destroyed his task had been carried out, and the cruisers were all running short of AA ammunition – *Dido* had shot off over 70 per cent. Cunningham in his memoirs is critical of this decision but it had, at any rate, the merit of preserving the Force intact for the time being. King, on the other hand, had not made contact with the enemy during the night and, in obedience to the Commander-in-Chief's instructions, his weary ships swung north with the dawn, following the predicted approach route of the convoy and heading straight into the complex of bomber airfields that crowded the archipelago.

For three hours the flotilla was under continuous air attack. Very few

---

[1] At the time it was thought that the Germans must have suffered losses exceeding 4,000 dead, and this assertion is repeated both in Churchill's and in Cunningham's accounts, published after the war. However, we know from XI Air Corps report that the total strength of the convoy was well under this figure at 2,331. The daily reports to 12th Army GHQ show that, although on 22 May (morning) there was a warning that 'the loss of about 50 per cent of the convoy must be accepted', by that evening a total of 770 men had been rescued, and this rose on 23 May (evening) to 1,400. On 28 May this number had risen to 1,665 including 21 Italians and 'It is expected that this number will be increased slightly as not all the islands have been searched yet.' The final report, dated 4 June, shows the losses to have been 309 killed. NZOH Appx V, 487.

of the crews had had any sleep during the night; many of them could hardly stand upright in the turrets as the ships swung from side to side, weaving and yawing in evasion, dazed by the repeated concussions of bombs exploding alongside and the endless rattle of the pom-poms. At half past eight a solitary caique was seen and sunk, and soon after nine a small merchant vessel was also seen. The cruisers were now less than forty miles from Milos and still travelling at 20 knots; Ios and Thera, where there was a German seaplane base, had been left to starboard.

For another hour King held his course, the ships cleaving the flat blue water, shadowed by the aircraft, carrying always above them the mantle of white smoke from the bursting anti-aircraft shells. Then, at ten o'clock, when they were barely twenty miles from Milos, a destroyer was sighted, with four small craft behind her in line astern. The *Kingston*, detached to attack the line from the other side, saw a second enemy destroyer steaming at maximum speed to 'cross the T' of the approaching flotilla and laying down smoke. Behind the smoke *Kingston* could see scores of caiques, all crammed with soldiers. At least, after their morning's ordeal, Force C had come upon the second convoy. This group contained even more soldiers than that dispersed by Glennie and, had they reached their destination, the beaches west of Heraklion, it is probable that the town's defenders would have been overwhelmed within a few days.

However, at this very moment, when the convoy was within his grasp, Admiral King decided that with his ammunition almost exhausted he dared sail no farther northward, and ordered his ships to break off the engagement and turn west for the Kithera channel.

Cunningham, meanwhile, had also been informed of the enemy convoy, and of King's contact with it, from a long-range reconnaissance Wellington which was reporting direct to Cairo. When he read King's signal he was appalled, and immediately sent the order: 'Stick it out. Keep in visual signalling touch. Must not let Army down in Crete. It is essential no seaborne enemy force land in Crete.'

But already it was too late. The convoy had turned back and scattered, the caiques fading into the smoke screen to disperse among the numerous creeks and islets – and over 5,000 German soldiers were spared their lives.

Of King's action Cunningham wrote in his memoirs:

> the decision to retire, I think, was a faulty one. It is probable that the safest place was in amongst the enemy convoy, and retirement could not better the most unpleasant position in which he found himself. Also the destruction of that large convoy could have justified severe losses.

And now, with it not yet midday, Force C was faced by the most terrible prospect – a four-hour voyage to the Kithera channel, with the sun high in the sky and the Luftwaffe bases at thirty minutes' flying time. They had been cruelly frustrated at the last moment of the chance of closing with the enemy, of the chance to die in a combat that would at least have been a worthy occasion. The Force could make no more than 20 knots as the *Carlisle* was capable of only 21 when steaming at maximum speed. Soon the *Naiad* began to show the effect of four sticks of 500-pound bombs that had straddled her. Her plates were bulging, and one bulkhead after another was filling with water. Her speed was reduced to 16 knots, and two of her turrets were put out of action. As each ship was damaged so the vulnerability of the whole flotilla increased, for speed was reduced and with it the ability to take evasive action. For four hours the tortured squadron struggled to the west. Ammunition was now so low that the gunners were forbidden to fire at shadowing aircraft and told to hold their fire until the attackers were actually started on their dive. This was yet another trial for the spirit of men whose nerves had been stretched taut for forty-eight hours of continuous alert.

The moment that he heard that King's force was heading west, Cunningham had realised their plight and coolly ordered Rawlings to take the battle fleet on an easterly course to meet him, so that for the last part of the voyage their firepower would reinforce the waning strength of Force C. Glennie's cruiser squadron, Force D, had joined the main battle fleet during the morning and, in spite of their depleted condition, Rawlings decided to bring them along with him.

The result of this was that by early afternoon there was committed in the narrow and perilous Aegean the whole of effective British naval strength in the Middle East.

The two capital ships, *Warspite* and *Valiant*, disposed between them of twenty-four 4.5-inch heavy anti-aircraft guns, and they made up a major part of the fleet's firepower. Doubtless it was on account of this, because of their size and importance, that the Luftwaffe singled them out for special attention. The Stukas would line up at 3,000 feet, then come down in pairs, sometimes diving below 1,200 feet before releasing their bombs. Near misses did not trouble the big ships, although their repeated concussions dazed the crews. But they were slower at the helm than the cruisers and soon enough the inevitable happened – *Warspite* was hit by a heavy bomb, an 1,100-pounder, that struck her amidships on the starboard side, knocking out all the 6-inch and 4.5-inch turrets and the fire-control system.

This occurred almost at the very moment that the two formations joined. From that time the overall command had passed to Admiral King, who was senior to Rawlings, and a whole series of misfortunes led one to another. First the *Greyhound*, returning after having been detached (in spite of the Commander-in-Chief's instructions that ships were not to be detached singly or in pairs) to pursue and sink a caique, was set upon by a squadron of Ju 88s. She was hit by two bombs simultaneously and sank in a quarter of an hour. King thereupon ordered the destroyers *Kandahar* and *Kingston* to pick up survivors, and signalled to the cruisers *Gloucester* and *Fiji* to stand by and give them support.

Gloucester and *Fiji* had expended over three quarters of their ammunition, so they were hardly in a position to give very effective cover, but they obeyed without demur. King had no knowledge of their ammunition state as they had only just come under his command and their hourly returns had been going to Rawlings. However, when Rawlings learned of their mission he signalled to King, warning him of their vulnerable condition. King thereupon ordered the cruisers to leave *Kandahar* and *Kingston* and rejoin the battle fleet.

Thus by half past three, the fleet, which had formed a formidable whole less than an hour earlier, was once again split into three parts. Separate from the main mass were the two destroyers, searching for survivors from *Greyhound*, and between them the pair of cruisers, practically defenceless and steaming at full speed to catch up with the battle fleet, which was itself withdrawing at over 20 knots. The Luftwaffe soon discovered which of these alternative targets was the most suitable, and upon this they concentrated. After half an hour of intensive dive-bombing, during which she was hit three times, the *Gloucester* was ablaze, with all her forward guns out of action and reduced to a hesitant 12 knots. The *Fiji* decided that she must leave her comrade and, after throwing her Carley rafts overboard, she took up full steam again in an effort to catch up with the fast receding battle fleet. The *Gloucester* was never seen again.[1]

The hapless *Fiji* struggled on. Since being detached to cover the two destroyers, she had fought off twenty quite separate bombing attacks and was now reduced to using practice ammunition. The end came gradually. At 6.45pm a single Bf 109 came in on a shallow dive and dropped its bomb alongside. It blew in the cruiser's bottom and she came to a standstill, listing heavily and with her engine-rooms flooded. Half an hour later she was again hit, by three bombs in succession, and the list increased. For an hour she wallowed in the gentle swell, with the crew working the pumps by hand until, at 8.15, she turned over and sank. By now, though, *Kandahar* and *Kingston*, who had miraculously survived their passage, were on the scene. It was dark at last and they could heave to and lower boats. In this way 523 of *Fiji*'s complement were rescued.

That afternoon Cunningham had been reinforced by the one remaining fresh unit left in the Mediterranean – Lord Louis Mountbatten's 5th Destroyer Flotilla, comprising five of the latest K class ships, which had lately been sent from the United Kingdom to Malta from where they were to engage in the blockade of Tripoli. After briefly making contact with Rawlings and King, they were ordered, directly by Cunningham

[1] In his memoirs, p. 371, Cunningham wrote of the *Gloucester*: 'She had endured all things, and no ship had worked harder or had more risky tasks. She had been hit by bombs more times than any other vessel, and had always come up smiling. As she left Alexandria for the last time I went alongside her in my barge and had a talk with her Captain, Henry Aubrey Rowley. He was very anxious about his men, who were just worn out, which was not surprising as I well realised. I promised to go on board and talk to them on their return to harbour; but they never came back. I doubt if many of them survived as they were murderously machine-gunned in the water. Rowley's body, recognisable by his uniform monkey jacket and the signals in his pocket, came ashore to the west of Mersa Matruh about four weeks later. It was a long way round to come home.'

from Alexandria, to pass back through the Kithera channel that evening and patrol the north coast of Crete. It was originally intended that the battle fleet should lie off to the south during the night and then move north in formation at dawn to support the 5th Destroyer Flotilla with its firepower, while Mountbatten withdrew. However,

> . . . on the night of the 22nd we had a report of the 'state' of the close-range ammunition from Rear Admiral Rawlings, from which it appeared that the battleships had expended all they had. We knew that the ammunition of the cruisers was at a very low ebb, so all forces at sea were ordered to Alexandria to replenish. Actually a mistake occurred in Rawlings' signal, and whether it was phonetic or just bad writing I do not know. Anyhow the first copy of the signal shown to myself and the Chief of Staff indicated that the battleships were 'empty' of short-range ammunition, whereas the typed copy distributed the next morning had the word 'plenty', which was correct.

The result of this was that at dawn the destroyers of Mountbatten's flotilla were racing for the Kithera channel at full speed, with the prospect of over four hours' daylight sailing ahead of them and the prospect of fire-support, or rescue should they sink, excluded. Except for Force E, three destroyers under Captain Mack, which had carried out a night patrol east of Heraklion and were withdrawing in the opposite direction, through the Kaso Strait, there were no other ships of the Mediterranean Fleet at sea on that morning.

Mountbatten's flotilla was twice attacked between six and seven o'clock, but they were among the fastest ships in the Navy and their speed and energetic manoeuvring kept them from being directly hit. But in the third attack, by twenty-four Ju 87s at 8am, their luck ran out. *Kashmir* was hit by two bombs, her magazines exploded and she sank in two minutes. *Kelly*, in which Mountbatten had his flag, was struck by an 1,100-pounder amidships, while steaming at 30 knots under full helm. She listed heavily to port and capsized while still moving through the water. After floating upside down for half an hour she, too, went to the bottom. In defiance of the general orders issued to every ship, *Kipling* (Commander A St Clair Ford) slowed and began to search for survivors, although under continuous air attack. She remained on the scene for three hours, and had to endure no less than six separate attacks by formations of up to twenty aircraft. In spite of this, 279 men and officers were rescued, including Mountbatten himself who, some accounts have it, was hauled out of the sea on the end of a boathook. On her way back to Egypt *Kipling*, with her decks crowded with survivors, was attacked by forty bombers during the afternoon, and she used up so much fuel taking evasive action that when finally she arrived off Alexandria on the night of the 23rd/24th she had to be towed in to harbour.

With the smashing of the 5th Destroyer flotilla, Cunningham had literally no ships remaining in his command that were 100 per cent serviceable, but on the 23rd he had received a message from the Admiralty reiterating that 'the outcome of the Battle for Crete would have serious repercussions, and that it was vitally important to prevent seaborne expeditions reaching the Island in the next day or two, even if this resulted in further losses to the fleet'.[1]

Cunningham replied that the withdrawal of the fleet to Alexandria had been forced upon him by the necessity to refuel and restock with ammunition, adding that the fleet was operating 400 miles from its base and that it was 'impracticable' to have any considerable force in the Aegean on the night of the 24th, although two destroyers which were landing urgent supplies at Suda that night had instructions to sweep westwards after discharging their cargo. On the night of the 24th/25th he hoped to be able to send two cruisers and two destroyers back into the Aegean. He added that

> The operations of the last four days have been nothing short of a trial of strength between the Mediterranean Fleet and the German Air Force . . . I am afraid that in the coastal area we have to admit defeat and accept the fact that losses are too great to justify us in trying to prevent seaborne attacks on Crete. This is a melancholy conclusion, but it must be faced. As I have always feared, enemy command of the air, unchallenged by our own Air Force, and in these restricted waters, with Mediterranean weather, is too great odds for us to take on except by seizing opportunities of surprise and using the utmost

[1] Cunningham, *Memoirs*, 374.

circumspection. It is perhaps fortunate that HMS *Formidable* was immobilised, as I doubt if she would now be afloat.[1]

The Chiefs of Staff now intervened in these exchanges, and notified Cunningham that in their view the situation was being allowed to 'drag on',[2] that unless 'more drastic action were taken' the enemy would be able to reinforce the island to a considerable extent. 'If air reconnaissance showed enemy movement by sea north of Crete, the fleet would have to operate in that area by day, though considerable losses might be expected . . . only experience would show how long the situation could be maintained, and that time was the dominating factor.'

It seems reasonable to identify the Prime Minister's hand behind these messages to Cunningham. Churchill was viewing the battle from a distance. But he would have been mindful, it may be suggested, of how the pusillanimity of the admirals had thwarted his purpose at the time of the battle of the Dardanelles. He would also have been disturbed – for the *Bismarck* episode was unfolding over these critical days – by the loss of the *Hood* and the fact that in this encounter the *Prince of Wales* had broken off the action and allowed the German ship to escape. All these things must have preyed on his mind as he urged Cunningham to take greater 'risks'.

In fact, the position as set out by Cunningham in his reply was stark in its simplicity.

It is not the fear of sustaining losses, but the need to avoid losses which will cripple the fleet without any commensurate advantage which is the determining factor in operating in the Aegean . . . The experience of *three days* in which two cruisers and four destroyers have been sunk, and one battleship, two cruisers and four destroyers severely damaged shows what losses are likely to be. *Sea control in the Eastern Mediterranean could not be retained after another such experience.*[3]

With the advantage of hindsight we can know that all these gallant ships and their crews were squandered to no purpose. Certainly it is true

[1] Churchill, *The Grand Alliance*, 259.

[2] Cunningham, 375.

[3] The italics are mine. AC. Passage quoted in part Cunningham, 376, more fully, Churchill, 260–61.

that the sacrifices of the Navy prevented the enemy making a seaborne landing in Crete. But of what use was that? What difference would it have made if the German convoys had landed? As it turned out, hardly any. A shortening of the campaign by two, perhaps three days.

But that was no fault of the Navy. They did their best, and they did give to Freyberg and the garrison those two nights of grace, the 21st and the 22nd, when both sides knew that the Germans depended for everything on the stony, cratered square mile that was Maleme airfield, strewn with the wrecks of broken Junkers, defended by exhausted paratroopers. The War Diary of Mountain Division records that on the evening (21st/22nd), 'the situation seemed to be balanced on a knife-edge – a heavy concentrated British counter-attack would force the defenders to fight for their lives.'

It was to preserve for the soldiers this opportunity that so many sailors had drowned.

ELEVEN

THE COUNTER-ATTACK

T he Germans were strongest at Maleme, but even here their situation was, on the night of 21/22 May, highly precarious. The men of 7th Parachute Division and of the Assault Regiment, who had made the initial landings, were by now utterly exhausted. No system of reliefs had been put into operation, and many of them had not eaten for twenty-four hours. In many areas they were also short of ammunition and water. The fresh troops of 5th Mountain Division, who had begun to arrive during the afternoon, were appalled by the state of the airfield and its defenders, and they themselves were being forced to take cover immediately on landing. Due to congestion on the airstrip itself numbers of the transports were being directed to put down on the road which ran along its southern edge and even on the vine terraces that surrounded it, but less than half the aircraft which landed in this way were able to return.

> . . . They lay there immovable, like giant captured birds, and slowly the work of destruction by the British artillery was completed. With the aid of a captured Bren Carrier a group of paratroops and aircraft personnel did their utmost to clear the landing-ground, but the wreckage still constituted a severe obstacle to further landing operations. If the following day were to bring further losses of landing space the problem of supplying the defenders would become acute. Already a number of officers in the Quartermaster's department of the General Staff were of the opinion that reinforcements and supplies should strictly be seaborne . . .[1]

The commander of I Parachute Battalion has described how that night he was woken by his orderly with the news that a great sea battle was

[1] Von der Heydte, 116.

being fought. With his staff he climbed '. . . breathlessly to the top of "Great Castle Hill" as quickly as we could. What we saw from there was like a great fireworks display. Rockets and flares were shooting into the night sky, searchlights probed the darkness, and the red glow of a fire was spreading across the entire horizon. The muffled thunder of distant detonations lent sound to this dismal sight. For about twenty minutes we watched, until suddenly the fireworks ceased . . . very depressed we returned to our Headquarters.'[1]

Freyberg and his staff, too, had been spectators of this scene, and their reaction was one of elation. Geoffrey Cox has described how they were standing on the hillside in which the Creforce HQ caves had been tunnelled, and Freyberg turned to his CGS, Brigadier Stewart, and said, 'Well, Jock, it has been a great responsibility.' There seems little doubt that with the knowledge that the counter-attack planned at the afternoon's conference was at that very moment going on, and the enemy seaborne effort smashed, he thought the battle for the island had been won.

In fact, though, the counter-attack had not yet started. Nor, indeed, had its essential and complicated preliminaries been completed. It was to be a 5th Brigade affair, planned and commanded by Hargest, under whose orders Puttick had placed 28th and 20th Battalions. From the outset its conception carried certain features that were, to say the least, highly unpromising. These lay in two separate categories. First, the administrative complications that surrounded the three-stage relief required to bring 20th Battalion into the line and, second, the combat plan itself which had been hung on the shape of the New Zealand 'line', as it then was. This resembled a capital 'L' of the Greek alphabet, with vertical face on the north–south axis and a long west–east throw-back on the northern or right flank that covered the coastal area and the road from Maleme to Platanias.

In this region a number of enemy parachutists were still lodged in houses and dug in behind walls and ditches, and during the day they had been joined by advance guards from the main body. They were too weak to present any offensive threat but their presence there meant that any

[1] Von der Heydte, 108.

advance over this ground would be opposed and, in the confusion of darkness, liable to take up several hours. Hargest had fixed the start-line for his two fresh battalions to the west of the River Platanias, and this meant that they would have to traverse over a mile and a half in depth of enemy-occupied territory before they were level with the old 23rd Battalion positions and the Brigade proper – before, that is to say, any threat to the airfield would really be developed.

That evening Hargest called a conference at his headquarters at which he propounded the plan. Lieutenant Colonel Dittmer, who commanded the Maoris, raised the question of possible delays caused by enemy pockets in the ground between the start-line and Pirgos, and suggested that detachments from 23rd Battalion of the Field Engineers – whose positions overlooked this area – might be sent down to clear it in advance of the main body. However, it was decided that 'it was too late for any clearing up activity'.[1] Puttick, to whom this decision might have been referred, had not thought it necessary to attend the conference in person, but had sent his GSO, Lieutenant Colonel Gentry.

Another curious feature of Hargest's plan is the extreme restraint shown in making use of the force available. By the time that the 20th and the Maoris were up level with the rest of 5th Brigade there would be a strength of five battalions[2] facing the enemy. If all these had been moved forward together the chances of driving the enemy back to the Tavronitis would have been very good, but, in fact, the commanders of these battalions had not even been asked to Hargest's conference. A vague consolidation rôle had been allotted to the 21st, on the extreme left, but they were not notified of it until 12.40am. 'As an afterthought' the 23rd Battalion were told of a possible 'mopping-up rôle' for which they must hold themselves ready, and this information reached them in the early hours of the 22nd.

For the 20th and the Maoris no formal operation order appears to have been issued, its place being taken by 'Notes for COs', a copy of which is reproduced in the New Zealand Official History. From this it can be seen

[1] NZOH, 199.

[2] It is true that the 22nd amounted in strength to only half a battalion, but there were a number of other troops, engineers etc in the line performing a combat rôle.

that the 'advance' and the 'attack' were differentiated, the former fixed for a starting time of 0100 hours, the latter (by which was presumably meant the crossing of the Sfakoriako and the assault on Pirgos) for 0400 hours. The two battalions were to march on parallel lines, the 20th north of the road, the Maoris to the south of it. Along the road itself, and forming the junction of the two battalion flanks, would be three light tanks. There was to be a rest period of thirty minutes in Pirgos itself before the troops formed up for the next stage of the operation, which was to be the clearing of the airfield by 20th Battalion and the recapture of Hill 107 by the Maoris. Final evidence of Hargest's optimistic attitude may be found in paragraphs (5) and (6) of this strange document which ordered the Maoris to withdraw to Platanias as soon as the operation had been completed and entrusted the defence of Hill 107 'with posts thrust forward to command the aerodrome' to the 20th Battalion alone. When one battalion had failed in just this task – defence of the hill and airfield – on the first day of the assault, it is hard to see how the same number of men, exhausted after a difficult night attack, could have achieved this against an enemy nearly twice as strong. But there is no record of any orders to the three other battalions to move forward and support the 20th if it should prove successful in the first stage, and if there had been any in Hargest's mind it is reasonable to assume that he would have issued them that same night, for the difficulty of communication during the daytime, especially from his distant headquarters at Platanias, would have made their dissemination on the 22nd a highly uncertain business.

This, then, was the plan for the most critical operation in the whole battle. It cast a heavy burden on infantry of the 20th and 28th Battalions, with their arduous approach march and two successive attacks against a stronger enemy, but they were equal to it. Like every other soldier on Crete, they were keen to be let loose against the enemy, tired of hanging about under constant air attack, confident from their brief and successful clashes with the parachutists of their superiority.

But the whole essence of the planning was speed of execution. The hours of darkness were limited. Every minute of the night, before the Luftwaffe patrolled once again at tree-top height, was priceless.

The 2/7th Australian had no transport of their own, and spent the afternoon of 22 May waiting for the lorries which were to be sent from a pool at Suda. The second in command of the Battalion, Major Marshall, has described the events of that day:

> During the afternoon the transport arrived in dribs and drabs from all sorts of sources . . . The drivers were all unnerved by the bombing and the threat or sound of planes and were sheltering away from their trucks as they considered the vehicles targets . . . I hoped to get away at 5pm and speeded things up. Odd planes had been over our area all day and nothing had happened. Just as we had completed the embussing of the battalion in their areas, with the exception of D company whose drivers were still coming in, some enemy planes discovered us. They were concentrating as well on a supply dump about a mile further on nearer to Neo Khorion. Everyone else was ready except D Company so I left Halliday to hurry them on and I started off with the planes still around. It followed on our idea from Greece that the best way is just to go on in the face of an attack . . . We whizzed down the road and passed the food dump and breathed again. Then we turned a corner and found half a dozen planes above with the obvious intention of attacking us somewhere. I stopped the columns until I was sure Savige with A Company had caught up and then we sailed on. It was rather exhilarating. The planes had now obviously got on to us, but the road was winding along a valley and there were few straight stretches. The planes cruised about these straight stretches waiting for us . . . Twice I watched a plane single us out, bank and turn to machine-gun us along the straight, and I told the driver to crack it up. It then became a race to the curve . . . we streaked along and I hoped the battalion was following.[1]

In this way the Australians travelled westwards. The leading companies made reasonable progress for the first two hours, but it was dark by the time that they got to Suda. Here they found the town with many fires burning from the day's air-raids and time was lost in detours. They were misdirected on the road out of the town and had difficulty in finding 20th Battalion HQ, which was on the western side of Canea on the

[1] AOH, 235.

126

Kladiso river. It was well after midnight before the first arrivals, A and B Companies, reported to Burrows, and those behind were delayed even longer by misunderstandings over the passwords and by still further losing the way under the very strict blackout conditions that were enforced.

This delay had been particularly irksome for Dittmer, who had got the Maoris onto the start-line at 11.30, and was still more frustrating for 20th Battalion itself which had yet to move forward and whose move to the start-line would occupy at least another two hours after the relief. Dittmer had twice asked Hargest to bring the 20th up to the start-line without waiting for the Australians to appear, and on the second occasion Hargest had telephoned to Puttick for authority to permit this. However, Puttick refused this request on the ground that a sea landing might be attempted in 20th Battalion's area that night – in spite of having witnessed, together with every other member of Creforce, the smashing of this attempt by the Navy a short time before.

Burrows had also, and independently of 5th Brigade, asked Puttick for permission to move his battalion, or at least part of it, without waiting for the 2/7th, and had been refused. However, the very moment that the first Australian appeared Burrows himself set out for 5th Brigade HQ, leaving instructions that the battalion was not to wait as a whole for the 2/7th but that the companies were to move forward and follow him 'as relieved', ie one by one – and it is probably this order of Burrows, given on his own initiative, that made it possible for the counter-attack to go in at all.

When Burrows got to Hargest's headquarters it was after two o'clock, and the Maoris had been waiting for three hours. The attack plan was explained to him, as was some perfunctory description of the ground that he was expected to cover. By a quarter to three only the first two companies of the 20th, C and D, had arrived, and Burrows decided that, if the attack was to get anywhere before daylight, 'there was no option but to put in the attack with the two companies only'. At this, Hargest underwent a rapid change of opinion and 'felt doubtful whether the plan could be carried through at all'.[1] He thereupon telephoned Puttick once more, and was told that the attack must go on.

[1] NZOH, 215.

At half past three then, over two and a half hours late, the two battalions moved off to the attack, with the three light tanks clanking down the road between them, paced by a section of Maori infantry who had been detailed to protect the tanks from Molotov cocktails and other types of short-range attacks by the enemy.

Almost immediately the New Zealanders found that the Germans were much thicker on the ground than had been anticipated. Nearly every cluster of houses contained a group of parachutists, all of them equipped with machine-guns, while others were concealed in the drainage culverts or among the vine terraces. The attackers

> went on meeting resistance in depth – in ditches, behind hedges, in the top and bottom storeys of village buildings, fields and gardens on road . . . The wire of 5th Brigade hindered our advance. There were also mines and booby traps which got a few of us. We did not know that they were there. There was tommy-gun and pistol fire, and plenty of grenades and a lot of bayonet work which you don't often get in war. The amount of MG fire was never equalled. Fortunately a lot of it was high and the tracer bullets enabled us to pick our way up and throw in grenades. We had heavy casualties but the Germans had heavier. They were unprepared. Some were without trousers, some had no boots on. The Germans were helpless in the dark. With another hour (of darkness) we could have reached the far side of the 'drome. We captured as it was a lot of MG's, two Bofors pits were over-run and the guns destroyed. The prisoners went back to 5th Brigade.[1]

On the left the Maoris had had an easier passage because the ground south of the road was commanded in daylight by the guns of the 23rd Battalion and the Engineers, and most of the parachutists in this area had retreated northwards to the coastal strip where they were in the path of 20th Battalion. Even so, there were enough snipers about to slow down the momentum of the advance. By the time the Maoris reached the crossroads north of Dhaskaliana it was already daylight, and there was no sign of the 20th. It was now plain that if the strongly fortified village of Pirgos was to be attacked at all this would have to be done under

[1] Report by Captain Upham, VC.

conditions very different from those envisaged in the 'Notes for CO's'. The three tanks which had come up with the Maoris had halted. 'The tanks were one behind the other on the road just east of the road junction and to my mind at the time were very dubious about the whole show.'[1] Captain Dawson, Brigade Major of 5th Brigade, who had met the attackers at this rendezvous, decided that as there was no sign of the 20th Battalion he would go back to Hargest and report '. . . it was well after daylight by then, and my impression was that we could not accomplish much with the attack from then on – because of the strafing from the air that was going on. Situation seemed unstable and unsatisfactory.'[2]

Shortly after Dawson had left Burrows appeared, still with only two companies leading, and he and Dittmer decided to put in the attack on the village immediately. C Company of the 20th was to go for the houses on the north side of Pirgos while D was to go straight across to the eastern boundary of the airfield itself. The Maoris would skirt its southern edge and swing up to make a direct assault on Hill 107. The tanks, and their section, would attack directly down the road into the centre of Pirgos and, it was hoped, assist in the distraction of the enemy from the two threats on his flank.

The tanks ran into trouble straight away. They were thin-skinned Mark IIs (it will be recalled that the two 'I' tanks had been lost in the 22nd Battalion counter-attack on the first afternoon) and their only armament was a pair of Vickers heavy machine-guns in the turret. They were vulnerable to the German 20-mm anti-tank gun and in addition to this they had to face a number of captured Bofors anti-aircraft guns being used by the enemy in a close-support rôle.[3]

The leading tank was hit and set alight almost immediately, the gunner and the commander being killed, although the wounded driver managed

---

[1] Report by Captain Dawson, quoted NZOH, 219.

[2] Ibid.

[3] As early as 1936 the Germans had realised that the very high muzzle velocities required to propel shot six or seven miles upwards into the atmosphere would be still more deadly when used against armour at ground level. Their success in adapting the 88-mm needs no reiteration here, and against the Vickers Light tanks the Bofors were equally effective. XI Air Corps report mentions that captured armour-piercing ammunition in Greece was flown out to Maleme for use in the Bofors.

to reverse it back to a bamboo grove where there was some cover. The troop commander (Lieutenant Roy Farran) had turned his own tank in here a few minutes earlier to avoid a Messerschmitt that was strafing the road, and had broken one of the bogeys. He signalled to the third tank not to go on alone, and decided to transfer the bogey from the damaged tank to his own. But this meant sending back three miles to Squadron HQ for fitters and a wait of at least three hours while the bogey was changed.

Tactically the effect of the tanks *débâcle* was that the centrepiece on which the two battalions were hinging had been removed, and each battalion was now operating independently. On the extreme right D Company pressed right on up to the edge of the airfield, in spite of steadily increasing opposition and heavy casualties. When they got there there was only one officer remaining unwounded, Lieutenant Maxwell, who has described the scene:

> . . . there were stacks of aircraft, some crashed, some not. I remember Private Amos saying, 'I've carried this anti-tank rifle all this way and I am going to have one shot.' He fired two shots into an aircraft and made a mess of it.
>
> Broad daylight – at this time we had come under the most intense mortar and MG fire with the clear ground of the 'drome in front of us . . .[1]

C Company on its left was held back by the Germans in Pirgos village where they badly missed Farran and his troop of tanks. As the New Zealanders penetrated into the square the parachutists ran back along the roofs of the houses, dropping grenades into the streets as they went. Others went underground as the attackers passed through, then came up and fired on them from behind. C Company were too weak to deal with every cellar and it was hoped that 23rd Battalion would have been following on their heels in fulfilment of the mopping-up rôle that had been allotted to it. But, with the exception of A Company which had detached and was following the Maoris on the left flank, Leckie, for the third day running, made no move with his battalion.

[1] Report by Captain Maxwell, quoted NZOH, 218.

In the meantime, the Maoris were engaged in bitter fighting to the south of the village. It was broad daylight now and the Luftwaffe was exerting its fullest efforts, constantly harassing them. As they pressed deeper, they came under cross-fire from the German positions on the lower slope of Hill 107 as well as from the houses on the fringe of Pirgos.

We must get forward and get above and round the Germans whose bullets and mortar bombs were cracking round us. We could at times see German machine-gunners running up through the trees. We collected in small groups and worked forward. Men were hit, men were maimed. The din of the fight was incessant. There seemed to be German machine-guns behind all the trees. If we could silence one or two immediately in front we might break through.[1]

The bravery of these Maoris, outnumbered, struggling forward against four or five times their own firepower and under repeated air attack, was quite incredible. And always at their head was their CO, Lieutenant Colonel Dittmer. 'At one point he came across some of his men whom the heavy enemy fire had forced to ground. "Call yourself bloody soldiers," he said, and went forward. His example was not lost, the men got to their feet and the attack went on.'

Major Dyer described how the enemy tried at one stage to mount a counter-attack and 'the red Nazi banners erected on poles before they came at us. The Maoris in a scattered mob under the trees going forward to meet them crying, "Ah! Ah!" and firing at the hip. The Huns with their fat behinds to us going for their lives down the gulley and then our job to hold the Maoris in. When one considers what the Maoris had been through, and the position and the state we were all in and think of the spontaneous nature of that charge – the ancestral fighting urge was a truly magnificent thing.'[2]

As the morning wore on Brigadier Hargest, with an imperfect picture of the situation in his mind, became increasingly optimistic. The brief bout of nervousness which had led him, the previous evening, to ask Puttick

[1] Report by Major Dyer, quoted NZOH, 220.

[2] NZ Div War Diary, quoted OH, 229.

for permission to cancel the whole attack had gone. In its place he developed the private theory that the Germans were evacuating Crete. At 10.42 he sent a message to Division: 'Steady flow of enemy planes landing and taking off. May be trying to take troops off. Investigating.' Shortly after this two events occurred that might have been expected to temper his optimism, although they do not seem to have done so. Farran's tanks returned and reported the strength of the resistance in Pirgos and the disposal of the infantry, and accounts came in of Germans landing motorcycle and AFVs from the aircraft that were landing in this 'steady flow'. In spite of this Hargest's next message read: 'From general quietness, and because eleven fires have been lit on 'drome it appears as though enemy might be preparing evacuation. Am having further investigations made. Do any other reports from other sources show further evidence of this?'[1]

Division made a noncommittal reply: 'No other indications as you suggest, but it is possible'. Still hopeful, Hargest signalled at 12.30 that 'men had been seen to run towards planes before they took off' (these were, in fact, unloading parties).

The dispelling of this illusion may well have been responsible for Hargest becoming more despondent than he would otherwise have been, or the situation warranted. But this did not come until the late afternoon. The first sign that optimism was on the wane came back to Division at 1.25pm when Hargest told them: 'Recent messages make situation confused. M (the Brigade Major) going to investigate. Troops NOT so far forward on left as believed. Officers on ground believe enemy preparing for attack and take serious view. I disagree but of course they have closer view. Will visit your HQ when M returns.'

In fact, the attack had petered out during the morning and both 20th and 28th Battalions were at a standstill and under increasing pressure from the Germans, who had brought up three fresh companies of II Battalion, 85th Mountain Regiment. The New Zealanders had done magnificently against a much stronger enemy, and with every kind of physical limitation on their movement and communication. Now they

---

[1] The Ju 52 was not capable of carrying any AFV. It is more likely that observers were mistaking the small Jeep-like version of the Volkswagen for an AFV.

were exhausted and they were short of Bren ammunition, mortar bombs and grenades. They could make no further progress, even at night-fall, without substantial reinforcement. Major Burrows, who was still handicapped by operating with only a three company strength leading, decided that only a modified version of the original plan had any chance of succeeding, and started trying to bring his battalion across the front into the Maori area so as to assist Dittmer in an attack on Hill 107.

Captain Upham, who was sent with Sergeant Kirk to bring in the furthest company, which had penetrated to the eastern edge of the airfield, found plenty of activity of the kind that had fostered Hargest's optimism, although he had good reason to put a different interpretation upon it.

> The mortar and machine-gun fire on the open ground was heavy, and we were lucky to get back alive. When we reached the 'drome the planes were landing (some leaving 'drome too) and the parachutists were jumping out and getting straight into battle for the Germans were counter-attacking on the right flank.

By midday Burrows had managed to get his men south of the road, but he learned that all four companies of the Maori Battalion were pinned down by enemy fire and could get no further without stronger mortar and infantry support. The Regimental Aid Post was crowded with wounded of both sides, and had run out of medical dressings. After a conversation between Burrows and Lieutenant Colonel Dittmer the latter went back to 23rd Battalion HQ and asked Lieutenant Colonels Leckie and Andrew to support him in a renewal of the attack that afternoon. This was reasonable enough for 23rd Battalion had hardly been engaged at all so far and there were three intact companies of the 22nd. It was desirable to keep up the pressure on the Germans while they were still put out of the course of the night's fighting during the time that elapsed while the situation was being appreciated at the distant 5th Brigade HQ in Platanias. However, these two commanders, who had so far done little to show the same qualities of aggressive leadership as Dittmer, decided that '. . . the best course was to hold what ground they had, and stop the enemy infiltration that was constantly going on'.

This decision meant, in effect, that the counter-attack had come to a dead stop. And with it was reached the third, and last, major crisis in the battle for the island. On the first day, before 22nd Battalion had withdrawn from Maleme, and on the second, when the plan for the counter-attack was being formulated, there had been a chance for Freyberg, or for Puttick, or for Hargest, to so affect the course of the battle by their orders and actions that it might yet have been won. Now, on the third day, there was still that chance. But this was the last opportunity and when it had gone the fate of Crete would be sealed.

TWELVE

WITHDRAWAL TO UNPREPARED POSITIONS

General Freyberg's 'Report on the Battle of Crete' is still a secret document.[1] It is not available to historians, other than the two officially appointed by the Australian and New Zealand Governments, and those extracts from it which have been made public by these authorities are neutral in character and add nothing to what we can readily discover from a reading of other material. But what we cannot learn from any other source is Freyberg's attitude of mind. We may guess, though, at the frustration felt by this brave and aggressive man as the battle developed; at how much he must have regretted his initial diffidence over interfering with his subordinate commanders; at his bitterness, as, rendered practically impotent by the steadily deteriorating communications, he felt the pattern of defeat becoming hourly more apparent.

At 5pm on 22 May, the afternoon following the failure of the first counter-attack, Freyberg called a conference and – it is the first time that the phrase is used in the New Zealand Official History – 'gave his order' for a fresh counter-attack. The swollen 5th Brigade would now take part, *en bloc*, together with two fresh battalions from 4th Brigade, the 2/8th Australian and the 18th New Zealand.

Puttick accepted this, but when he got back to 4th Brigade HQ he found reports of enemy activity against Galatas.[2] This cannot really have amounted to much, even in the form in which it reached Puttick, but the idea made him apprehensive of his left flank and rear. Then, when he spoke to Hargest, he found that the brigadier had reverted to a mood of pessimism. Hargest 'represented that his troops had been severely

[1] At the time of writing. AC.

[2] New Zealand Div Report, para 97, said that 'the road between 4th and 5th Brigades is "commanded" by an enemy detachment including a machine-gun.'

attacked, were considerably exhausted, and certainly not fit to make a further attack'.[1] What led Hargest to this opinion – one which he had formed without visiting his Brigade front at any time during the battle – is not clear. But he must have expressed it to Puttick at greater length than is recorded in the Divisional diary because at the end of their conversation Puttick had decided not only that 5th Brigade was unfit to take part in any further attack, but that it should be withdrawn from its positions immediately.

Puttick then came back on the telephone to Freyberg and told him of the 'new situation'. Freyberg was very reluctant to authorise a total evacuation of the old 5th Brigade position and it was at first considered that the 18th Battalion and the 2/8th Australian might relieve Hargest and enable him to pull his men back into the coastal area to reorganise. But Puttick pointed out that two battalions could hardly be expected to hold what five could not, and so finally Freyberg agreed in principle to the withdrawal. He told Puttick that he would send down Brigadier Stewart to Divisional Headquarters and that together they could draw up the plan in detail.

The orders were quickly agreed. They were for a complete evacuation of the prepared positions along the Dhaskaliana ridge. This movement was to be covered by the gallant Maori Battalion which would, in due course, reoccupy its old positions around Platanias, with the rest of 5th Brigade (less 20th and 22nd Battalions which were to go under 4th Brigade) herded in echelon behind it. 'All moves were to be completed by daylight if possible.'

This decision, whatever the detailed plan of carrying it out, meant acceptance of the loss of Maleme and thus, inevitably, of the island itself.

It seems to have been occasioned by two things. First, Hargest's seriously underrating the stamina and spirit of his own Brigade; second, Puttick's concern over the supposed threat from the enemy in the Prison Valley. It is necessary, therefore, to examine briefly the situation there for once the 5th Brigade withdrawal had been carried out the Prison Valley would no longer be a separate front but would

---

[1] NZ Div Report, para 97.

fuse with the main enemy mass that was advancing eastwards from Maleme.

The German force in the Prison Valley had not been reinforced since the first day's fighting, and its total comprised the three battalions of Heidrich's 3rd Parachute Regiment and the Engineer Battalion. A small quantity of supplies were being dropped to them each afternoon on the flat ground near the reservoir, but these were kept to a minimum, owing to the demands of the fighting at Maleme, and what they received did not keep pace with expenditure. On 22 May von der Heydte, commander of I Battalion, recorded that 'Nothing had changed during the past twenty-four hours. The ammunition and food situation had not improved. What little ammunition we had received during the previous day had already been used up, and food was virtually unobtainable. The soldiers were hungry, and in the awful monotony of waiting their morale sank.'[1] Heidrich realised that it was of the first importance to make contact with Ramcke and with 5th Mountain Division to the north, and with this end in view he formed a battle-group from the Engineers and elements of III Battalion and sent it off in a northerly direction and across the lower slopes of Signal Hill – wild, rocky country that was unoccupied by either side. This force under Major Heilmann had as its main purpose the 'establishment of contact with the German forces east of Maleme'[2] and was not in sufficient strength to undertake any more aggressive rôle. But it is undoubtedly their movement, reported that afternoon by scouts of 10th Brigade, that caused Puttick to take fright and support Hargest in recommending that no second attack should take place. As a cover for Heilmann's movement, and so as to preserve an aggressive posture against 10th Brigade, Heidrich had ordered two attacks to be made during the day. These were made by two or three companies at a time and directed against the Galatas heights to the flank of the brave Petrol Company that had fought so successfully on the first day.

The Germans were well supported by heavy mortars and by relays of

---

[1] Von der Heydte, 118.

[2] XI Air Corps report.

ground-strafing Bf 109s which flew up and down the ridges, firing at the defenders' gun flashes. After about half an hour they succeeded in establishing some machine-guns on Pink Hill, which had been left in no man's land after the previous fighting had died down and the situation began to look threatening. The battalion reserve, only fifty strong, was being readied to move forward when

> There came a terrific clamour from behind. Out of the trees came Captain Forrester of the Buffs, clad in shorts, a long yellow army jersey reaching down almost to the bottom of the shorts, brass polished and gleaming, web belt in place and waving his revolver in his right hand. He was tall, thin-faced, with no tin hat – the very opposite of a soldier hero; as if he had just stepped on to the parade ground. He looked like a Wodehouse character. It was a most inspiring sight. Forrester was at the head of a crowd of disorderly Greeks, including women; one Greek had a shot-gun with a serrated edge bread knife tied on like a bayonet, others had ancient weapons – all sorts. Without hesitation this uncouth group, with Forrester right out in front, went over the top of the parapet and headlong at the crest of the hill. The enemy fled.[1]

The German attack had been going so well that Heidrich had attempted to develop it by a supporting movement to the east of Cemetery Hill, but here, too, the day was saved by the intervention of the Greeks, this time under Captain HM Smith.

> . . . they surged around and went on with great enthusiasm – at the trot or steady jog yelling '*aera*' or something like that, which I was told was the *Evzones*' war-cry. It was very effective, and the whole show was the most thrilling moment of my life.

These two counter-attacks, and the quality of the resistance put up by the Greeks at Kastelli and by the Cretan gendarmerie at Rethymno town – to cite examples taken at random – suggest that their valour and military capacity had been seriously underestimated by their allies. In spite of their record against the Italians in Greece and, indeed, against

[1] Report by driver AQ Pope, 4 RTM Coy, quoted NZOH, 235.

the Germans in Macedonia, the prevalent view was to regard them as militarily negligible. In fact, when granted the rudiments of trained leadership and a distribution of captured weapons, the Greeks were only too eager to take on the strongest enemy formations, which they did with great dash and spirit. Had the course of the battle been differently conceived by the senior officers on the island, the Greeks might have been used with great effect in a counter-offensive – perhaps making the frontal attack with the New Zealanders operating on the flanks.

As it was, their double intervention and its success had left the Germans utterly dispirited. Derpa, whose II Battalion had carried out the attacks, had earlier expressed his misgivings to Heidrich about their practicability.[1] He had been allotted all the reserves of ammunition and hand-grenades, including those held by the other two battalions. When the attacks collapsed 3rd Parachute Regiment was left practically defenceless. The following day (23 May) the CO of I Battalion wrote that

I had handed over all my available supplies to II Battalion the previous day. This could have meant disaster for my own battalion if the expected supplies were not sent up to us; should the British then have launched an attack we could have held out scarcely an hour.

But the 'British', by which title the enemy referred indiscriminately to all Commonwealth troops, were not attacking. The tireless Captain Dawson, who had been sent out once again by Hargest to take his orders to the forward battalions of 5th Brigade, arrived at the headquarters of the 23rd at dawn.

He arrived – very exhausted. It was full daylight. He said he had some

[1] Von der Heydte has described the interview, which he witnessed: 'The Regimental Commander, whose nerves were stretched to breaking point, did not wish to listen to any such misgivings. He cut short the commander of the II Battalion, shouted at him and accused him of being a coward. Deeply hurt, the sensitive and chivalrous Commander turned pale. Even from his tightly pressed lips all the blood seemed to have been drained. After a momentary pause he saluted. "It is not a question of my own life, sir," he replied. "I am considering the lives of the soldiers for whom I am responsible. My own life I would gladly give." These were the last words I ever heard him utter.' (Derpa was mortally wounded in the attack.) Von der Heydte, 120.

'very surprising news' for me. My remark was 'What? Have they tossed it in?' (Wishful thinking I'm afraid; but I *did* feel that we had made a mess of them the day before. And the morning was so quiet and peaceful, with not a 'plane in the sky as yet.) Dawson said, 'We are to retire to the Platanias R line. Will you get in touch with all Battalions. The withdrawal was supposed to start half an hour ago.' I gave Dawson my blanket and told him to have a sleep. I would wake him up in good time.[1]

When Dittmer was told that all his hard won gains were to be forsaken and that his battalion, which had borne the heat of the fighting the previous day, was detailed to act as rearguard he was furious:

I went extremely rude about being left in such a manner, but had little time to go into the reason for it. I knew that the enemy would see other units going over high ground to the East and then 28th Battalion would catch it.[2]

And so, with full daylight once more, 5th Brigade was again on the move. But now a change had come over the men, and soon it was to affect the whole of Creforce. The scent of victory had gone, and in its place there spread a draught of rumour. Their bravery and their determination were unaffected. But the elation, the feeling that at last they were going to teach the enemy a lesson; that they, confronting the Germans for the first time on terms that were more or less equal, could take revenge for their comrades who had died in Greece; could by one valiant stroke stop short the German army and wipe away the memory of Namsos and Dunkirk – these hopes faded. The smell of defeat was abroad.

We withdrew under orders soon after midnight, carrying our wounded on improvised stretchers down the steep cliff face and then along a difficult clay creek bed to the road. Then we marched until nearly dawn. I was very impressed by the continued discipline of the men. Mile after mile we trudged. Everyone was tired. All were vaguely

[1] Letter from Colonel Leckie to DM Davin, 12.4.51.

[2] NZOH, 252.

resentful, although none of us could have put a finger on the reason. Those who could bear the strain better carried the rifles and Bren guns of those who were fatigued.[1]

The severely wounded had to be left behind, and only two of the 75-mm guns were got away. The artillery did not get their orders until 4am and it was impossible for the outlying troops to remove their guns in time to withdraw under cover of the main body. Two 3.7-inch howitzers and three 75s were disabled and abandoned, their crews being allotted to 28th Battalion to fight as infantry. Even the rearmost troop only managed to extricate half their strength for one truck and limber went over a precipice and another broke its towing attachment.

The Maoris had to stop three times and fight pitched battles with their pursuers for the Germans were following closely, towing their captured Bofors with pairs of Volkswagens and then manhandling them up to the line, often as close as two or three hundred yards.

By 2pm the withdrawal had been completed – at least in so far as it had been envisaged in Hargest's orders of the previous night – but once it had been carried out the Germans on the coast could make immediate and effective contact with Heidrich's 3rd Parachute Regiment that was poised to the south of Galatas. It was a matter of hours before the New Zealanders, who were bunched on the tongue of land between Ay Marina and the Platanias bridge, would be forced to withdraw inside the perimeter of which the Galatas heights were the keystone.

That morning the Prime Minister had sent General Freyberg a message, 'The whole world is watching your splendid battle, on which great events turn.' By the same signal, to Wavell, he was more specific:

Crete battle must be won. Even if enemy secure good lodgements *fighting must be maintained indefinitely* in the island, thus keeping enemy main striking force tied down to the task. This will at least give you time to mobilise Tiger Cubs and dominate situation Western Desert. While it lasts it also protects Cyprus. Hope you will reinforce Crete every night to fullest extent. Is it not possible to send more tanks and thus reconquer any captured aerodrome? Enemy's exertions and loss

[1] Report by Lieutenant Thomas, quoted NZOH, 263.

141

in highest class troops must be very severe. He cannot keep it up forever . . .

But the possibility of 'reconquering' territory had now passed. The best that could be hoped for was to prolong the resistance in the hope that the battle might have ended, in the light of German strategic preparations elsewhere, in a sort of infantry stalemate. The enemy would have had to withdraw the paratroopers and the bulk of von Richthofen's Air Fleet for the attack on Russia. A quiescent deadlock, such as existed around the Tobruk perimeter, might have resulted.

For when Puttick and Hargest had persuaded Freyberg that the counter-attack ordered by him for the 22nd was not practical, all hope of a clear-cut victory went with it. Three days, and three opportunities, had already passed. Now it was a gamble. If it failed Crete was lost, it is true, but the gamble was not even taken. The final chance had been discarded and no inspiring messages, no last-minute expenditure of matériel, or ships, or aircraft, could turn the battle for Crete into a victory. The question was, simply, how serious would be the defeat?

THIRTEEN

THE BATTLE OF GALATAS

Throughout 23 May the German strength increased. With the retirement of 5th Brigade Maleme had become fully operational and in the late afternoon the first fighters were transferred there. This meant that from the following day standing patrols of ground-strafing aircraft could be maintained throughout the period of the aircraft's endurance as the combat zone was less than five minutes from the runway – a damaged aircraft could glide from Canea to Maleme on a dead engine.

In addition to the Bf 109s, the enemy landed fresh troops and equipment in strength. These included I and II Batteries of 95th Mountain Artillery Regiment with 95th Anti-tank Battalion and twenty 50-mm anti-tank guns. Fifty-fifth Motorcycle Battalion also arrived on that day and the first battalions of 141st Mountain Regiment. The arrival of the latter meant that within twenty-four hours the whole of 5th Mountain Division would be in the line[1], as well as all the surviving parachutists. Ringel, the Commander of the Division, who had landed the previous evening, now set about consolidating his command and laying his plans for the later stages of the operation.

His arrival was a move to regularise the situation, and although there were many senior German officers who still doubted the value and practicability of the whole affair at least when Ringel took command it became professional business. For now, although Lohr still held nominal command, executive control was taken out of the hands of the Luftwaffe and had become a Wehrmacht responsibility. Ringel lost no time in asserting his authority over the parachutists. He informed Heidrich that from now on West and Centre Groups were both under

---

[1] Information regarding the enemy dispositions is taken from 4th Air Fleet report, quoted NZOH, 278.

his command and would be known as Ringel Group. All the parachutists who survived from Group West were formed into a single strong battalion formation under Ramcke and placed on the extreme left flank on the coast road.

Ringel's orders from IV Air Fleet were: (i) to secure Maleme airfield; (ii) to clear Suda Bay; (iii) to relieve the paratroops at Rethymno; (iv) to make contact with Heraklion; and (v) to occupy the whole island.

The instructions and their order of priority were never varied, and were to have an important and, for the British, a happy result in the later stages of the fighting. However, on the morning of 24 May Ringel had only just managed to achieve the first of his objectives, and was laying his plans for the fulfilment of the second. These plans provided for a concentric attack on the Galatas heights, with the intention of breaking the New Zealand resistance in their positions before the town and then pursuing the defenders into Canea, with a direct attack on Suda the following day (26 May). The main thrust would come from the Mountain troops in the centre of the arc – 'in all planning the greatly diminished strength of the paratroops had to be taken into consideration' wrote the diarist of 5th Mountain Division War with satisfaction – but Ringel had also planned an ambitious 'right hook' by using two battalions, the I and III of 85th Mountain Regiment, and supporting forces to take Alikianou, which was still holding out, although defended only by the 8th Greek Regiment[1], and to strike right across the hills and cut the Suda–Rethymno road in the rear of the New Zealand Force.

On this same day, 24 May, while the fresh German forces were getting into position, Wavell and Cunningham received another message from the Chiefs of Staff to the effect that

Our difficulties in Crete are great, but from all the information we have so are those of the enemy. If we stick it out enemy's effort may peter

---

[1] Kippenberger tells how, before the attack, when the preliminary dispositions of the New Zealand Division and forces under command were being made, he told Puttick that 8th Greek were 'only a circle on the map', and that 'it was murder to leave such troops in such a position'. The reply was that 'In war, murder sometimes has to be done.' In fact, far from being 'murdered' the 8th Greek fought with such valour and for so long that they played a substantial part in securing the safe evacuation of the main body of Creforce. (Kippenberger, *Infantry Brigadier*)

out. It seems to us imperative that reinforcements in greatest strength possible should be sent as soon as possible to island to ensure destruction of enemy already landed before they can be seriously reinforced. The vital importance of this battle is well known to you and great risks must be accepted to ensure our success.[1]

Freyberg's own view, also expressed on that day, was deeply pessimistic. In his Report he wrote: 'At this stage I was quite clear in my mind that the troops would not be able to last much longer against a continuation of the air attacks which they had had during the previous five days. The enemy bombing was accurate and it was only a question of time before our now shaken troops must be driven out of the positions they occupied. The danger was quite clear. We were gradually being driven back on our base areas, the loss of which would deprive us of our food and ammunition. If this heavy air attack continued it would not be long before we were driven right off our meagre food and ammunition resources. I really knew at this time that there were two alternatives, defeat in the field and capture, or withdrawal. Without tools, artillery and transport we could not re-adjust our rearward defences.'[2]

It is plain from this text that already, on the fifth day of the battle, Freyberg was considering 'withdrawal', not just as a possibility but as an inevitable sequel to the battle. Whether, and how soon, he communicated this conviction to Puttick is something about which we have no information, but there is evidence – in a letter from Puttick to Hargest on 26 May[3] – that Puttick regarded it as the determining factor in Division on the 24th and 25th, and it may reasonably be inferred that, even before the battle of Galatas broke, Puttick was certain as to what its outcome would be.

The Galatas heights were a naturally strong position, and the most favourable ground on which to fight a defensive battle in front of Canea. They are relatively shallow eminences – none of them over 400 feet – but their proximity to sea level makes them seem higher. They lie in the form

---

[1] Churchill, *The Grand Alliance*, 260.

[2] Quoted NZOH, 340.

[3] NZOH, 294.

of a curved bow, with the town of Galatas in its centre. In the north, a little over half a mile from the coast road, is the summit of Red Hill, and from this the bow curves south-east to include Wheat Hill, Pink Hill and, at its tip, the bare mound of Cemetery Hill, swept by the fire of both sides and in no man's land. Across the bow, in its centre, was drawn an arrow, Ruin Ridge, with its tip, Ruin Hill, the highest of the quintet, lying a quarter of a mile west of the arc.

The strength of the forces allotted by Puttick to this position was effectually little greater than two battalions – to face an enemy attack by at least five battalions of which three were fresh. The whole of 5th Brigade had been withdrawn into reserve, together with the 20th and 28th Battalions, and no move had been made to bring forward any of the fresh troops from the Suda area. This meant that the Galatas heights were held in the south by the gallant Petrol Company, still on Pink Hill, and a motley group of dismounted drivers and gunners, the whole taking its name from the commander, Major Russell; in the north, from Wheat Hill to the sea, by the Composite Battalion, another force of weary auxiliaries with stout hearts but no proper infantry training.

These dispositions are most easily explained if Puttick had already decided that he could not make a real stand at Galatas but intended to use the troops there as a screen behind which the main body could be withdrawn still further. This interpretation is reinforced by his positioning of the two strong Australian battalions – 2/7th and 2/8th – on the flank as a hinge on which the withdrawal might pivot. Even so, withdrawal from the Galatas heights must eventually have led to abandonment of Canea and Suda Bay, a very drastic step to consider before full-scale evacuation of the whole island had been authorised.

Throughout 23 May the forward troops of 10th Brigade could see the enemy arriving on the southern slopes of Signal Hill, two and a half miles to the west, and getting into their positions for an attack, but the New Zealanders had few weapons and virtually no ammunition with which they could reach them and held their fire. That afternoon Major Lomas, the medical officer of the Composite Battalion, told Kippenberger that 'morale was going down' and that 'during the day we had an increasing number of cases of slightly wounded men being brought in by three or four friends in no hurry to go back'.[1] In view of this, and of the imminence of a German attack, Kippenberger made a personal tour of inspection 'and was forced to the reluctant conclusion that it [the Composite Battalion] was in no condition to meet the heavy attacks that must come soon'.[2] He drove back to Divisional Headquarters and saw Puttick, who agreed to release 18th Battalion to take over the right flank. The 18th moved into position on the night of 24/24 May and at the same time the command structure of the area was reorganised, the front becoming a 4th Brigade responsibility with Inglis having the overall command. Inglis kept his own headquarters back at the Galatas turn-off on the coast road and Kippenberger remained forward as 'sub-area commander'. This arrangement was a sensible one and had the added advantage of preserving on this vital but weakly held position the two ablest and most vigorous of the New Zealand commanders. Their subsequent conduct of the battle cannot but heighten speculation as to the probable outcome of affairs at Maleme had they held command there in the opening stages.

When the 18th moved into position on Red and Wheat Hills the Composite Battalion was drawn back and placed on Ruin Ridge. Most unfortunately, Colonel Gray, the CO of the 18th, did not occupy Ruin Hill, the commanding knoll that jutted out from the perimeter, during the night as he felt that his battalion was already, with the Composite now completely out of the line, dangerously strung out. (It was responsible for the whole front from the shore to the right of Russell Force.)

During the 24th, then, the enemy moved forward and occupied Ruin Hill with three companies of I Battalion, 100th Mountain Regiment, and dug in nine heavy mortars on the reverse slope. An exploratory attack that afternoon soon showed that enemy cross-fire from Ruin Hill could make Red Hill practically untenable and, by driving the defenders off it, threaten the flank of Wheat Hill in a like manner. On this occasion, though, the relatively fresh 18th Battalion fought well, holding the flanks of the break-in without giving an inch, and Colonel Utz decided Galatas

[1] Kippenberger, op cit, 63–4.

[2] Ibid.

was 'so strongly defended that the assault would have to be deferred until the next day, after a thorough softening up by Stukas'.[1]

This postponement of the attack is a tribute to the bravery and resolution of New Zealanders in the front line but, in fact, the Galatas position was anything but 'strongly defended'. Only 18th Battalion was reasonably fresh – Russell Force and the 19th Battalion had been in their positions since the day of the invasion – and there was no reserve worth speaking of to repair the breaches that must occur if this tenuous line should be simultaneously and concentrically assaulted. The Composite Battalion, who might have filled the rôle of a sort of close-up Brigade Reserve, were still in poor shape. That morning Kippenberger had 'managed to walk along the whole of the Composite Battalion's new line and get them something like reasonable positions. I also tried to put a little heart into some of the officers, but too many had only the idea they had done their bit and should be relieved. It was only too clear that the unit had little fighting value left.'[2]

All other formations were east of the Galatas turn-off and it would not be easy to move them quickly up to the 'heights' in daylight. Of these the only unit that was directly under Inglis's orders was the remains of the 20th Battalion, now in a sadly depleted state. The evening before Kippenberger had seen their last platoons coming back from Ay Marina, 'looking dazed and weary to exhaustion, and for the first time I felt the coming of defeat'.[3]

The German plan was for a succession of blows at different points along the perimeter, rather than a simultaneous attack, as this would allow them to concentrate their firepower on each sector in turn. It was to be led off by Ramcke Group in the north, leading with two battalions – Stentzler's and Gericke's. It would then be taken up by II Battalion of 100th Mountain Regiment under Schury, with I Battalion (Schrank) following on its heels, and a final push in the evening by Heidrich's parachutists in the south. The 100th Mountain Regiment was under the command of Colonel Utz and had the main rôle. In fact, its strength was

---

[1] Neuhoff, Interrogation, 1945.

[2] Kippenberger, op cit, 65.

[3] Ibid 59, 61.

much greater than the nominal two battalions indicated by its order of battle for all the supporting units, mobile, anti-tank and heavy weapons detachments, came under Utz's command.

Ringel had originally hoped that Utz would be able to develop his attack on the evening of the 24th, but after the failure of the exploratory attack by I Battalion Utz had refused to go any further without developing his build-up. During the night this proceeded. A company patrol from 18th Battalion counted no fewer than eighteen separate heavy machine-guns firing tracer in their area alone – a greater strength than that at the disposal of the whole of the 18th Battalion. In contrast to this, Colonel Gray found that his mortar ammunition was reduced by 10am on the morning of the 25th to ten bombs. When he sent for more he received another thirty – with a note to the effect that they were the last remaining in the entire brigade.

Nevertheless, with his last reserves of mortar ammunition Gray had been doing good work among the enemy, particularly the men of Ramcke Group who came under observation from Red Hill as they were forming up for the attack. By now the Germans had a healthy respect for the New Zealanders.

'Never before [the fighting in Crete] had we run up against men who would stand and shoot and stay to fight it out – disciplined troops who could hold their fire until the last moment.'[1]

And so for a variety of reasons Ramcke Group were late in getting started, and the air support which had been promised Utz was diverted against the north of the line to support the parachutists. At 12.20pm, zero hour for II Battalion, the preliminary air bombardment had not gone in. Schury obediently led his men off, but progress was disappointing and at 12.45 Utz signalled Ringel, 'When do we get Stuka support?' Getting no answer, he again asked, at 1.30pm, 'Request an immediate answer whether there will be any more Stuka attacks. The battalion is waiting.'[2]

He was then told that raids would take place at 4.30 and 4.45 that afternoon. This information was a further factor in slowing down the

[1] Interrogation (Murphy).

[2] 5th Mountain Div War Diary.

enemy advance in the centre as the men were reluctant to press too deeply into the New Zealand positions, unless it were on a broad front, for fear of being caught in their own bombardment during the afternoon. Without a successful assault on Wheat Hill or Pink Hill, they found that all probing movements in the valley were pinned down by fire from the two heights. In this way the New Zealanders managed to keep their front intact through the afternoon until, about four o'clock, the parachutists of Ramcke Group, aided by an intense volume of mortar fire (estimated by Kippenberger at twenty a minute) in addition to support from several captured Bofors and some 50-mm anti-tank guns firing HE at point-blank range, succeeded in driving in the positions of the northernmost company of 18th Battalion next to the coast road. That morning Inglis had brought up the two remaining battle-worthy companies of 20th Battalion and placed them in the olive groves north of Galatas. Now, as the situation seemed critical, they were ordered up to the breach with orders to counter-attack and restore the position. Fierce fighting was now ranging along the whole front, and it was probably this counter-attack which led an enemy officer to write:

These hammer blows seem to affect the New Zealanders like mineral baths. Frantic, hellish fire keeps raking us whenever we raise our heads – they even try a desperate counter-attack on the left of No. 1 Company. They want at all costs to get out from under the Luftwaffe without giving up the hill. So their only chance is to 'withdraw' forwards.[1]

For a moment the situation seemed stabilised, but Kippenberger had now used his last reserves. He had literally no men left with which to repair breaches in the line. And now it was half past four, the hour fixed for the main Stuka bombardment of Galatas town in support of Schury's attack. For half an hour the dive-bombers kept up their bombardment, supplemented by intensive fire from light artillery and mortars on Ruin Hill, and even the whole of II Battalion, including the reserve company, was launched against Wheat Hill. Kippenberger was to recall:

[1] Interrogation (Murphy).

[I] went forward a few hundred yards to get a view of Wheat Hill and for a few minutes watched, fascinated, the rain of mortar bursts. In a hollow, nearly covered by undergrowth, I came on a party of women and children huddled together like little birds. They looked at me silently with black, terrified eyes.'[1]

Twice in the next hour runners came back from the company on Wheat Hill to ask Kippenberger himself for permission to withdraw, and each time they were sent back with refusals. He had already been compelled to peg back the north of the line, with the two reserve companies from the 20th holding the northerly tip of Ruin Ridge. Red Hill, as had been seen the previous day, was untenable and so now the front, from being a semi-circle, had taken on the shape of a triangular wedge with is apex pointing directly at the enemy and standing between them and Galatas at Wheat Hill.

Matters were now looking grave, for John Russell reported that he was being hard pressed, and a trickle of stragglers was coming back past me. I sent Brian [Bassett, the Brigade Major] on foot to tell Inglis the position and say that I must have help. There were nearly 200 wounded at the Regimental Aid Post, close to headquarters. Our two trucks worked incessantly, taking them down to the Advanced Dressing Station in loads like butchers' meat.[2]

Around 7pm it seemed as if once again the crisis was passing as the sound of firing had slackened, but then those at Battalion Headquarters noticed that the trickle of stragglers had turned to a stream, 'many of them on the verge of panic'. Wheat Hill had been overrun and the two companies to the right and left had been levered off their positions. Now there was a gaping hole exactly in the centre of the New Zealand line, and nothing with which to plug it. Kippenberger 'walked in among them and shouted, "Stand for New Zealand," and everything else I could think of' in an effort to halt the men. Although they were not yet under fire from the enemy, the whole area was criss-crossed

[1] Kippenberger, op cit, 64.

[2] Ibid, 65.

THE FALL OF CRETE

with overs – spent bullets on a falling trajectory – and people were still getting hit. At any moment the Germans were expected to emerge from the olive groves that ran down from the col between Wheat and Pink Hills.

With the help of two sergeants, Sullivan of 20th Battalion Intelligence section and Andrews, RSM of the 18th, Kippenberger rallied the men and sent them back to reform on the Daratsos Ridge. He sent runners north to warn the companies on the right flank that they should fall back into place as a continuation of the new line, which was now to run north-east in front of the village of Karatsos, and then remained by the side of the road with Andrews until the latter was wounded[1], directing the retreating men of the 18th to their new positions. The last to come out was Colonel Gray 'looking twenty years older than three hours before'. By now a few scratch formations, borrowed by Inglis and sent up post-haste in response to the urgent message brought him by Dawson, began to make their appearance. These included 4th Brigade Band, the Kiwi Concert Party – a sort of Divisional Music unit 'half orchestra, half Naafi' – and a Pioneer platoon. These Kippenberger put into position immediately round his headquarters, which were themselves forward of the main line. The first regular fighting formation to arrive, A company of 23rd Battalion, he sent to make a junction with the troops of the 20th that were still intact on the extreme right.

It was now twilight, and it seemed as if the Germans were slackening their assault. Their fire had abated and only light scouting parties were probing the summit of the col. The new line, like the short-lived second one, had a triangular form, with its right flank running parallel with and just below the Daratsos ridge where the shattered 18th were reorganising. Galatas town itself was now on the edge of no man's land. Its southern flank was formed by Russell Force and the 19th, who had held fast all day, and its tip was formed by the last hill in the chair, Pink Hill – still in the hands of the valiant Petrol Company, a unit that must have

[1] 'Andrews came to me and said quietly that he was afraid he could not do any more. I asked why, and he pulled up his shirt and showed a neat bullet hole in his stomach. I gave him a cigarette and expected never to see him again, but did, three years later, in Italy. A completely empty stomach had saved him.' Kippenberger, op cit, 65.

killed more Germans per man on its strength than any other on the island.

In fact, the third stage of the German offensive, the attack by Schrank Group, was yet to come. It had been delayed by the resistance that Schury's Battalion had encountered in their attempts on Wheat Hill, and the very heavy casualties that all his units had suffered made Utz hesitate about ordering the third stage so late in the day. He finally decided that if the New Zealanders were given the night to recover, he would have to start the operation all over again as a three-stage affair on the 26th, and considered doing this, leading off with Schrank Group and working northwards.

This would have meant, though, that the *coup de grâce* would be delivered by Ramcke's paratroops, an idea to which Utz was not sympathetic, besides placing the whole offensive a day behind schedule and getting out of phase with the outflanking movement in the south by 85th Mountain Regiment. Accordingly, he reinforced Schrank with his last fighting formation, the Engineers from III Battalion, and ordered that the attack was to start immediately, while II Battalion to the north was to penetrate into Galatas town.

And so, after a day of savage fighting, the weary Russell Force were once more attacked, this time in overwhelming force, and within half an hour Pink Hill had fallen to the enemy. The Petrol Company, with only enough ammunition to keep one machine-gun operative, fought to the last.

> One fellow as tall as a tree climbs out of a slit trench. He has pulled two egg-shaped hand grenades. One of them explodes prematurely and takes off his left hand, but he still throws the second one to the feet of the Germans only three paces away.[1]

As Russell Force was driven back they found that their right flank was in the air as there were no troops west of Galatas to which they could join. Men from II Battalion were now pouring over the col into Galatas and it seemed as if they would roll up the whole southern half of the position, including 19th Brigade. Kippenberger decided that 'it was no

[1] Neuhoff, Interrogation, (Murphy).

use trying to patch the line any more, obviously we must hit or everything would crumble away'.

When the first news of the collapse of the Wheat Hill position and the fall of Galatas reached Inglis, he managed to get some few more reinforcements sent forward. These included two light tanks (the same two, under Lieutenant Farran, that had supported the unsuccessful counter-attack on the 22nd) and two more companies of the 23rd Battalion. When the tanks arrived, Kippenberger told them to go straight on into the village and return to him and report its condition. They clattered off obediently and intense firing could be heard shortly afterwards. In the meantime, the two companies of the 23rd had arrived and halted by the side of the road. Kippenberger thought that 'they looked tired, but fit and resolute. I told the two Company Commanders that they would have to retake Galatas with the help of the two tanks. No, there was no time for reconnaissance; they must move straight in up the road, one company either side in single file behind the tanks, and take everything with them.' Stragglers and walking wounded were still streaming past and, seeing the men fixing bayonets, some of these stopped to join in. For about a quarter of an hour the men waited by the side of the road, and then the sound of firing in Galatas died down and the two tanks could be heard approaching. Farran put his head out of the turret and said, 'The place is stiff with Jerries.' Kippenberger told him that 'I had two companies of Infantry, would he go in again with them?' Certainly he would, but he had two men wounded, could they be replaced? I turned to a party of Sappers who had just arrived and asked for volunteers. Two men[1] immediately volunteered, the wounded were dragged out and they clambered aboard. I told Farran to take them down the road and give them a ten minute course of instruction, and that we would attack as soon as he came back. My batman went off to John Gray with a message that we were counter-attacking and an order to join in.'

[1] These were Privates Lewis and Ferry. Of Farran, Ferry said, 'This one-pipper bloke was a man of action, he gave us many words of instruction and few of encouragement, finishing up in a truly English manner "Of course you know you seldom come out of one of these things alive." Well, that suited me all right – it seemed a pretty hopeless fight – and a couple of my bosom friends had just been knocked.' Quoted NZOH, 311.

Soon Farran and the second tank with its novice crew were back. The two companies of the 23rd had had their orders, given in the best amateur traditional style of the British Commonwealth:

'D Company will be attacking on the left of the road, and we have two tanks in support but the whole show is stiff with Huns. It's going to be a bloody show but we've just got to succeed. Sandy, you will be on the right, Tex on the left. Now for Christ's sake get cracking.'[1]

Farran yelled to the other tank to follow him close up, then ducked down into his turret and slammed the hatch. It was dusk now, and the noise of battle had abated. Only the sound of small-arms fire could be heard from the direction of 18th Battalion positions on the coast. In the failing light the two tanks creaked off and the infantry followed, first at a walk, then breaking into a run as a column closed up on the outskirts of the town.

As the movement got underway all sorts of men who had got cut off from their units and would not be left behind tried to join in. Lieutenant Thomas recalled that 'There was the fair Forrester, with only a rifle and bayonet, bare-headed – and that great lump of foot-balling muscle William Carson (late of the Petrol Company) with a broad grin, licking his lips saying, "Thank Christ I've got a bloody bayonet." ' Thomas also told of how, when he rejoined his platoon, 'their numbers seemed greater. Looking closer in the gloom I made out several unfamiliar faces. "We've got some reinforcements, Sir," said Sergeant Templeton. "These chaps are from the 18th and 20th and want a crack at the Hun." A tall Lance-Corporal stood up, "Is it OK, Sir?" a little anxiously, "the bastards got my brother today." '[2]

As the tanks burst into the village a second time the Germans were caught off balance for they thought that they had repelled the first assault so successfully that the fighting was over for the night. And now, as the infantry reached the first buildings of the town,

their whole line seemed to break spontaneously into the most blood-curdling of shouts and battle cries. Heaven knows how many colleges

[1] NZOH Report by Lieutenant Thomas, 313.

[2] NZOH Report by Lieutenant Thomas, 312.

and schools were represented by their '*hakas*', but the effect was terrific – one felt one's blood rising swiftly above fear and uncertainty until only the inexplicable exhilaration quite beyond description surpassed all else.[1]

It was quite dark now, and from the south Lieutenant Colonel Gray was cutting across to join the attack with what men he had been able to scrape together from the remnants of the 18th. He has recounted how 'I shall never forget the deep-throated wild-beast noise of the yelling charging men as the 23rd swept up the road.'[2]

Farran got his tank into the square, where it careered wildly round twice, shooting at the doorways of the houses. Fire poured on it from all sides, and against the sky he could see the German distress rockets calling desperately for help. Soon mortar bombs began to fill the square and one of these landed on the rear of the tank, the explosion concussing the crew and blowing Farran half out of the turret. Just in time the first of the infantry appeared. They had been held up in clearing the cellars and alleyways as they made their way forward, and had soon given up this precaution, preferring to keep up the momentum of the advance. They had been told to go no further than the square, but on arrival there, and finding that the enemy was keeping up a steady fire from the buildings on the other side, they decided to charge again:

The consternation at the far side was immediately apparent. Screams and shouts showed desperate panic in front of us and I suddenly knew that we had caught them ill-prepared and in the act of forming up. Had our charge been delayed even minutes the position could easily have been reversed. By now we were stepping over groaning forms, and those which rose against us fell to our bayonets, and bayonets with their eighteen inches of steel entering throats and chests with the same hesitant ease as when we had used them on the straw-packed dummies in Burnham. One of the boys just behind me lurched heavily against me and fell at my feet, clutching his stomach. His restraint burbled in his throat for half a second as he fought against it, but stomach wounds

---

[1] Report by Lieutenant Thomas.

[2] Lieutenant Colonel Gray to DM Davin, 26.7.41.

are painful beyond human power of control and his screams soon rose above all the others. The Hun seemed in full flight. From doors, windows and roofs they swarmed wildly, falling over one another – there was little fire against us now.[1]

By midnight the New Zealanders had completed the reconquest of Galatas, and the companies were positioned to repel an enemy attack at dawn. They had suffered terrible casualties – only four subalterns were left standing and of these two were wounded – but they had restored the line and shown, once again, the superiority of the New Zealander in close combat. It is certainly ironic to recall that this unit, 23rd Battalion, was the one designated to come to the rescue of the 22nd at Maleme on the first day when it was restrained by the hesitations of the officers of 5th Brigade. On that night, fresh and opposed by an enemy half as strong as they tackled at Galatas, there can be little doubt as to what the outcome would have been, and the subsequent course of the battle for the island.

The description of the battle may best be closed with an enemy judgement on its significance:

We were fully convinced that this was much more than a local counter-attack; it was a general counter-offensive along the whole line which we had been expecting for some days. The appearance of tanks confirmed this view and we were quite sure that the whole battle was turning against us. The men had reached the limit of their endurance. My commanding officer had just been killed. Our morale was very low. We were both amazed and relieved that the counter-attack after clearing the town of Galatas advanced no further and that the enemy appeared to be retiring.[2]

[1] Report by Lieutenant Thomas.

[2] CSM Neuhoff, Interrogation (Murphy).

FOURTEEN

RETREAT

The fact that there was no follow-through to the Galatas success may be ascribed to three factors. First, as will shortly be seen, the exchange of messages between Puttick and Freyberg became muddled, and the texts themselves out of date in relation to the matters to which they referred. This led to confusion. Second, the actual disposition of the troops, particularly of the fresh units like the Welch Regiment and the Northumberland Hussars, made their employment in an immediate forward move a difficult business and was bound with certain personal and administrative problems that can now be seen to be of little account but which may have bulked large at the time – such as the putting of English troops under New Zealand Brigadiers, the denuding of General Weston's command, and so on. Third (and undoubtedly the facts cited above were a function of this), one cannot avoid the view that Freyberg and Puttick were both early convinced that a stand-up fight to the finish in the face of the overwhelming enemy air superiority was suicidal, and that they were, at any rate from the 25th onwards, anxious to secure authority to evacuate the islands as soon as possible.

Nothing is plainer from a study of the fighting in Crete than the fact that the senior New Zealand commanders (with the honourable exceptions of Inglis and Kippenberger) consistently underrated the fighting power of their own men. At Galatas they had very nearly fought the Germans to a standstill. Had the Australian battalions, who had a quiet day on the 25th, been ordered to attack at dawn on the 26th, and the two fresh English units been put in the centre in a counter-attack with strictly limited objectives – the restoration of the line of the heights, with the inclusion of Ruin Hill – it is just possible that the enemy would have been forced to recognise a stalemate.

But, equally, in considering Freyberg's position, with the advantage of hindsight, we must remember that it was hard for him to conceive of the enemy pressure slackening. He could not see the battle in a strategic context – not, at least, from the enemy side – with the realisation that to their maximum effort hours were vital, before the demands of Barbarossa reduced their air strength, compelled the withdrawal of their finest troops and caused the flow of supplies to dwindle.

At the very moment that the battle for Galatas was at its climax Freyberg was writing a cable to Wavell:

> To-day has been one of great anxiety to me here. The enemy carried out one small attack last night and this afternoon he attacked with little success. This evening at 1700 hours bombers, dive bombers and ground strafers came over and bombed our forward troops and then his ground troops launched an attack. It is still in progress and I am awaiting news. *If we can give him a really good knock it will have a very far-reaching effect.*

But just as Freyberg was writing the last words a message came from Puttick saying that 'Heavy attacks about 2000 hours have obviously broken our line', that 'Enemy is through at Galatas and moving towards Daratsos', and that 'Reports indicate that men (or many of them) badly shaken by severe air attacks and TM[1] fire. Am afraid will lose our guns through lack of transport . . . Am exceedingly doubtful on present reports whether I can hold the enemy tomorrow (26th)'. When he received this report Freyberg struck out the last sentence of his draft telegram (in italics above) and substituted: 'I have heard from Puttick that the line has gone and that we are trying to stabilise. I don't know if they will be able to. I am apprehensive. I will send messages as I can later.'

To Puttick he wrote,

Dear Puttick,

I have read through your report on the situation. I am not surprised that the line broke. Your battalions were very weak and the areas they were given were too large. On the shorter line you should be able to hold them. In any case there will not be that infiltration that started

[1] Trench Mortar.

before. You must hold them on that line and counter-attack if any part of it should go.

It is imperative that he should not break through.

I hope that we shall get through to-morrow without further trouble.

B. Freyberg

Of course, while these exchanges were taking place the line had been restored; the enemy had been given the 'really hard knock' for which Freyberg was hoping; and the problem was how to speed its exploitation so that there might still be achieved the 'very far-reaching effect'.

It was well past midnight when Kippenberger, 'more tired than ever before in my life, or since', was making his way back to report to Inglis. Inglis had called the conference immediately because he realised that, if the counter-attack was to have any chance of restoring the position, it must be delivered that night and in as great a strength as possible. The only 'fresh' troops that he had available were the redoubtable Maoris – and they had only been out of action for less than twenty-four hours – and he felt that a full restoration of the position was beyond even their ability if they were sent in without support. Inglis's own view was that

The front was far too wide for a single battalion in a night attack; the terrain was cut across by vineyards and small ravines lying at angles to the line of advance; the Maoris did not know the ground; the rolling features made identification of the objective almost impossibly difficult; even if 28th Battalion were to make the objective it was a certainty that it would leave a lot of unmopped enemy in its rear, for it had not enough men to cover the area.[1]

That night, and for the last time, the battle of Crete hung in the balance. The motley, exhausted group of New Zealanders who retook Galatas had, by their bravery, presented an opportunity for leverage against the whole German position. If it was to be properly exploited this must be done by fresh troops in strength. Inglis, therefore, had asked Puttick to attend the conference in person so that he could decide what additional units he could allocate to the attack.

[1] Kippenberger, op cit, 68.

Puttick, however, felt unable to do this and sent Gentry, who was late arriving. The time passed, and while they waited all the commanders whom Inglis had called together came to realise that they were going to get no extra help. If the attack was to be put in that night they would have to mount it from their own resources.

Kippenberger has described how 'It was quite dark when we arrived at Brigade Headquarters and we stumbled around for some time among the trees. Inglis was in a tarpaulin-covered hole in the ground, seated at a table with a very poor light. Burrows, Blackburn and Sanders were already there. Dittmer . . . arrived a moment after me. It was clear to all of us that if this [the counter-attack] was not feasible Crete was lost. It was a difficult operation, perhaps impossible: darkness, olive trees, vineyards, no good starline, only 400 men in the battalion. Dittmer said it was difficult; I said it could not be done and that it would need two fresh battalions. Inglis rightly pressed, remarking that we were done if it did not come off: "Can you do it, George?" Dittmer said: "I'll give it a go." We sat silently looking at the map, and then Gentry lowered himself into the hole. Without hesitation he said "No" – the Maoris were our last fresh battalion and if used now we would not be able to hold the line tomorrow. There was no further argument; it was quickly decided that Galatas must be abandoned, and everyone brought back to the Daratsos line before morning.'

Of course, the contention that the 28th Battalion were 'the last fresh unit' which was available was only true in so far as it applied to 5th and 4th Brigades – the units, that is to say, who were actually in the line and fighting the battle. There still remained available to Freyberg the whole of the 1st Welch, the Northumberland Hussars and the 1st Rangers. It seems almost incredible that these battalions had not been put into the Galatas position at least twenty-four hours earlier, but they were, in fact, still in Suda Force under Weston, and not directly concerned with a battle which was being controlled by Puttick. This is yet another example of the tendency of many British commanders to commit their strength piecemeal, to think in terms of Forces, each responsible to, and usually carrying the name of, a separate commander of his area, an extension of the 'Jock column' principle that plagued their conduct of operations in the desert for years. The result of it was that these fresh troops were standing idle throughout the day and night of 25 May and the morning of the 26th at Mournies and, on Weston's orders, in the curiously conceived stop-line across the neck of the Akrotiri peninsula.

The following morning, the 26th, Freyberg decided at last to put these units under Inglis's command, making a 'New Brigade' out of them, and that they were to be used to relieve 5th Brigade. He summoned Inglis to his headquarters that morning and told him of this intention although Weston, who would now be left with practically no fighting formations under his command, was not present. But it was now too late. Puttick had decided independently that a further withdrawal must be made and he left at 11am for Freyberg's headquarters with the intention of putting the case in person. Evidently Puttick was confident that he would be able to persuade the Commander-in-Chief as to his point of view because, before leaving, he had sent a warning order to 5th Brigade that 'we are working with a British covering force, the night's operation should be an easy one'.[1]

However, on arrival at the quarry Puttick had a rude shock, and found that there had been yet further changes in the command structure. Freyberg told him that the line must be held as supplies were being landed at Suda that night. He went on to say that he had dropped the idea of a joint HQ and intended to put General Weston in command of the forward area. Puttick and the New Zealand Division would be under Weston.

The consequence of the appointment of a new commander at this late stage seems to have been an amplification of the confusion. When Inglis tackled Weston about the 'New Brigade', 'He was hurried and worried and very short with me: but I gathered that he intended to use these troops himself and not through me. In any event neither then, nor at any other time did he give them any orders through me, and I did not attempt to make confusion worse confounded by giving them any myself.'[2]

Indeed, it is curious how few orders Weston gave, considering the growing fluidity of the battle, the urgency of the situation and the seniority of his own position – second only to Freyberg himself. Three

[1] NZOH, 342.

[2] Letter from Inglis, quoted NZOH, 345.

times during the night of 26/27 May the New Zealand Division asked Weston for orders, but with no reply other than a message direct from Creforce, which carried the following – hardly helpful – text: 'You are under command LIFT (Weston) who will issue orders.' When he received this, Puttick set off in person once again, this time to Weston's headquarters. Here he found Weston in bed. When he asked why no orders had been sent Weston told him that 'It was no use sending orders as Div Cmd had made it very clear that NZ Div was retiring whatever happened.'[1] Puttick replied that orders were necessary so that he should know where to retire to and how best to co-operate with the other troops.

The upshot of this very odd affair was that Puttick brought back all the New Zealanders during the early hours of the 27th, but that the 'New Brigade', or Force Reserve, or however it was properly termed, was still going forward in obedience to its instructions of the previous afternoon. With daylight the force found itself unprotected on its flanks, and under fierce attack by an enemy strength over five times their own. In these conditions they were cut to pieces within a few hours. The last card in Freyberg's hand had been thrown away as casually as if it were valueless.

A few of the men managed to fight their way through the German ring, but when they got to Suda they were told by Weston 'not to attempt to organise but to push on in small parties to Sfakia'.[2] Now the retreat was indeed becoming precipitate.

As the situation on the island became more desperate so in London an awareness of the importance of the struggle mounted. On 27 May Churchill had telegraphed to Freyberg, 'Your glorious defence commands admiration in every land. We know enemy is hard pressed. All aid in our power is being sent.' And to Wavell, 'Victory in Crete essential at this turning point in the war. Keep hurling in all aid you can.'

Before the COS committee Churchill urged the sending of Beaufighters immediately, the despatch of further troops in fast Glen class ships to the south coast and continued pressure on Cunningham and

---

[1] Puttick's diary, quoted NZOH, 366.

[2] NZOH, 372.

Tedder to exert a maximum effort in their respective spheres.[1] To the Prime Minister, at least, the struggle for Crete had assumed such importance that he was prepared to overlook the basic tenets of British Middle Eastern strategy – that in all matters of priority the security of the Canal Zone and the demands of the army in the Western Desert must come first. Nor is this attitude wholly without justification for the enemy strength committed in Crete was nearly double that in Cyrenaica, and defeat there would have done greater harm to his prestige (though not perhaps to his strategic posture) than in Libya.

But Freyberg had decided that the battle was lost. On the morning of 26 May he cabled Wavell:

> . . . in my opinion the limit of endurance has been reached by the troops under my command here at Suda Bay. No matter what decision is taken by the Commanders in Chief from a military point of view our position here is hopeless. A small ill-equipped and immobile force such as ours cannot stand up against the concentrated bombing that we have been faced with during the last seven days. I feel that I should tell you that from an administrative point of view the difficulties of extricating this force in full are now insuperable. Provided a decision is reached at once a certain proportion of the force might be embarked. Once this sector has been reduced the reduction of Rethymno and Heraklion by the same methods will only be a matter of time.[2]

[1] The 2nd Battalion, Queen's Regiment, was embarked in the *Glenroy*, and the destroyers *Jaguar* and *Stuart* on 27 May, but was attacked by torpedo bombers and forced to turn back. Ten Hurricanes were flown to the aerodrome at Heraklion but of these six were shot down by the defenders who mistook their identity, two turned back and were never seen again – they did not have the petrol to return to Alexandria – the remaining two succeeded in landing but were destroyed by German aircraft the following day.

Of the Beaufighters COS (41) 189, quoted NZOH 329 shows Portal as saying that 'they would have to have their secret night-fighter apparatus removed and could hardly come into action before 31 May. It had to be remembered that they were not fitted for fighting in the tropics (*sic*), that they had no rear gunner, and that they could patrol over Crete for an hour at a time only. To do even this a whole squadron would be needed operating from Egypt. And because of lack of spares it would be difficult to keep them serviceable. He concluded that they should be sent only if their presence was likely to make a substantial difference to the outcome. It was finally decided that none should be taken from Fighter Command.

[2] AOH, 247.

When this message arrived Wavell was in Alexandria conferring with Cunningham, Tedder, Blamey and the New Zealand Prime Minister, Mr Fraser. At this conference they had decided to send an additional three battalions to Crete by destroyer and Glen ship during the next three nights. They also hoped to be able to disembark some new 'I' tanks at Heraklion if the quay was still usable.

When Wavell got back to his own headquarters and read Freyberg's cable asking for a 'decision at once', he did not accede to this request – which was, in fact, a plea for the authorisation of an evacuation which was already being planned and the initial stages of which had begun to be implemented. Instead, Wavell replied that if Freyberg could continue to hold on 'the effect of the whole position in the Middle East would be all the greater'. He went on to ask if, with the reinforcements which had reached him on the night of the 26th (the Commandos of Layforce) and with 1st Welch (which Wavell knew from the last report of dispositions to have been uncommitted: naturally he had no knowledge of their fate, with the 'New Brigade', that day), it might not be possible 'to push the enemy back or at least relieve the sector in greatest danger'.[1] However, if it was impossible to hold Suda after 27 May, Wavell suggested that Freyberg should use his freshest troops to cover his withdrawal on the night of 27 May, join up with the troops at Rethymno and block further enemy progress to the east. In this way it might be possible to hold out for some time still. 'If Freyberg would send the outline of proposals for carrying out such a plan he himself would do his best to help.'

This reply must have been very unwelcome to Creforce HQ because, in fact, orders for withdrawal to Sfakia (ie southwards, not eastwards to Rethymno as Wavell suggested) had already been formally promulgated in instructions that were sent out from Weston's own headquarters at 3am on the 27th. No immediate answer was sent back to Cairo, but a *situation report* mentioned that the line had been penetrated and that the men were falling back in disorder.[2] It also spoke of an 'ultimate plan' of falling back on Sfakia and Porto Loutro. Any idea of

[1] NZOH, 365 (from a copy sent to CIGS 26 May).

[2] It is not clear to what this refers. Unit reports show the line as holding well on 26 May. Nor do the Germans claim any penetration on that date. AC.

using the Commandos in an offensive rôle had been quickly abandoned for on arrival they were told to jettison their radios, motorcycles and all their heavy equipment, and to keep only weapons, ammunition and rations.

Then, that afternoon, Freyberg sent a further personal message to Wavell. He said that his force could not continue to function as such without air support. The Rethymno plan was out of the question and the only hope was to withdraw to selected beaches. '. . . His plan was to withdraw to Sfakia, fighting a rearguard action as he went. Since the bulk of his force were not front line troops and were now in a deteriorated state he would like General Wavell to try and spare some more Commandos . . .'[1]

When he had received this Wavell realised that the condition and attitude of the island's defenders was such that to send reinforcements there would be a waste of men. He asked the Prime Minister for permission[2] to authorise the evacuation, and this was granted.

Now would have to be paid the last instalments in the price of muddled strategy, neglected defence planning and tactical mistakes of the preceding months and weeks. And the currency in which that price was to be paid, as so many times in our history, was the blood and heroism of the Navy.

[1] NZOH, 366.

[2] His letter reproduced in full, Churchill, *The Grand Alliance*, 262.

FIFTEEN

EVACUATION

O n 28 May the bulk of Creforce had disengaged from the enemy and was making its way through the defile in the central massif that separated it from the port of Sfakia on the south coast.

The retreat bore many of the marks of a rout – 'on all sides men were hurrying along in disorder. Most of them had thrown away their rifles and a number had even discarded their tunics as it was a hot day. Nearly every yard of the road and of the ditches on either side was strewn with abandoned arms and accoutrements, blankets, gasmasks, packs, kitbags, sunhelmets, cases and containers of all shapes and sizes, tinned provisions and boxes of cartridges and hand grenades; now and then one ran across officers' valises and burst-open suit cases.'[1] Discipline, too, had become precarious, even in the presence of officers. Kippenberger has recounted:

At one point, half way through the march, the road forked and I was uncertain which fork to follow. I spread a map on the ground and turned a torch on it. Immediately there was a chorus of cries from the bank above: 'Put out that — light' and a man rushed up and kicked the torch out of my hand. I stood up and seized him by the throat, throttled him until he started to choke and threw him down. I then stated that if there were any more such talk I would open fire.

In the neck of the pass the fighting troops leap-frogged their way back, keeping the Germans at arm's length while behind them the mass of the garrison toiled their way higher and higher, then across the flat plateau of the plain of Askifou and down again through innumerable hairpin bends as the broken, dusty road twisted its way down towards Sfakia.

[1] Stephanides, 213.

The columns moved at night. During the daytime the men slept in the boulder-strewn countryside, crouching in primitive shelters, in drainage culverts and in caves. Many of them went all day without food or water for they had only what rations they carried with them, and the wells on the route were soon sucked dry.

In the first days of the retreat the marching columns would often be passed by trucks that careered along the narrow track, throwing up clouds of choking dust, laden to capacity with wounded and escorts. But as they climbed higher the lorries would run out of petrol, and the slower-moving columns on foot would come upon the abandoned vehicles and push them over the cliff to clear the way so that the gorge was dotted with broken, upturned trucks, like great khaki beetles with their stunted legs pointed to the sky.

The defence of this column was the responsibility of the Commandos, the two Australian battalions and the 5th New Zealand Brigade, who took it in turn to hold the pass while the others drew back through them. Gallant as this rearguard action was, it should be pointed out that the freedom from serious interference which Creforce enjoyed once the retreat had begun owes much to two other factors.

The first of these was the continuing resistance of the 8th Greek Regiment, in position at Alikianou and among the hills to the south. These men had been isolated since the first day of the assault, and from that time Creforce HQ seems to have given them up for lost. In fact, though, the Greeks had on that day worsted the Engineer Battalion of 3rd Parachute Regiment, recapturing Alikianou from them during the evening and improving their equipment with captured weapons. For the three days following they remained in the town, containing such local probing movements as the Germans thrust in their direction and harassing them with mortar fire. The War Diary of 3rd Parachute Regiment shows that during this period Heidrich was seriously concerned by the presence of this force so close to his flank and communications, and there is no doubt that this consideration would have weighed heavily with the Germans if the counter-attack which Inglis desired had ever been launched.

By 23 May, after the New Zealand withdrawal to the Platanias river line, General Ringel began to conceive the plan of a direct thrust across to the Koelaris river, deep on the southern flank of the British concentrations around Suda. An enemy situation map for that evening shows I Battalion of 85th Mountain Regiment, a fresh unit, probing in that direction. The following morning Colonel Krakau, the Regimental commander, arrived, together with the whole of III Battalion, and the attacks started. Throughout 24 May, and again on the 25th, the Greeks repulsed their assailants. By now II Battalion had also been brought up, and the whole Regiment was in action against this motley collection of Greeks, youthful cadets, gendarmerie and civilian irregulars. As fast as the Germans extended their flanks so did the Greeks, their sharpshooters picking off the enemy sections as they stumbled upwards across the rocky, unfamiliar mountainsides. By the evening of the 25th Krakau still had to report to 5th Mountain Division that there had been 'No change in the general situation'.[1]

It seems incredible that Creforce HQ should have given no thought to this long, vulnerable flank. Themselves bound to the roads, they must have believed that the same restrictions would apply to the enemy – a risky assumption after specially trained mountain troops had been identified. Perhaps it was thought that as the 8th Greek were believed to have disintegrated on the first day, and there was no sign of the enemy patrols crossing the range, the Germans considered such a move impracticable. Anyhow, whatever the reason, the obstinacy and heroism of this Greek unit was providential for they blocked a German move which, if successful, would have cut the road to Sfakia before a single man had travelled it.

The second factor that affected the strength of the enemy follow-through was that Ringel's own order of priorities was never altered by Student, and so he was left with the first duty of relieving Rethymno and Heraklion in preference to pressing along the road to Sfakia. Had the Germans pressed harder and in greater strength – they were little more than two battalions effectively – it is difficult not to believe that they would have brushed aside the thin and weary screen that kept them from what Freyberg described as

[1] It is not easy to build up a clear picture of this battle as most of the Greeks who survived it were killed later with the partisans. Only enemy sources are available and these, owing to the fact that the engagement was of an inconclusive nature, are scanty.

disorganised rabble making its way doggedly and painfully to the south. There were thousands of unarmed troops including the Cypriots and Palestinians. Without leadership, without any sort of discipline. Somehow or other the word 'Sfakia' got out and many of these people had taken a flying start in any available transport they could steal and which they later left abandoned. Never shall I forget the disorganisation and almost complete lack of control of the masses on the move as we made our way slowly through that endless stream of trudging men.[1]

But the screen held and on the first two nights of the evacuation nearly 8,000 men were taken off. Even on the third night the whole of 5th Brigade was got away under cover of the Commandos and the two Australian battalions.

The last formation it was intended to evacuate were the stalwart 2/7th Australian, the Bardia veterans whom Freyberg had wished to use in his counter-attack of 22 May and who, ever since, had been wasted away in patching and shoring and fighting innumerable small rearguard actions. When these men reached the ground behind the beach where the road petered out, they found the whole area in confusion and blocked by large numbers of non-combatant troops, only thinly officered, who were sitting and lying about in a resentful state. These men did their best to stop anyone getting through because rumour had got about (correctly, as is so often the case) that they themselves were not to be evacuated. However, in the absence of firm discipline, they were adopting the understandable but obstructive attitude of regarding themselves as the head of a queue which should not be passed by later arrivals and which would itself start moving when the beaches below became clearer. Brigadier Vasey has described how

When some little distance from the beach it was found that this road was blocked with men sitting down and many officers challenged anyone approaching wanting to know what they were. Other officers represented themselves as MCO's (Movement Control Officers) and eventually one of these said that only single

[1] Freyberg's report, quoted AOH, 253.

file was allowed through from that point and that [the Australians] would have to wait.

Vasey himself passed through with two of his staff officers but the others remained in this position 'for some time'. On the beach Vasey found that the blockage further back was beginning to take effect because 'it was noticed that the troops were not available on the beach when boats came in and there was considerable delay in getting the boats filled and away to the ships'.

Short of cutting their way through with the bayonet, there was nothing that the 2/7th could do except make a detour and attempt to find their own way down to the boats. This they did, traversing 'nightmare' country in pitch darkness and remembering from their experiences in Greece that it was a race against time. The Navy, whose deadlines were governed rigidly by the hours of darkness and light, could not wait. Major Marshal, the second in command, has described how

> I could have no mercy on them and I had to haze them and threaten them and push them into a faster speed. We crossed the road and stumbled on after Atock (on the Intelligence section) who was guiding us down the centre of this rocky valley. Falls were numerous but I would permit of no delay as I knew that time was against us. One of the A company men fell and refused to get up, wanting to be left where he fell and not caring whether he was captured or not. I pulled him up and supported him for the next five miles; every time he stopped he sagged and pleaded to be left.

At last the battalion reached the beach. Some of the head of the column were embarked in the boats that were waiting there and the remainder formed up in order along the shore. An officer on the last barge watched the battalion standing there, 'quiet and orderly in its ranks' – and this after a week of continuous fighting and marching on half rations – but

> Then came the greatest disappointment of all. The sound of anchor chains through the hawse. I found Theo (Walker) and we sat on the edge of the stone sea wall. He told me that things were all up and that the Navy had gone. All our effort and skill wasted.

The Australians' first reaction was a desire to fight their way down the coast in the hope that they might be picked up by the Navy at one or other of the fishing villages to the east. When, at first light, some of the base troops who were now wandering about on the beach began to fly white flags two of his NCOs came to Walker and asked, 'Shall we shoot them?'

They need not have bothered for at eight o'clock the first of the German aircraft appeared and did their work for them – cruising up and down the beach, firing indiscriminately – although by now there were white flags everywhere. Walker told his men that further resistance was hopeless, they must destroy their equipment and escape as best they could. He walked up to Komitadhes, where he surrendered to an Austrian officer of the 5th Mountain Division. 'What are you doing here, Australia?' he was asked, but when he replied, 'What are you doing here, Austria?' the answer that he got was 'We are all Germans'.

Later Walker and his adjutant were invited to dinner by a Colonel of the 7th Parachute Division. In his diary Walker recorded that 'He says our generals did everything to assist him. Cannot understand why we ever gave ground and did not attack. Neither can we. Said our counter-attack at Suda[1] was the only decent fight we gave them. Troops had a concert at night, finished up with "Rule Britannia" and "God save the King".'

The garrisons at Rethymno and Heraklion met with different fates. At Heraklion the ascendancy which Brigadier Chappel's men had established over the enemy and the existence of deep-water embarkation facilities encouraged Cairo to attempt an evacuation from the port itself.

In spite of his frightful losses, the exhausted condition of the crews and the worn-out state of the ships themselves, Cunningham agreed to attempt this in a single night, and allocated nine fast ships to the task. This was Rear-Admiral Rawlings's Force B comprising *Orion*, *Ajax*, *Dido* and six destroyers. The squadron sailed from Alexandria on the morning of the 28th, steaming due north for the Kaso Strait and on a direct course

---

[1] Presumably means Galatas. AC.

for the Stuka bases on the island of Scarpanto, which they had to pass at a distance of only forty nautical miles.

By mid-afternoon German reconnaissance aircraft had spotted them and reported their course and position. At 5pm the first Stukas appeared and the ships were under continuous attack from that time until dusk. Many of the Stukas made over five sorties that afternoon as the fleet came ever closer, steaming into the jaws formed by Kaso and Cape Plaka. The aircraft would fly straight back over the ever-shortening distance to their base, taxi the length of the runway and have their bomb racks rehung without even switching off. Both the *Ajax* and the destroyer *Imperial* were damaged, and the former had to return to Alexandria. When Force B arrived off Heraklion it was 11.30pm and more than half its anti-aircraft ammunition was spent.

The Germans, in rage and frustration at their defeat here, had been bombing the town in reprisal raids without cease for the last three days. It was

> one large stench of decomposing dead, debris from destroyed dwelling places, roads were wet and running from burst water pipes, hungry dogs were scavenging among the dead. There was a stench of sulphur, smouldering fires and pollution of broken sewers. Conditions were set for a major epidemic.[1]

In spite of the conditions the embarkation was completed, without any interference from the German troops, by 3.30am. All the British and Australians were taken off with the exception of a detachment guarding the roadblock at Khoudesion and the wounded in the dressing-station at Knossos, but no Greeks were embarked, nor were they informed of the decision to evacuate.

When Force B sailed it had two and a half hours of darkness – enough to allow it to make the passage of the Kaso Strait before the sun was high. Moreover, a rendezvous had been arranged with fighters from the Matruh airfields the moment the ships were within range. But a chapter of disasters lay ahead of them. First *Imperial*, whose steering gear had been damaged in the attacks of the previous evening, found it jamming

---

[1] Report by Captain Tomlinson. AOH, 291.

without warning, and narrowly avoided a collision with *Orion*. Rawlings detailed the destroyed *Hotspur* to take off the 400 soldiers from *Imperial* and then sink her and rejoin him at maximum speed. *Hotspur* had been selected because she was the fastest ship in the flotilla but, even so, rather than desert her completely Rawlings reduced speed to 15 knots while waiting for her to rejoin the squadron. This meant that it was not until six o'clock that he was passing through the Kaso Strait, and the moment when it was nearest to Scarpanto and the Stuka fields coincided with the first enemy searches at 6am. They were located almost immediately and within minutes there were over 100 dive-bombers in the air. The attacks became a continuous ordeal. As the vessels weaved and ducked in their efforts to avoid the bombs, the troops crowded on the open decks skidded and scrabbled from one rail to another. Shrapnel rained down upon them.

> As soon as the planes appear overhead you can feel the boat lift out of the water as she puts on speed. Then the deck rolls over at an angle of about 45 degrees. Then back it comes again and down goes the other side as she zigzags, turns and squirms at 40 knots, trying to spoil their aim. Down comes the Stuka and lets his bomb go at about 500 feet. The commander watches the bomb, judges where it is going to fall, turns his boat inside out and generally manages to dodge it. Meanwhile every gun is firing all the time and the noise is deafening. The 6-inch and 4-inch shake the whole boat and the multiple pom-pom is going like a steam-hammer. Four-barrelled multiple machine-guns mounted on each side of the ship add to the general din. Besides all these a lot of our boys had their Brens mounted on deck and were doing their best to add to the general row – occasionally as the bomb was coming down I glanced at the sailor sighting and firing the pom-pom and I didn't see the slightest sign of emotion on his face, even though the bomb only missed by three feet and lifted our boat out of the water.[1]

After half an hour the destroyer *Hereward* was hit and damaged so severely that she could no longer keep station with the force. Rawlings

---

[1] Corporal Johnstone, quoted Long, 292.

rightly decided that he could not reduce speed again and so the *Hereward* turned north in a painful effort to reach Crete before she sank. She was beached two miles north of Cape Plaka and gradually subsided in the sludge as she was abandoned. All those on board who survived were taken prisoner, many owing their lives to an Italian Red Cross seaplane, which circled low over them after they had abandoned ship and prevented two Stukas from attacking the lifeboats.

As the day wore on the plight of the ships became steadily worse. The RAF could not find them owing to the dislocation in schedules caused by the sinking of *Imperial*, and some of the cruisers began to run out of pom-pom ammunition. *Orion* was hit three times in two hours and her commander, Captain GRB Back, was killed. She was the most over-crowded of all the ships in the force, and this in turn led to frightful casualties being suffered in the confined spaces below decks when a bomb penetrated, while the congestion of dead and wounded that lay there prevented the proper functioning of the medical and firefighting pickets. One bomb which exploded on the mess decks killed 260 soldiers and wounded another 280. On board *Dido* 103 out of 240 of the Black Watch were killed.

All afternoon the RAF searched for the force without success, and the enemy attacks were continued until the ships were within a hundred miles of Alexandria. When finally they reached port at 8pm on the 29th over one-fifth of the Heraklion garrison had been killed or wounded.

At Rethymno there was no evacuation, and here the gallant Australians under Campbell and Sandover fought till the last. As at Heraklion they had completely worsted their immediate enemy. They had over 500 parachutist prisoners penned in the cage under Hill B and had buried another 550. Their morale was as high as ever, and as late as 29 May they were still attacking, although reduced to one day's reserves of rations.

But now their hour had come, as it did to Beddings's men at Kastelli. The day following, the 30th, very substantial German reinforcements appeared from Suda (an armoured battalion and elements of 5th Mountain Division) and by 10am Sandover's Battalion was under heavy attack from tanks and over 100 motorcycle combinations with heavy machine-guns. Campbell estimated that he could now carry out his task – to deny the airfield to the enemy – for only another hour and decided to surrender his force intact. Sandover, however, thought it better to make for the hills. He told his officers that 'all the men should be told that there was no chance of rescue or source of food, and then be given the chance of surrendering or going. If they wanted to go they'd better go quickly as the back road might be cut. I am going myself,' he said, 'we'll think what to do when we get out of this.'[1]

And so the force was split up. The Germans found those who surrendered 'not in any way dispirited, they were friendly and calm, just as if they had given up a sporting Test Match'. But that evening when a German major fell into conversation with Campbell, and tried to speak 'of the German cause, and why kindred nations should fight', the Australian's cool and tactful replies persuaded him that 'it was hopeless; the fight must be carried to a finish; God's iron plough, war, must tear up man's earth before the seed of the future can grow'.

[1] AOH, 274.

EPILOGUE

Immediately after the surrender large numbers of men filtered away from the beaches and prison compounds and made their way into the hills. At first the life was pleasant. The Mediterranean summer stretched before them. It was possible to sleep in the olive groves or in the scrub of the mountainsides and during the day they would forage for food. Many of them had small arms and ammunition, supplies from looted dumps were abundant and the enemy had neither the strength nor the administrative apparatus for a thorough policing of the island.

Then winter came. Snow fell in the high reaches of the Lefka Ori and a man who slept out alone might die of exposure. Food became scarce, shoes wore out, clothes turned to rags. The Germans were determined to clear the island and they reinforced the garrison with echelons of Gestapo and SS beginning a series of methodical drives, squaring off the island into sections which were then combed for the deserters – as the escaped soldiers were termed. The enemy used to shoot on sight. Villages that harboured the escapees were savagely punished, sometimes losing up to half their menfolk shot and left to die without burial.

But many of the soldiers, or their comrades, survived. In spite of everything, their spirit held, and below are their stories. Personal accounts such as these have an equivocal place in a military history. They disturb the narrative and have no bearing on the facts, and those concerned with the facts of the battle for Crete need read no further. But in terms of courage and fortitude, of the spiritual values that give significance to combat, these experiences are important. They are a complement to the battle and should be recorded – for, similar in concept yet with variations in pattern, they are the molecules of the whole, which is war.

On the day of the surrender, New Zealand, Australian and British soldiers found an abandoned landing barge near Sfakia which they put out of sight in a sea cavern. They sailed the barge out of the cavern on the night of 1 June; the Germans nearby opened fire but no one was hit. An Australian, Private Harry Richards, was skipper and a New Zealander, Private AH Taylor (HQ NZ Div) , was engineer. The following morning the barge was damaged when it ran ashore on Gavdhos Island but the damage was soon repaired. Richards appealed for volunteers to stay ashore and lighten the load and ten men stood aside.

When the petrol gave out, the men put up a jury mast and sail. The wind dropped and the boat drifted. The food ration was cut down to a small drink of cocoa for breakfast, and even this was soon finished. The men became weak; nerves were on edge and outbursts of unreasoning temper added to their misery. Planes flew over but the soldiers dared not wave in case they were the enemy. On 8 June they saw land immediately to the south. The barge drifted, maddeningly slowly, on to a rock beach near Sidi Barrani. The escapers stepped ashore right in the middle of a British camp and were given a great welcome.

One hundred and thirty-seven men, mostly Marines under Major R Garrett, RM, sailed an abandoned landing barge from Crete to Sidi Barrani. Two miles out on the first day, 1 June, they picked up a New Zealander, without any clothes, paddling along on a large plank.

This man was Private WA Hancox of 1st General Hospital. He and three other New Zealanders had missed final embarkation by minutes. The following morning they saw a rowing boat drifting two miles off shore. Hancox stripped off and starting swimming towards it, but three-quarters of the way out saw the boat taken by other soldiers. It was then the barge picked him up. Once on it, he could not go back to his friends on the shore.

Seven miles out the men saw bombers attacking the evacuation beach. Air attacks were dreaded but none came – the morning they set out another barge had been bombed and machine-gunned. Fuel ran out and blankets were rigged as sails. Often the men had to jump into the water and push the nose of the heavy barge around so that the sails could catch the breeze. Food was rationed to half a tobacco tin of water and a teaspoonful of bully beef a day. During the voyage a British soldier died of exhaustion and a Palestinian committed suicide. On 9 June the barge drifted ashore fifteen miles west of Sidi Barrani.

Private BB Carter (27 MB Bn) was caught by the Germans at Kisamos Bay, not far from where he had landed after escaping from Greece in a fishing boat. A German officer treated him kindly and gave him an easy job in his kitchen, but it did not last long. Within two weeks the officer went away and Carter was removed to the prison camp at Galatas. On 1 July he slipped out of camp in the dust of a passive convoy of trucks. Next day he reached Meskla and joined Private DN McQuarrie (18 Bn).[1]

McQuarrie had had a hard time. He was lying wounded in the hospital near Suda when the Germans arrived. Had it not been for the Cretans giving them food for two weeks, he and other patients would have surely starved to death. Life was no better at the prison in the Canea hospital and he saw men dying for want of food and care. Despite the shooting of an unlucky escaper half an hour before, McQuarrie escaped through an obvious gap in the barrier on 18 June. He had not gone far when he heard the fire of tommy-guns from the camp. Heading south, he reached Meskla, where he stayed with a friendly family for two weeks. He had plenty of food, sleep and care, but when he saw notices posted in the village threatening Cretans with death if they helped British soldiers he moved into the hills, where he met Carter.

The two hid for a while. They used to watch a German patrol going to Lakkoi every week in a car driven by a New Zealander. They did not worry because they knew the Germans were after eggs, not escapers. Carter and McQuarrie moved through Lakkoi and Omalo to the coast where two Australians joined them. At Suda the men found a derelict eighteen-foot dinghy and on 16 July they started to row across the Mediterranean.

The four escapers knew nothing about boats, they had little food and the dinghy itself was a wreck. They patched it up as best they could: the holes were blocked with socks, but they had to take turns to sit on the biggest hole near the stern while the others bailed water. Lashed oars

---

[1] McQuarrie died of wounds in the Western Desert on 2 December 1941.

were the mast and tied blankets the sail. A gale blew all the way. On the fourth evening the gale stopped and they found themselves just off Sidi Barrani. In ninety hours they had travelled 400 miles.

Soldiers waded out to help the escapers, but when they grasped the boat the top planking came away. Next day, when others tried it out to find out how such a broken-down craft had stood up to the long and hard voyage, the dinghy fell to pieces. Both New Zealanders were awarded the Military Medal.

After being captured in Crete and escaping from Kokkinia Prison near Athens, Lieutenants RB Sinclair (22 Bn) and Roy Farran (3 Hussars) were given berths on a caique bound for Alexandria with ten Greeks and three other soldiers. It was a small diesel vessel about thirty feet long with no mast. The Greek skipper had four days' fuel, just enough to reach Alexandria if everything went well. The chart was a school atlas and their only provisions a sack of crusts and a few onions.

The second night out, the relief man at the tiller took the boat well away from its planned course, a serious error when there was so little fuel. Then it was found that someone on shore had stolen three full tins. The course was corrected and on the fourth morning they pulled in to an island for fresh water. The same night, while they were going through the straits between Crete and Rhodes, a sudden storm blew up and for a day and a half the tiny craft battled against the mountainous waves. Thanks to the skill of the skipper, the boat rode out the storm. All the fuel had gone, the food also and nearly all the water, which was now rationed to one third of a jam tin a man each day. Makeshift sails were erected but were not much help. Paddling with planks was tried but the men were far too weak. On the seventh day the water gave out. A British seaplane dived over the caique and flew away. Everyone was happy, but no rescuing boat came.

By the ninth day the situation was desperate. The men could hardly move, and to speak, at best a croak, was agony. Spirits picked up when the engine was converted to distil fresh water from sea water, bits of wood and oily rags being used for fuel. In an hour enough water dripped through for each to have three mouthfuls. At night they heard ships' engines and lit flares. Three British destroyers approached. The last one edged alongside, and sailors came aboard and carried the men up the gangway. They reached Alexandria on 10 September, 1941. Sinclair was mentioned in despatches.

In the counter-attack on Maleme Aerodrome, Corporal END Nathan (28 Bn) was wounded in the hip and an eye. He went on a barge carrying wounded to Egypt, but off Kastelli enemy planes sank the craft. Nathan swam ashore, hid from a German patrol and started off for Sfakia. When he arrived there he saw large crowds of soldiers on the beach surrendering to the Germans. His wounds, his long trek and this last bitter disappointment were too much for him and he collapsed.

A family in a nearby village found him, carried him to their home and looked after him. Nathan stayed with the family for a long time. He learned the Cretan dialect and moved around freely, even among the German soldiers. He was questioned by the Gestapo but always convinced them that he was a Cretan. The third time he was before the Gestapo it was definitely proved that he was an escaped soldier. He was badly beaten up when he refused to give the name of the family who had befriended him.

Nathan went to a prison camp in Germany and acted as an English–Greek–German interpreter. In September 1944 he was repatriated to England from Germany because of his bad eye and was later mentioned in despatches. After the war he went back to Crete and married the Cretan girl to whom he was engaged while on the island, the daughter of the family that had sheltered him.

Ten days after they escaped, Privates WD Tooke and E Harland (18 Bn) broke back into the prison camp for extra clothing. The following night they were out again. Tooke then spent nearly five months trying to track down boats and submarines. Once he considered himself hard done by when he lost a card draw for a seat in a small boat, Private DRF MacKenzie (19 Bn) being the winner. He found out years afterwards that he had been fortunate as the boat had landed behind the German lines on the North African coast. Despite this accidental salvation, luck was against him and he was recaptured by a German patrol. MacKenzie writes:

A boat with six Greeks was leaving for North Africa and there was room for one soldier. As there were eleven of us, Dean Tooke produced a pack of cards and we cut for the place . . . I was the lucky man.

The boat, an eighteen-footer and well stocked, left on Thursday 18 September, 1941 and the voyage was uneventful, it being calm with just enough wind to keep us going. We had no compass, trusting to luck to get there. We first sighted land on Saturday evening, then our next sight was at noon on Sunday when we saw some buildings and a battle in progress, shells were bursting and dust columns from vehicles were rising. We were sailing parallel to the coast, the battle was on our right and we veered to the left, thinking we were passing Sollum which we had heard was the front line. Late in the afternoon some Blenheims crossed our front from the left and bombed something on our right, so completing the illusion. At midnight we landed. A red flare went up in front of us, the moon was bright and we saw several parties standing at close intervals and a patrol advancing along the beach – they were Germans. They had watched us all day and were waiting for us. The following two days we went from one German post to another. While in one not far from Tobruk, Rommel came in and spoke to the major. I parted from the Greeks at Derna and was sent to Benghazi, where I met Ted Smith and MacGregor who had escaped from Greece, only to be picked up, like me, by the enemy.

Driver P Brocklehurst (Div Sup) heard from the villagers ('It was uncanny the way the Cretans received their news by bush telegraph') that two other escaped New Zealanders were coming to the village. They were Drivers WHW Haslemore and WR Bullot (both Div Sup). Three other New Zealanders also lived in the district, Corporal SG Truesdale and Drivers LM Chinnery and JF McAnally – all from the same unit, the Divisional Supply Column.

In September 1941, when the Germans started their determined drives, the party had to break up and keep moving from one place to another. In between times they looked for boats. Haslemore and others set off late in 1941 in a lifeboat salvaged from a sunken Italian ship, but the overloaded boat was swamped. Once Haslemore and a Welshman were walking across the hills to their hideout when they saw two New Zealanders picking oranges in an orchard. 'From a distance I recognised one as Ray Stuck [Private RHC Stuck, 23 Bn] whom I knew before the war.' In April 1942 a man who appeared to be trustworthy and who had promised Haslemore and others a boat passage led them into a German trap.

Constant raids and alarms in the area of Suda convinced the villagers that the Germans knew they were sheltering an escaped soldier. The soldier, Private AW Gleeson (22 Bn), had been there ten months but now he had to move to a safer place. With his dog, a great companion, he went off to the hills. One day Gleeson badly wanted a smoke so he went into a wineshop in a close-by village. Too late he saw two German soldiers there. They picked him as an escaped soldier, took him over to their table and gave him wine and food. 'They were decent enough blokes and we had a merry time.'

Driver AHH Lambert (4 RTM) was unlucky with submarines. At Sfakia he waited a week for one; at another rendezvous the Greek agent, Colonel Papadakos, told him and other escapers that there had been a leakage of news and that it was not safe to wait any longer. Yet another time he was in touch with an organised party but was away when the submarine made its hurried pick-up, and he was one of the 140 who waited at Treis Ekklesies. In the year that Lambert was free he roamed from one end of Crete to the other, having many narrow escapes from capture.

Life was hard. 'Anyone left in Crete felt in the depth of despair and we had little happiness, though there were one or two lighter moments . . .' Lambert accepted the cold, the hunger and other miseries as part of his hunted life. Generally he and his companions had just enough to live on, though there were times when they starved and were glad indeed to eat such things as slugs. Once when desperately hungry they called on the nearest police station and demanded a meal, which was gladly given them. Sickness was an added affliction. Cretan friends nursed him back to health during these hard times. Clothing was fairly easily picked up but was not warm enough for the rigorous winter, and they found it impossible to obtain boots. Their boots quickly wore out and they had to do all their walking on bare feet. Lambert was well treated by the Cretans and remembers them with affection.

At a village on the western side of Mount Ida Lambert and Lance Corporal ET Goodall (4 RTM) were given up to the police by an informer. The police hated arresting them but had to do so for fear that the informer might betray them also to the Germans.

On 16 April, 1945 Driver PL Winter (Div Pet Coy) came safely through the American lines in Germany. His first escape, from Galatas prison camp, had been easy. While two old Cretan women were throwing pieces of bread over the wire to the hungry soldiers, he and Driver HF Mace (Div Pet Coy) slipped unnoticed from the camp. A few weeks later the two looked miserably down on the camp; at their lowest in health and spirits, they were returning to the imagined security of prison life. A passing Cretan was horrified at this and induced Winter to go with him to the village of Meskla, where he handed the New Zealander over to the care of a family. Mace continued on his way to Galatas, but it was not long before he, too, was talked out of his intention, though he had to go back to the camp a few months later to get hospital treatment for a bad attack of jaundice.

Winter and Private JP Smith (18 Bn) were captured by a German patrol. Back at Galatas camp the day-to-day round was relieved by the arrival of a shipload of sick and wounded New Zealanders from the battle of Sidi Rezegh in North Africa. At Salonika, *en route* to Germany, Winter sickened and was left out of the train drafts. He spent his time with the others talking and planning escapes. His chance came when returning from a working party. He dropped from the truck, ran off and hid in a cellar.

The same night he knocked at the door of a cottage to ask the way to the coast. The man of the house guided him back to a building in the city, and just in the nick of time Winter realised it was the police station. He moved along country tracks, was fed and sheltered by the Greeks and finally reached the small village of Hierissos where, he was told, he could hire a boat passage. This was about April 1942. There were plenty of promises of boats in this and other villages but nothing ever came of them. He then started a slow trek south. Once he was arrested as a vagabond and jailed for a few days. South of Olympus he was captured again. A youth acting as his guide took him to the mayor of a village, who, promising to help him, told him to wait in the café until his return. He returned with the police and Winter was arrested.

Prison life was callous and brutal. The Italians tied handcuffs around Winter's legs, cooped him in a filthy cell for three days and then sent him trussed up to the Larissa concentration camp. The place was indescribably dirty, lice-ridden and overcrowded; the inside guards carried heavy rubber whips. Torture was common. In the special compound Winter met Privates JD Ridge (19 Bn) and TG McCreath[1] (20 Bn). Ridge had evaded capture at Corinth and had been free some time, while McCreath had jumped the train on the way to Germany. Another New Zealander, Private C Corney (25 Bn), who had escaped in Athens, joined them there. Soldiers convicted of 'espionage' or 'sabotage' were kept in the main compound with the Greeks, among them Private W Ditchburn (25 Bn) and Gunner GF Mills (7 A-Tk Regt).

Winter and an English officer, Captain 'Skipper' Savage, who had been sentenced to thirty-six years' imprisonment for 'espionage', planned to escape during siesta time when the guards generally dozed off. On the day chosen they unpicked their way through the twenty feet of the barbed-wire entanglements and were crawling over the open space to the outer wire when one of the guards woke up and forced them with shots to return the same way. The two were tied to posts and flogged – forty lashes with the heavy rubber whips on their bare backs.

The prisoners were tied in pairs and sent to Patras for shipping to Italy. The one bright spot was the comfort of meeting more New Zealanders. One of them, Private JE Wainwright (25 Bn), was well known for his artistry in annoying the guards. He went even so far as to organise a successful strike. Another New Zealander was Sapper JL Langstone (6 Fd Coy) who, passed over as dead by the Germans at Corinth, was nursed back to health by the Greeks. For most of the sixteen months he was free he lived in a monastery with Private RO Petrie (19 Bn). In

---

[1] Escaped in Italy in 1943 and was mentioned in despatches.

September 1942 Winter was shipped to Italy, and on the Italian capitulation in 1943 was sent on to Germany.

When Winter was returned to the prison camp at Galatas, he heard sad news of his friend, Private JA McClements (18 Bn): 'There had been a raid on the village of Meskla but all the soldiers staying there had been forewarned and had made for the hills. Jim McClements and others lived for a time in a cave, where finally (on 3 September, 1941) they were found by the Germans. Jim McClements was at the mouth of the cave cooking over an open fire. There was a shot and those inside rushed out to see Jim, with blood running from a wound in his arm, standing with his hands raised facing a patrol of Germans. Another German fired with a tommy-gun and Jim fell to the ground wounded through the chest. He was still alive and when the Germans came up he said, "Don't shoot," whereupon a third German shot him through the head.'[1]

Private C Corney (25 Bn) became skilled in the ways of an escaped soldier during the eight months he was free in Crete. But luck was against him when his broken Greek and strange accent (good enough to pass the ordinary German) gave him away to the Greek interpreter of a patrol. On the way to Germany his prison convoy stopped at the Athens transit camp, and from there he escaped with Privates JR Stuart and AH Zweibruck (19 Bn). In Athens Corney met a baker who said he knew of a submarine calling at the coast. The baker fixed a meeting place where Corney was to be picked up by car. The car took him straight to the Italian police headquarters.

At the ill-famed Averoff prison, in which he was held for five months, Corney was annoyed by an Italian medical orderly called 'Bianco', a cripple whose sadistic amusement was hitting prisoners with his stick. He met Private GIT Tong (19 Bn) here and was distressed to see the large number of running sores on his head and ears. Tong had been free in Greece for sixteen months and the Italian police, thinking that he had something to do with the widespread espionage and sabotage, interrogated and lashed him mercilessly. They forced his arms through the

[1] Narrative (unpublished) by PL Winter.

186

slats of a chair, punched him on the ears with closed fists and hammered him with a heavy wooden baton until it broke. At Larissa, the next camp, inhumanity and cruelty was still Corney's burden. He was there when his friend, Driver Winter, received forty lashes for trying to escape. The following morning he saw an Italian sergeant ripping the bandages off Winter's back and expressing delight at the sight of the lacerated skin. From Patras, Corney was shipped to Italy to a prisoner-of-war camp. Zweibruck and Stuart were both recaptured and Stuart was later executed by the Italians.[1]

The Cretan family of Kandisachis in the village of Spaniakos looked after Private WE Wheeler (19 Bn) for about a year and a half. Soon after escaping from Galatas camp in June 1941, Wheeler and two other New Zealanders, Gunners EJP Owen and RA Gover[2] (both 5 Fd Regt) were guided to the village and remained unmolested until September 1941, when large German forces searched the island for escaped prisoners. This and other raids passed the New Zealanders over, thanks to the help given by the Cretans. With raids, informers and bogus agents, times became hard and the Cretans a little jittery as the Germans did not hesitate to shoot, burn and imprison when they found anybody helping escaped soldiers. Yet all New Zealanders could be sure that a good Cretan was never a traitor.

A ship's captain offered to take a load of prisoners to Alexandria if they gave him enough money to buy a boat. This was done and the soldiers met at the appointed place. While waiting for darkness, they saw a German spotter plane crash into the sea in front of them and saw the pilot paddling to the shore in a rubber dinghy. Ten minutes later three aircraft flew overhead and they were sure that the pilots had seen them and had radioed back. Friends told Wheeler some days afterwards that the skipper had taken the boat to the Greek mainland.

At the end of October 1942 Wheeler went to a cave not far away, in which there were twenty soldiers, to discuss escape prospects. He stayed a day or so, but one morning the Germans made a lightning raid and captured the lot. Wheeler underwent a twenty-four-hour interrogation by

[1] See p. 198.

[2] Escaped in Italy in 1943 and was mentioned in despatches.

187

the Gestapo. He never left the room. He sat in the same chair, was allowed no rest and, as soon as one of the five questioners stopped, another carried on the relentless chain.

Wheeler made three breaks from his German prison camp and was free for about eight weeks each time before he was recaptured. Just before Christmas 1944 he escaped into Czechoslovakia and was sheltered by a family, members of a partisan organisation, until the arrival of the Russians in May 1945. He married a Czech girl. Both went to England and from there came home to New Zealand.

In September 1941 a smuggler's boat carried Gunner WJ Griffiths (5 Fd Regt) from Crete to Greece where, he thought, the chances of escape were good. Griffiths had spent four months in Crete scouring the beaches for a boat, but had had no luck. Greece was not much better, as he found out: 'Spent some weeks with malaria and lost a good deal of constitution. Then had yellow jaundice and finished up living in a monastery in the mountains to recuperate . . .'

In June 1942 Griffiths went by sea to Athens where he lived with a family, moving around freely. A professor from the Athens University obtained a place for him on a boat going to Smyrna on 23 July, 1942. The night before it was to sail the Gestapo raided the house and took Griffiths away. He had been betrayed – the one and a half million drachmas' reward for the capture of an escaped soldier was too much of a temptation for someone who knew his plans.

After two unsuccessful breaks from German prison camps, Griffiths got away on his third attempt and came through the American lines to safety.

Sergeant AC Barker (4 RTM) hid in Crete until September 1941. He then rowed over to Greece, where he and an Australian who had joined him lay up in a village until May 1942. Three *carabinieri* surprised them one night when they were taking a walk. They refused to surrender. The *carabinieri* opened fire and the escapers fired back and killed one. The Italians combed the countryside. The two were swift and elusive in dodging the patrols, but in July 1942 they were betrayed by pro-Axis Greeks.

Barker would not talk, or 'confess' as the Italians put it, and for five days the guards tortured him. They gave him no food or water, tied him to a chair and punched and kicked him throughout the days. The two were moved to Xilocastron concentration camp, where they lived for three weeks in appalling conditions. In October 1942 Barker and the Australian appeared before a court which, after a farce of a trial, condemned them to death. The Italians chained them hand and foot for twenty-four days and then by the hands only for another seven days. On the way to Bari in a ship they and other prisoners were chained in gangs of twelve. Bari prison, where they stayed a month, was filthy and crawling with lice. Food was scarce and the prison staff stole much of it. At Sulmona prison Barker and the Australian were put in the dungeons and kept apart from the other prisoners. By this time Barker's sentence had been commuted to thirty years' imprisonment.

In September 1943 the prisoners rioted, the cells were opened and Barker escaped into the hills near Pratola, where he hid for twenty days. He and two other soldiers found a guide who offered to take them down to Allied lines. They had a narrow shave once when they were stopped by Germans at Pietro in Valle and forced to dig gunpits along with thirty Italians. On 23 October, 1943 Barker came through Allied lines at Castropignano. He was awarded the MM.

During the fifteen months Driver EJA Phelan (4 RTM) spent in Crete, he made sixteen attempts to track down seaworthy boats. Twice he actually set out – the first time the boat sank under him, and on the other occasion the engine broke down. In a determined effort to catch him, the Germans terrorised the family and relatives of his Cretan friend, a robber in the Robin Hood style.

Phelan and four Australians, heavily armed, overpowered the crew of a large vessel and took it out to sea. When they pulled in to the island of Gavdhos at dawn to repair the engine, two German planes machine-gunned the boat. German guards chased the soldiers across the island, caught them and sent them back to Crete, where they were grilled by the Gestapo for four weeks.

His next prison was in Athens. He was not there long before he made a break, reached the hills and was cared for by a band of fugitive Greeks.

They called themselves *andartes* (guerrillas) but, in fact, were an idle, drunken crowd living by stealing and by sponging on relatives. Still, they looked after Phelan and never betrayed him. He was captured again when his fair complexion gave him away.

Phelan was moved to a prison camp in Germany. In the summer of 1943 he determined to escape. This was difficult. He was on the black list, was closely watched and was not allowed to go out on working parties. He changed identity with another soldier and went to work in a cement factory close to the village of Lidice. The Czech workers there who ran an escape organisation listed him as an intending escaper. The organisation was destroyed when a recaptured Palestinian soldier turned informer. Fourteen of the underground group were shot.

Soon afterwards Phelan escaped on his own and travelled to Prague by a series of local workers' trains. One day he went to a cinema to keep out of the way. A propaganda film was being screened and it was so full of Nazi strutting and fiction that Phelan laughed, whereupon a Gestapo agent sitting nearby arrested him for disrespect to the Reich. His real identity was discovered and back to camp he went for a spell in the punishment cells.

Phelan met another New Zealander, Sergeant BJ Crowley (4 RTM), and both planned a further escape. Phelan's luck was out when he sickened and went to hospital. Crowley and an Englishman carried on and in the end reached Sweden. Phelan organised another escape party, this time with Driver E Silverwood (4 RTM) and an English soldier. They made the break on 23 December, 1943 and, posing as foreign workers, travelled by train to Berlin. During a bombing raid on the station they slipped unnoticed onto the train to Stettin, and on arrival there dodged the strict check by going out on the heavily guarded waterfront looking for Swedish boats. After days of hide-and-seek a friendly Swede smuggled them on his boat and stowed them away until Stockholm was safely reached. Crowley was awarded the DCM, Phelan and Silverwood MMs.

Driver WJ Siely (Pet Coy) was shocked by the brutality of the reprisals taken by the Germans on Cretans suspected of helping escaped soldiers. He hated to think that these people might have to suffer on his account, and although he escaped three times, this thought always made him return to the prison camp.

In October 1941 Siely was moved to Stalag VIIIB at Lamsdorf in Germany, where he posed as a corporal. In the summer of 1943 he helped thirty-two prisoners to escape from a working party at Stranberg but was frustrated in his own attempt by being arrested as an agitator. After a punishment of seven days in the cells, he was sent to Arbeitskommando 399 at Oberwichstein.

Here he filed the window bar in his billet and was free for four days. At the next working camp (Freiwaldau) he and two other soldiers prised open the trapdoor in the theatre of their Lager and managed to reach Olmutz, in Czechoslovakia, by train before being recaptured by the Gestapo. The next attempt was made at Parschnitz, where he was working on the railway track. On the first favourable opportunity Siely and another soldier went to a nearby shed and climbed through the rear window. Both walked across the Czechoslovak frontier, only to be betrayed by the wife of a Sudeten German whom they had asked for help.

At a cement factory in Munsterburg Siely and a British soldier made careful and thorough plans for escape. On 14 July, 1944 they pulled a bar from the window of the washhouse in their billet; they then walked to the railway station and caught the train to Breslau. They travelled by train all the way to Stettin and their forged identity passes were never questioned.

In Stettin they met a Frenchman who hid them in his Lager. Soon they were negotiating with two Swedish seamen for a passage on a boat. On 24 July the Swedes smuggled the two soldiers and two Frenchmen on board and hid them in the airshaft of the main funnel. They stayed there for five days. The escapers were put ashore at Kalmar, in Sweden, and reached Stockholm on 1 August, 1944. Siely was awarded the DCM.

On 21 December, 1943 Private HA Hoare (23 Bn), who had been wounded and taken prisoner in Crete, climbed the fence of the Unterbenstatten (Austria) labour camp in daylight. He crossed the border of Hungary and within five days was in Budapest. There he was arrested and imprisoned in the old castle at Szigetvar which had been turned into an internment camp.

When the Germans marched into Hungary in March 1944, Hoare

escaped from the castle but was caught three days later and sent to the prison at Zemun. Although he was most persistent in cutting the barbed wire entanglement, he was always unlucky to be caught in the act. One day Allied bombers came over and destroyed, among other places, the prison camp. When the bombers had finished and the danger was over, Hoare and two other prisoners escaped.

The patriot forces in the locality took the escapers under their wing. Hoare repaid their friendship by serving with them for three months. On 20 July, 1944 a plane took him back to Allied lines in Italy. He was awarded the MM.

Private PE Minogue (20 Bn) first escaped from a party working at the stables in Salonika.

'One day there were no guards about, so I dropped my broom and walked down the road. I walked very slowly to the corner, then took to my heels and only stopped when out of breath. A few minutes later a woman from a house beckoned me. I went in and she gave me clothes to change into. She went out into the street and beckoned me again. I followed for half a mile when another woman took over. She led me to her home where her family gave me food and money. An hour later the same woman guided me to the house of Madame Lappa and I met two Aussies and three Tommies there. That night I went to a family to stay – their names were Costa and his wife, Koula, and their son, George. It was like heaven, I had everything.

'On the twelfth night George said, "Hurry, get ready, you are going to Cairo." He led me to another house and I saw the Aussies and Tommies again. Madame Luppa, the brains of the outfit, came and told us we were going on a submarine. She guided us to the outside of the town where she handed us over to two men. These men took us up to the third floor of a big building by the docks. One asked if we would like coffee or whisky. We said "whisky". He produced a bottle of Scotch and we were drinking a toast to success when we heard "Hands up!". What a shock, there at the door were two Gestapo men with guns out. I've seen this sort of thing in the pictures but never dreamed it would happen to me.'

Back at Salonika prison camp Minogue joined his friend, Private PR Blunden (20 Bn), and several others who had worked in the stables. They knew they were going to Germany by train and they prepared for escape by collecting all sorts of handy tools.

'At six when it was dusk we cut a hole in the side of the cattle truck, put a hand through, undid the wire holding the catch and pushed the door open. There were twelve altogether, I drew fourth place and the train was going twenty-five miles an hour when I jumped. Peter and I went back to Salonika to warn the people about the submarine. Next afternoon we saw our friends and were just in time to save twenty soldiers from the submarine fraud.

'Madame Lappa took us to Madame Tousula's home where we stayed for six months. While there we became very friendly with Bill Flint [Private W Flint, 18 Bn], who was living at another house. Food was soon extremely hard to get in Salonika and I moved back to Costa and Koula because two in one home was too much of a struggle. Costa and Koula were going without for me and I didn't like that. One day I said I was going to visit Peter. Instead, I hit the trail out of town. I walked all night. I passed through a village at two in the morning when a Bulgarian grabbed me and handed me over to the police.'

Minogue found out that of the twelve who had escaped Blunden was the only one who was still free. In the camp Minogue took part in digging a tunnel under the barracks of the camp leader (a British sergeant major). It was almost finished when the guards rushed in and went straight to it. The soldiers were sure that the sergeant major, a toady of the Germans, had betrayed them. On yet another train journey to Germany Minogue escaped, this time with seven others. He and an Australian named Sid decided to walk down through Greece and find a boat to take them to Turkey. The Australian insisted on going into a strange village in daylight and the people thought they were Germans posing as escaped prisoners. The Greeks did eventually find out who they were but only when it was too late to do anything. The soldiers were then in the custody of the police and the Gestapo had been notified.

Salonika prison closed down and the few prisoners left were locked in cattle trucks for the trip to Germany. The sergeant major was there – he travelled in the carriage with the Germans – and he suggested that those who wanted to escape should travel in the second truck.

'Late that night we were sawing away when the train suddenly stopped and guards ran up to us and shone torches on the hole. They battened up the hole and took our saw but we still had a file. Once everything appeared settled, we filed the wire off the window. Johnny Leach [Gunner JJ Leach, 4 Fd Regt] was second through the window. I was about to follow when the train slowed down and, after a few minutes, stopped. The guards came down the left side, spotted Johnny, and started running. Johnny ran around the back of the truck to the other side past where we were. Then the guards on the right side saw him; Johnny turned again to run and they shot him in the back. He lay outside our window and we heard him say that they had got him in the back and then had put the boot in. He lived five minutes. They took us out of our truck and put us in the other. And so I landed in Germany.'

Eight months later Flint arrived in the prison camp and Minogue learned of the happenings in Salonika. Blunden was taken off Greece a few weeks after Minogue had left Costa's house. Within a short time of this, the Gestapo raided Blunden's old place and Flint was eventually tracked down. Flint heard that the Greek women, Lappa and Tousula, and also several others were sent to German concentration camps.

'Bill Flint and I were cobbers all through Germany. He would escape, get picked up, do a stretch in the cells, and away again he would go. I know he was away about eight times. We had a final flutter towards the end of the war and managed to come out through Prague and Pilsen.'[1]

In July 1941 Private CC Nicholl (19 Bn) and Private W Gilby, an Australian, saw a boat well out to sea. Thinking that there might be people on it who, like themselves, might want to escape from Crete, they piled their gear on the beach and swam out to it. They grasped the side and in broken English and by signs asked the two Greeks on board to take them to North Africa. The Greeks made no move to pull them in. They talked, then screamed and finally picked up sticks and hit the soldiers until they had to break away.

They swam back to the beach but were no sooner there than Nicholl collapsed. Gilby dressed him and watched him during the night. By

---

[1] Blunden received the MM for his escape and Leach, who was killed on 24 April, 1942, was awarded posthumous mention in despatches.

morning he knew that he would have to get him to shelter and aid. Nicholl was in agony with severe pains in his stomach. They set out over the mountains but Nicholl was too weak and in too much pain to walk any distance. Gilby then carried him for eight miles to a village where there were Germans. The sick man was immediately put to bed. Gilby sat beside him all the time and was with him when he died two days later.[1] Gilby was sent to the prison camp.

In September 1941 Gunner O Cole (5 Fd Regt), Private FM Blank (23 Bn) and four other soldiers hid in a gully when they heard the Germans were making a drive to round up soldiers still free in Crete. The Germans surrounded the gully and the soldiers, seeing that they did not have a chance, came out with their hands up. The Germans lined them up. On a signal from the officer a guard fired a burst from his tommy-gun and shot two of the men. Cole was killed outright, as was also an unknown soldier.

On the morning of 25 August, 1941 three escaped New Zealanders lay down to rest in a dry creek bed in Crete. A German patrol surrounded them and opened fire; the escapers surrendered. Gunner RG Dry (5 Fd Regt) was badly wounded and the others dressed his wounds. The Germans tied the hands of the two unwounded New Zealanders, Driver CFH Snell (4 RTM) and Sergeant SH Richards (19 Army Tps), and refused their offer to carry Dry between them.

Some of the Germans stayed behind with Dry. The others moved on with the prisoners and came to the top of the ridge. There Snell and Richards heard shots coming from the direction of the creek bed. The Germans who had stayed behind caught up. All the guards then stopped and passed a New Zealand army paybook around from hand to hand. In June 1942 another prisoner of war reported that Dry had been shot and killed while escaping. Dry was awarded posthumous mention in despatches.

Warrant Officer RH Thomson, DCM, who had been captured in Crete and moved to Salonika prison, missed the train drafts to Germany by

[1] On 7 July, 1941.

using the old soldier dodges of doctors' chits, feigning sickness or just by being absent when the drafts left. There came a time, however, when he had to go on the train. But he went prepared and from a belt around his middle hung knives, files and pliers belonging to him and other hopeful escapers.

The cattle truck he was in had an opening covered with barbed wire high up in the side. He cut the barbed wire carefully and tucked in the ends at the bottom. While he was doing this six soldiers in the next truck sawed a hole through the wood, but when they jumped from the bumper of their truck the guards opened fire and killed four and wounded one; the other made a clean break. From then on two German soldiers rode on the bumper, a few feet away from Thomson, guarding the sawn hole. The night was full of more stoppings, more shooting, more examinations. When one German was taken off the bumper and the other was out of sight, Thomson squeezed through the opening, dropped flat on the track and lay still until the train was out of sight.

He eventually reached Salonika and, after being rebuffed by several householders, met four young Greeks who promised to take him in their chartered boat to Alexandria. The day before sailing two Greeks betrayed him and had him arrested by the Germans, who recognised him as an escaped soldier by his army boots.

In his basement cell in the Salonika prison Thomson was troubled with dysentery and had to go often – under escort – to the latrine at the end of the corridor. He worked out a plan of escape. He developed a limp, carried a boot in his hand and then at the chosen time hit the guard hard on the back of the head. Instead of collapsing, the guard bellowed, swung around and hit Thomson over the head with his bayonet. In a minute the corridor was full of abusing and punching Germans.

Thomson's hands were tied with wire, and as soon as the officers had left the three guards of his section dashed into the cell and hammered him with heavy sticks. They poured water on the floor to stop him resting and every hour they took him outside and beat him. Twenty or more Germans came along in the morning to look at the '*Engländer Schwein*' and they cheered and clapped while the three guards rained blow after blow on him.

Thomson was then put on board a train for Germany. The guards were instructed to keep a close eye on him so they put him in their carriage in a small compartment with a little seat and a window beside it. A guard sat in front of him with his rifle and bayonet at the ready. After a time the Germans closed the door, being content to make sudden and surprise checks on their prisoner. Thomson worked his hands free of the wire, and retied them so that they could be quickly slipped free. He opened the window and closed it, then he waited. He dropped from the train (it was travelling fast over open country) and landed on the jagged stones by the track. Skinned and bruised – his left hip was the only part unhurt – Thomson set out on foot and finally reached Salonika.

Thomson moved slowly northwards from village to village, and when he met Private JC Mann (18 Bn) he stayed with him. It was winter, the people were friendly and the two escapers were weak so they decided to lie up until spring and then continue their journey. It was during this time that Second Lieutenant Thomas (23 Bn) came and stayed with them for nineteen days. Thomas went south and in the end managed to escape from Greece. Four months later the two friends started walking for Turkey. They reached the Struma river, where some smugglers promised to ferry them across to Bulgarian-occupied Greece, but an old man induced the smugglers to hand them over to the police. On the night of their capture they lowered themselves out of the high window of their prison by knotted canvas strips but had the misfortune to walk into the arms of a returning patrol. They worked on the padlock of their next prison and would have escaped if the Germans had not come to collect them.

On the train to Germany from Salonika prison Thomson was tied hand and foot to the seat and had one guard by day and two by night during the ten days' journey. In Germany he was court-martialled and sentenced to eight months in a punishment prison. Thomson was mentioned in despatches.

In an Italian prison camp Private AB Wright (18 Bn), who had been captured in Crete, made careful preparations for escape. He collected and saved food, had a wire-cutting tool and had copied a map of Italy and the Balkans. The night of 8 February, 1942 was black and stormy and it was snowing – the night Wright was waiting for. He picked a shaded patch of the barbed wire between two searchlights, lay low until the outside patrol had passed then cut a way through the first fence. An inside sentry spotted him and fired without warning. Wright died almost immediately. He was awarded posthumous mention in despatches.

On 7 February, 1943 Private JR Stuart (19 Bn) was executed in Athens by the Italians on the charge of 'political conspiracy, political defeatism, holding of arms and violence against the military'.

Stuart was badly wounded in Crete, but early in 1942 when well enough he escaped in Athens from a prison convoy bound for Germany. Little is known of his life in Greece. When he was recaptured he was immediately recognised by the Italians as an escaped prisoner who had resisted arrest. In May 1942 an Italian secret policeman stopped Stuart and his friend Tony Handkinson, a civil internee, in an Athens street. There was a gunfight and the Italian was wounded in the leg. Handkinson was caught at the same time and both stood trial before an Italian military tribunal. They were condemned to death by shooting.

While awaiting trial Stuart was locked up in the dreaded Averoff civil prison. He was cruelly treated but bore his suffering with courage and never gave way to despair. Once he and a Commando captain were given thirty lashes for attempting to escape. Another time Stuart and his cell mate, both desperate with hunger, were badly beaten by the guard. Stuart had a severe internal haemorrhage and was left in an underground cell for weeks. After another attempt he was beaten in his cell every two hours and the floor was flooded with water to stop him resting.

Corporal FIA Woollams heard of Stuart when he came to Averoff prison and later had a talk with him. 'When I met him he was still suffering from severely mutilated hands and arms. He showed me his legs, which were now a queer colour, having been absolutely blue . . .'

The sight of Stuart was saddening. 'Jack Stuart and his mate [in an attempted escape] were now spending their time in and out of hospital. They both looked wrecks, and could only creep about like very old men. Jack was the worst case of the two . . .'

At dawn on 7 February, 1943 Stuart was taken from his cell and shot. The prisoners heard that he was steadfast and died bravely. The Director of Averoff prison saw the execution and told the Swiss Chargé d'Affaires how impressed he was by Stuart's attitude and bravery.

Staff Sergeant T Moir and Gunner DC Perkins (4 Fd Regt) escaped from the Galatas prison camp and spent weeks searching the coast for boats. They headed inland, there to find the mountain villages swarming with escaped soldiers. They knew the Germans would soon raid the locality so they headed for the rugged and sparsely populated west coast. The village folk, though poor, were most hospitable. Moir gives an instance: 'On one occasion, when they discovered us, sleeping off the effects of several liberal draughts of wine taken during the heat of the day, under a grove of olive trees not very far from the village, we were plied with so much food and wine that after three days we managed to continue on our way only by sneaking off during the dead of the night during a lull in hospitality. We carefully avoided villages during the next three days until our supply of food ran out.' They roamed the hills for weeks to get the lie of the country, then settled and became attached to two or three villages in a small area.

Moir and Perkins were always on the watch for boats, and many times they set out, only to be forced back again by the weather or by the many reefs on the coast or the wretched condition of their craft. Once they were lucky to escape drowning. The escapers moved freely around the western end of the island and were often chased by the Germans. In one German drive they were machine-gunned from a range of 200 yards and had a hectic game of hide-and-seek with a patrol of eight Germans for the rest of the day.

In April 1942 (not many soldiers were then still free in Crete) Moir and Perkins followed up separate leads on likely boats. At Mesara Bay there were fourteen boats under German guard. Accessories such as oars and sails were kept in a locked shed; the owners slept in boats but the German guard was away at the entrance to the bay. Moir planned to steal one of these boats. Perkins was then haggling with a man for the hire of a boat and had reasonable prospects of getting it. Moir continued with his plan and Perkins arranged to meet him with his boat in a familiar cove. If Perkins's deal fell through, he intended to join Moir's party.

The appointed night was so pitch black that the soldiers lost their way.

Next night they met and, amidst much shouting and waving of arms by the owners, selected a good boat and sailed it unchallenged past the German post. By morning they were snug in the cove waiting for Perkins. They waited two days but he did not turn up. They searched all his usual haunts but he could not be found. The wind changed to north-west and to delay longer would be dangerous. The high wind and rough sea gave natural protection from nosing aircraft, and several planes, German and British, flew over them. On the late afternoon of the fourth day, after sailing 300 miles, the party landed on a small beach a few miles west of Sidi Barrani.

Three months later, Moir met Perkins in Cairo and heard his story. Perkins went down on the night arranged, saw no one and thought Moir had got away. He then returned inland and heard when it was too late of the party's departure on the following night. A short time afterwards Cretan friends told Perkins that there were Germans in British uniforms wandering around the district. Perkins traced the men and found, as he had suspected, that they were Commandos off a Greek submarine. Perkins and other soldiers on the spot were given a passage in the sub-marine to Egypt.

After his escape Moir worked for Military Intelligence. He went on several special service operations and in February 1943 volunteered to go back to Crete to collect soldiers in hiding. By May 1943 he was in touch with fifty-one soldiers and had arranged their escape, but the evacuation date was altered and he had the worry of keeping a large body of men in one place for over a week. The Germans heard of this party, and although the fifty-one men were taken off, Moir walked into a police patrol containing an interpreter who was not deceived by his Greek as the usual German patrol would have been. There were fourteen New Zealanders in the party which Moir organised and all were mentioned in despatches for their courage and determination in not submitting to captivity. This was one of the final rescue operations from Crete.

After interrogation, Moir was sent off to Germany, marked as a dangerous prisoner. He was cooped up with three other bad prisoners for thirty-two days in a small cell in a prisoner-of-war camp for Russians. They forced the door and an outer window but were caught in the act of getting through the three sets of double barbed-wire fences around the camp. They were then placed in the punishment cells without boots or bedding and allowed only one pair of underpants and a singlet each.

In the next camp Moir and another New Zealander, Bombardier MJC Robinson (4 Fd Regt), volunteered to go to a working camp within striking distance of the Hermagor Pass into Italy. The two broke camp in June 1944 and headed for the coast, hoping to find a boat to take them to southern Italy. When they reached the mountains where the partisans were fighting, the place became alive with German troops. On the seventh night out the escapers were caught while trying to cross a bridge. The river was wide and swift and the bridge had appeared to be unguarded. They were sentenced to solitary confinement and then sent back to the ordinary camp.

After a month of near starvation in Galatas prison camp, Lance Sergeant GM Davis and Signalman MF Knight (Div Sigs) broke camp and spent a day foraging for food. The Cretans were so friendly that the night after their return to camp they went through the wire again, this time for good. The first few days were spent with their newfound friends. They then moved to the village of Lakkoi, where great numbers of escapers were hiding in a nearby gorge. The two New Zealanders heard that they were waiting for sea transport to pick them up. This was not true, and as the villagers were finding it hard to feed the men Davis and Knight moved on to the village of Meskla. An English-speaking Cretan took them into his home and they lived there for the next ten months. Within a few weeks the Germans put in their first big sweep to capture escaped prisoners, but the family hid the two safely in a small gully.

In April 1942 they joined three other New Zealanders – Privates R Huston and CJ Ratcliffe (19 Bn) and Driver J Symes (Div Pet Coy) – and an Australian in a hideout in caves halfway to Canea, where they lived for a year. Friendly villagers supplied them with food. At times they were forced to raid gardens under the guidance of a Cretan, who directed them to homes of German sympathisers or of people who had plenty. In April 1943 the Germans swooped down on one of the caves just after dawn. Somebody had betrayed them. Davis, Huston and Ratcliffe[1] were caught

---

[1] Ratcliffe escaped later and was reported safe with the Allied forces on 28 September, 1944.

and were sent to prison camps in Germany. The Germans knew that there were five soldiers altogether but they missed the two caves where the other two were hiding.

At that time Staff Sergeant Moir was going over the island collecting soldiers still in hiding, and shortly after the German raid he located the three survivors. They left Crete in May 1943.

After a course in sabotage and guerrilla warfare, Gunner Perkins was landed in July 1943 near Koustoyerako to act as second in command to another British agent, Major A Fielding. He spent some time becoming familiar with the White Mountains area and set up his headquarters in Selino on the south-west corner of the range. At this time (September 1943) there was widespread unrest among the Cretans, culminating in the abortive and expensive revolt led by Mandli Bandervas, who retreated from the east end of the island to the west. The Germans then carried out large-scale reprisals all over Crete. Koustoyerako suffered severely, being burnt out on 2 October. The villagers took to the hills and Perkins, better known to the Cretans as Kapitan Vassilios, formed them into a well-armed organised force about 100 to 120 strong. This force held the area above Koustoyerako while the Germans occupied the area below.

Perkins arranged air drops of supplies and arms from Allied planes. He was especially active in carrying out night raids on German positions, aimed usually at recovering sheep and cattle which had been taken by the Germans. The Germans often sent patrols up into the hills to find out the strength of the guerrillas. On one of these occasions Perkins lured a patrol of twenty men up to Alladha and surrounded them in a stone hut. He crept up, threw a hand-grenade in and killed ten. The rest were taken prisoner and shot. In this fight Perkins was wounded, the bullet hitting him in the neck and travelling down his back. A Cretan butcher traced the bullet with his knife and cut it out. Perkins continued his work of organising other bands of guerrillas, all of which took their orders from him. During this time he was promoted to the rank of staff sergeant.

He received orders in February 1944 to go to the village of Asigonia and join Major Denis Ciclitiras, another British agent. On the first day of the journey Perkins and his party of four Cretans fell into a German ambush. Perkins, in the lead, was killed instantly. One of the Cretans, Andreas Vantoulakes, was also killed outright, while the two brothers Seirantonakes, both wounded, threw themselves over a steep cliff and hid at the bottom. The remaining Cretan, Zaziakes, was badly wounded. Lying in the open, he held the fifty Germans in the patrol back for three hours until darkness, when he managed to escape and join the other two Cretans.

The Germans took Perkins's body to Lakkoi and buried it just outside their barracks. By his kindness and help to the Cretans and by his daring exploits against the Germans, Perkins was well known throughout the island. The Cretans kept his grave covered with flowers. A photograph received from Crete in April 1951 shows a small girl about to lay a wreath of flowers on Perkins's grave. The following was written on the photograph: 'Grave of the most fearless of fighters ever to leave New Zealand, known to all Cretans as the famous Kapitan Vassilios. Killed over 100 Germans single-handed during the occupation. Led a guerrilla band, and fell from machine-gun fire in February 1944, near Lakkoi – the last gallant Kiwi killed in Crete. This man is honoured by all Cretans.'

PUBLISHED SOURCES

BRUCE, COLONEL RNBD, OBE
Chronicles of the 1st Battalion the Rangers, 1939/45, KRRC.

BRUNSKILL, BRIGADIER GS, CBE, MC
'The administrative aspect of the campaign in Crete', *The Army Quarterly* LIV, 2.

BUCKLEY, CHRISTOPHER
Greece and Crete, 1941, HMSO, 1942.

CHURCHILL, WINSTON S
The Grand Alliance, Cassell, 1950.

CIANO, COUNT
Diaries, Heinemann, 1947.
Diplomatic Papers, Odhams, 1948.

CUNNINGHAM OF HYNDHOPE, ADMIRAL OF THE FLEET, LORD
Memoirs, A Sailor s Odyssey, Hutchinson, 1951.

DAVIN, DM
Official History of New Zealand in the Second World War, 'Crete' (Dept of Internal Affairs, War History Branch, 1953).

DE GUINGAND, MAJOR GENERAL SIR FRANCIS, KBE, CB, DSO
Operation Victory, Hodder and Stoughton, 1949.

GRAHAM, LIEUTENANT COLONEL, FCC, DSO
History of the Argyll and Sutherland Highlanders, 1939/45, Thos. Nelson, 1948.

HARMELING, LIEUTENANT COLONEL, HENRY
'Tanks in Crete', *US Army Combat Forces Journal*, Vol 4, No. 7.

HEYDTE, BARON VON DER
Daedalus returns, Hutchinson, 1958.

HIPPENBERGER, MAJOR GENERAL SIR HOWARD
Infantry Brigadier, OUP, 1949.

HOVE, R VON
Achtung Fallschirmjäger, Duffel Verlag, 1954.

LIDDELL HART, CAPTAIN BH
The Other Side of the Hill, Cassell, 1948.

LONG, GAVIN
Australians in the War of 1939/45, Series 1, Vol 2, Canberra, 1953.

PAPAGOS, GENERAL
The Battle of Greece (Tr. P Eliascos), Scaziglis, Athens, 1949.

SCHMIDT, LIEUTENANT COLONEL TC (US Army)
'The Fighting Forces', XXVI, 2.

SHIRER, W
The Rise and Fall of the Third Reich, Secker and Warburg, 1960.

STEPHANIDES, THEODORE
Climax in Crete, Faber, 1948.

STUDENT, GENERAL KURT
'Crete', *Kommando*, South African WO, March 1952.

WILMOT, CHESTER
Struggle for Europe, Collins, 1952.

WILSON, FIELD MARSHAL, LORD
Eight Years Overseas, Hutchinson, 1950.

VARIOUS
Kreta, Der Kuhnsten Sieg, Steirische Verlagsanstalt, Graz, 1942.

Author s note. I am also greatly indebted to help in conversation with two New Zealanders, Geoffrey Cox and DM Davin.

The personal experiences recounted in the epilogue are taken from the appendix to the New Zealand Official History.

INDEX